D1570630

# Sex and Salvation:
# Virginity As A
# Soteriological Paradigm
# in Ancient Christianity

Roger Steven Evans

UNIVERSITY PRESS OF AMERICA,® INC.
*Dallas • Lanham • Boulder • New York • Oxford*

Copyright © 2003 by
Roger Steven Evans

UNIVERSITY PRESS OF AMERICA,® INC.

4501 Forbes Boulevard
Suite 200
Lanham, Maryland 20706
UPA Acquisitions Department (301) 459-3366

PO Box 317
Oxford
OX2 9RU, UK

Library of Congress Control Number: 2003116843
ISBN 0-7618-2769-2 (paperback : alk. ppr.)

This book is dedicated to my wife, Christine,
and my two sons, Justin and Aaron.

# Contents

# Preface

In the summer of 2001 as I was doing research on-line for my class on Gender and Sex: Issues in Ancient Christianity, I began to discover a growing number of documents dealing with the issue of virginity. I began to mark these documents, and when the number reached eight, I began to read and analyze them. Themes began to emerge and be repeated. Biblical texts used to support arguments for Christian virginity were quoted over and again. And general views on sex and women's sexuality also were repeated. I decided to highlight these texts in my class, and continued to do research. In the end I discovered over twenty-five catholic gnostic and pseudopigraphical documents dealing specifically with virginity written in the first six centuries c.e. This did not include references to virgins in other various Christian writings, nor early canon law dealing with the subject of virginity.

Most, if not all, of the ethnic and religious, ancient, Mediterranean cultures expected their young women to remain virginal until the wedding night. What makes these documents so fascinating is that these writers were not just telling their young maidens to remain virginal until marriage to their husbands. They were calling for a commitment to life-long virginity, to forgo marriage and children, and to claim Christ as their only husband.

Early Christians were constantly thinking and writing about eternity, i.e., escape from this evil world, salvation from sin, etc. The writers of these documents on virginity were also interested in teleological concerns, and explained to their readers that there were eternal consequences associated with the decision to commit to a life of virginity. And while scholars have explored various early Christian soteriological paradigms, Virginity as a way of salvation, has not to date been identified as one of those paradigms. However the overwhelming plethora of evidence (epistles, letters, apologies, stories, canon law), irresistible by virtue of its volume, concerning early Christian virginity, both in theology and practice, brought together and analyzed in this book, will cause scholars to reengage the subject of early Christian understandings of salvation.

The belief in virginity as a way of salvation cannot be dismissed as just another "work" proscribed by the early church Fathers as a way of earning God's favor. Not only does the practice of virginity give virgins access to God in ways that no other good work does, but virgins, at least by the fourth century, seem to have their own salvific powers. They, in fact, are believed to be saviours; sometimes for their communities, and sometimes for their families. The questions of why this happened when this happened has not yet been thoroughly examined. It is interesting to note, however, that this growing elevation of the powers of virgins coincides with the rise of the status of "ever virgin Mary." It also coincides with the "conversion" to Christianity of hundreds of thousands of people in the Roman Empire; many of whom may have had female saviours in their pantheon of gods.

It is hoped, then, that this book will cause other scholars and students of history to recognize the interest in human sexuality that often occupied the interests of many of the early Christian leaders, and how it was believed that a persons sexual history could very well either haunt or bless the believer throughout eternity.

# Acknowledgments

It is rare today to find a scholar who works in isolation, alone with his or her thoughts and a few collected or selected manuscripts. Few of us have that luxury, and I am not one of them. Many people aided in bring this book to fruition, and deserve mention at the beginning of this study.

First I want to thank my mentors; Rev. Ted Bartter for teaching me to take theology seriously, and Drs. Joseph Lynch and Ted Gregory at Ohio State University for teaching me not only how to "do" history, but how to be a historian. Rev. Bartter continued to introduce me to authors who were not only out of my denomination, but out of my discipline. He taught me that the truly wise person is the one who can hold two opposing opinions at the same time. Dr. Lynch's ever-ready, invaluable, council has allowed me to navigate through the sometimes difficult and sometimes unclear road to publishing an academic work.

I want to thank my dean at Payne Theological Seminary, Dr. Larry George, for his constant encouragement, not only through the writing, but the through the search for a publisher as well. His feedback on my writing style is especially appreciated.

Finally, I want to thank my family for listening to me try to explain what it was that I was doing, and giving me important insights into this neglected aspect of early Christian theology.

# Introduction

The early Christian ascetics were not the first to practice an ascetic lifestyle. A life of rigorous moral discipline, lived either publicly or privately, for either philosophical or religious reasons, practiced by both pagans and Jews, is fully attested to by the ancient writers. The writings of the Stoic pagans and the Essene Jews, as two examples, reveal a desire to live a life free from the passions of life. Broadly speaking, the Stoics practiced this ascetic life because it was the virtuous thing to do. It more readily allowed them to live lives of ἀπαθή. The Stoics decision to live this life had very little to nothing to do with the will of the gods. The Essenes' asceticism, on the other hand, arose out of a religious zeal, and was part of a belief system in which sexual asceticism was demanded by and pleasing to God.

An analysis, then, of the writings of pagan, Jewish, and Christians ascetics reveals enough differences in motives, practices, and goals with regards to sexual asceticism to dissuade an attempt at drawing a straight philosophical or theological line between either the pagans and Christians or the Jews and the Christians. And for these ascetics it is the issues surrounding virginity where some of the more evident differences are revealed.

Our evidence will reveal that in actual numbers, virginity was practiced by many more Christians than pagans or Jews. While the reports of hundreds and even thousands of Christian virgins living in their own homes and in communities throughout the Roman empire must be read cautiously, there is no corresponding evidence that virginity enjoyed the popularity among the pagans or the Jews that it did with the Christians. And while it can be assumed that there were pagans who practiced life-long virginity, there is no evidence to support a belief that it was widespread, or that it numbered in the thousands or even hundreds. The overwhelming majority of people living in the far-flung Roman empire lived lives which included marriage and children. This is what people had done for millennia. We have no evidence that the general populace was ever encouraged to commit to a life of virginity; to forgo marriage and children. Even the pagan ascetics do not call for people to remain virginal their entire lives. They simply urged people to live lives free of the controlling passions of greed and sex, which they believed would bring their lives into ruin.

While there is better evidence of Jewish virginity, it was confined to a segment of a small sect living in the southern Judean desert. Philo and Josephus, writing about the Essenes, indicate that virginity was practiced by the Essenes. And while that may be true, the Essenes literature itself, gives instruction to those in the community who are married and who have children. There is no evidence in any Jewish community, either Palestinian or diasporic, that people were expected or actually practiced life-long virginity.[1]

However, the evidence from Christian sources tell an entirely different story. The idea (or belief) that Christians could (or should) reveal their devotion to Jesus Christ through the renunciation of sexual relations appears in the first half of the first century. In chapter 7 of his first letter to the believers in Corinth, the Apostle Paul attempts to answer questions which have come to him concerning the practice of virginity.[2] In the second century Clement of Alexandria (c.150-215), the *Epistle of Polycarp* (c.150), Ignatius of Antioch (c.35–c.107), two epistles of Pseudo-Clement (2nd c.), and Tertullian (c.160–c.225) testify to the continued existence, and growth of virginity in the wider Christian communities in Asia, Africa and Europe. In the third century besides Origen (c.185–c. 254), Cyprian of Carthage (c.200–258) and Methodius of Olympus (d. c. 311) each write two documents on virginity. The great explosion of literature on virginity, however, appears in the fourth century represented by Ambrose (c.339-397), Ambrosiaster (late fourth c.), Basil of Caesarea (c.330–379), Cyril of Jerusalem (c.310–386), Epiphanius of Salamis (c.315–403), Eusebius of Caesarea (c.260–c.340), Gregory of Nyssa (c.330–c.395), Jerome (c.342–420), and John Chrysostom (c.347–407). Fifth century documents penned on virginity were written by Augustine (354–430), the pseudopigraphical *Epistle of Titus, the Disciple of Paul, on the State of Chastity* (early fifth c.), Pseudo-Athanasius (fifth c.), Severian of Gabala (d. after 408), Socrates Scholasticus (c.380–450), and Sulpitius Severus (c.360–c.420). And finally in the sixth century there are the letters of Caesarius of Arles (469/70–542) and Leander of Seville (c.540–c.600).[3]

Further evidence is testified by papal decrees and canons devoted to issues of virginity in early synods and ecumenical councils. Popes Damasus I (366-384), Siricius (384-399), Innocent 1 (401-417) and Leo 1 (440-461) issued decrees on clerical celibacy, as did the councils of Turin (398), Carthage (390), Orange (441), and Tours (461).

If we add to this already impressive evidence the insistence (or at the very least urging) of virginity among the Christian Marcionites, Montanists, Manicheans, Encratites, and Gnostics, we can conclude that the sexual practices of Christian believers, both catholic and non-catholic, were very much a part of the growing sexual ethos of the Christian movement.[4]

The Gnostics have left scholars an abundance of evidence which reveals their preference for virginity. The importance of this is that many of the Gnostic documents, where virginity is discussed, pre-date many of the catholic Christian documents concerning virginity. Questions of borrowing and influencing are discussed in ch. 5 around this issue.

When attention is given to the motives for committing to a life of virginity, the differences among the pagans, Jews and Christians is also evident. There is no evidence that pagan ascetics committed to a life of virginity because of a dramatic religious conversion experience. Nor is there evidence that pagan virgins made this decision based on an understanding that this is what the gods wanted. Most likely the decision to live a life free from the pull of lust and sex was based on ethical and/or moral considerations. This was a life that was pleasing to them, a life that was best for the local and wider communities, and one that was in keeping with the teachings of the philosophy to which they accepted and studied. It was a *reasonable* life which was relatively unaffected by the vicissitudes and whims of fate. It was steady, secure, and safe.

It is perhaps more difficult to ascertain the motives of the Essene virgins to commit to a virginal life. However, if we work from the commonly held belief in the ancient world that sexual intercourse was cultically polluting, and if the Essenes believed that they were the only covenant people of God, and that worship of God happened (at least partially) through cultic rituals, then we can arrive at a belief that sexual intercourse by the only covenant people of God would be polluting to the entire community that would be motive enough. Yet, since virginity was not practiced by the entire community, it is difficult to come to any firm conclusions about sexual practices to which all in the community assented.

The motives that lie behind the Christian practice of virginity are well attested to. And as the practice of virginity grew, and as more Christian authors turned their attention to virginity, the list of motives grew. These will be fully discussed in the book, but a short list here includes the desire to attain Christian perfection, escape the troubles of marriage and childbearing/childrearing, to receive abundant blessings from God, to imitate the virginity of Christ, Mary, and the angels, and to never be out of the presence of Christ. But perhaps the most compelling reason many of the Christians in the first six centuries chose virginity, was because of the growing belief that virgins were assured of salvation. By the time we arrive at the fourth century, a theology of

sex—a sexual hierarchy—had been informally developed; a theology which
had soteriological consequences. At the top of this hierarchy was virginity,
followed by chastity, then marriage, and finally fornication. By the fourth
centuryVirgins had almost reached divine, immortal status. Jerome even
promises the virgins that they will not die, but will pass onto another blessed
state; one of which only they, precisely because of their virginity, have access
to. Virgins, by the fourth century have become more blessed than the martyrs
of the first four centuries. They are holy saints, and as saints, they can intercede before God for their families and their communities. Some even speak
of virgins becoming saviours. Therefore, to hold out this possibility to women
(and most of the documents are addressed to women), who by the fourth century have little or no venues in which to publicly express their spirituality,
must have been a very powerful incentive to accept the virginal life. This was
a way to publicly express to God and to the rest of the Christian community
their absolute, complete undivided devotion to God. The virgins are promised
accolades in this life and the next.

   This was true not only for the catholic virgins, but for the Gnostic virgins
as well. Practicing virginity would be, for the ascetic Gnostics, a logical expression of their belief that all things of the "flesh" were polluted, fallen, and
a hindrance to rising through the divine eons to reach the divine γνῶσις, and
to become one with the Divine Λόγος.

   As with the numbers of virgins in the pagan, Jewish, and Christian communities, and as with the motives behind the adoption of virginity in these
three communities, the goals of each reveal a marked difference.

   Pagan virgins' goals often depended on the philosophy they followed. Neo-
Platonist virgins may have seen virginity as a way of reaching a higher state
of existence. Stoic virgins may have adopted virginity as a way of reaching
ἀπαθή. However, regardless of their specific goals, these pagan virgins
found the "normal life;" a life defined by marriage and children as unacceptable, and found virginity as the only way to escape the "troubles" associated
with that life.

   The Essene virgins viewed all of humanity as hopelessly fallen and unre-
deemable. They rejected the Judaism practiced by the various sects in Jerusalem,
Palestine and the Diaspora. The Temple in Jerusalem had been cultically polluted beyond cleansing, and they (the Essenes) were the only true Israel left.
Armed with this cosmology, the Essene leaders began to gather around themselves others of like faith. This cosmology also forced them to find a place to live
and practice their faith unmolested, and more importantly, untouched by the rest
of the fallen world. This need for isolation eventually found its way into their
theology and in the way they lived their everyday lives, which is expressed by
documents found in the caves above the Dead Sea. And since they were the only

true people of God, their lives had to be lived in different ways. One of the ways to differentiate themselves from the rest of fallen Israel was to systematically excise from their lives that which was common to the rest of the Israelites, including their sexual practices. These Essenes were following a pattern that exclusivistic, morally rigorous religious groups have displayed throughout history. Not only was the rest of Judaism theologically and cultically polluted, but they were morally polluted as well. Therefore, as a different people, some of the Essenes believed that one of the most significant ways of displaying their moral difference (superiority?) was to adopt, and even demand, virginity. Neither God nor the rest of the Essene community could doubt their level of commitment to this righteous, God-ordained, movement. Their righteousness was their gift to God, and their righteousness was best expressed by their commitment to virginity.

Achieving personal righteousness is part of the language that scholars use when exploring the goals of Christian virgins. As is language that speaks of separation from the "normal" world; a world that many early Christians also saw as unredeemingly fallen. The normal expectations of people living in this normal world was that they would marry and begin producing children. This life, however, and marriage in particular, came under an increasingly hostile attack from some within the Christian movement. The Christian writers supporting virginity were evangelical in their denunciation of marriage. And while they could not totally condemn marriage, when they compared it to virginity, marriage looked like the choice of the weak and less-committed Christian. God had not called Christians to this "normal" life, but to a better, superior life; a life completely devoted to God; a life undisturbed by the "cares" of a spouse and children; a life of continuous prayer, none of which was possible while engaging in sexual intercourse. The goal, then, of the Christian virgins was to establish themselves as a distinct people, over against the normalcy of this world.

A goal of all Christians, not just virginal Christians, was salvation; salvation from sin, from this world, and salvation to heaven. Christian virgins believed that that goal was best achieved through the adoption of virginity. At least from the second century Christians were being told that virginity was more pleasing to God than marriage. This led some to translate that proposition into this belief: "If virginity is more pleasing to God than marriage, and since I, as a Christian, want to please God, and since God rewards those who please Him, then I can win God's greatest approval by committing to virginity." Virginity then becomes meritorious, which, in fact, some of the authors explicitly state. Virginity, in this theological construct, becomes another good work. And, at least by the fourth century, "good works" were deeply embedded into most still developing soteriologies.

Finally, modern scholars are not in possession of enough reliable evidence to conclude whether the majority of early Christian virgins were male or female, but it bears repeating that most of the documents penned in support of virginity throughout the first six centuries were directed at women. If they were not specifically addressed to women, the language of the authors unmistakenly reveals that they had female virgins in mind. Further, by the very fact that these documents survived, implies that these epistles and letters had a wider reading than just single virgins. Someone or some ones found in these documents important beliefs that were valuable to all Christians, not just Christian virgins. Therefore, what was being said about virginity was read or heard by many eyes and ears.

In these documents, not only do we hear the praise of virginity, the warnings of abandoning virginity, and instructions to virgins, but we also hear a theology of gender. No one would be surprised if they found in these documents evidence of doubt concerning the commitment made by these female virgins. In spite of the praise and elevation of virgins; in spite of the glory and promises made to virgins, there is always present a worry that these virgins, because they are women, are unreliable. The readers and hearers of these documents are introduced to a hostility towards all women that these authors could not hide. Indeed, many did not even attempt to hide their attitudes, which range from patronizing to outright hostility. Warning after warning is issued to the female virgins of the danger of succumbing to even one thought of lust or self-righteousness.

Some modern scholars have suggested that many of these women chose virginity instead of marriage to escape the control of men; the common practice being that most women went from the control of their father to the control of their husband. However, the evidence clearly indicates that the early church Fathers, who took an interest in female virgins, had no intentions of allowing these "female" Christians to take control of their spirituality or their lives. Waves of instructions flow from the pens of these authors about how female Christians are to live; from what they are to wear, how they are to neglect any hygienic care for themselves, to what they are to think, what they are to read, what they are to pray, where they are to go and not to go, whom they are to be seen with, etc. And these instructions to the female virgins are not suggestions. They are in fact demands, the neglect of which, brought serious, divine retributions.

Females, simply, were not safe. By their very existence they were a temptation to men; especially men who had made a commitment to God. These men believed that because women were, by nature, sensual, lustful, tempting and alluring, that they were the instruments of Satan, used by Satan, to cause men to abandon their commitments to God. This included single unattached women, married women who regularly engaged in sexual intercourse with their husbands, and widows who had once tasted the pleasures of the flesh. Women who either could have sexual intercourse, were having sexual intercourse, or who had in the past had sexual intercourse were seen as dangerous. These women, because they were women, could at any time, fall under the control of their own womanness, and abandon themselves to the sexual lusts that constantly burned in them. And in the process they would take many men, even Christian men, into the flames of hell.

Therefore, virgins, were the only safe women. However, it was not enough for them to commit themselves to a sexless life; a commitment they publicly made to God and the Christian community, but they had to completely abandon their femaleness. Not only did they have to become sexually unavailable, but they had to change the very essence of their being. They, in fact, had to become spiritual males, for as males, they were safe. And we will hear many of the authors speak of how virgins have either created a new gender, or they have become men, for only men have the spiritual strength to maintain a commitment to virginity. Women, as women, could never make and maintain this commitment. Therefore, female virgins in the early church were "other." They were not like everyone else, and the traditions and myths that continued to grow around these virgins of God, were so powerful that they carried through the Middle Ages, Renaissance, Reformation, Age of Enlightenment, the Industrial Revolution, and still exist in the post-modern world of the twenty-first century.

## NOTES

1. Evidence for Essene virginity will be fully discussed in Chapter 2.

2. See 1 Cor 7.25–38. Most biblical scholars believe that Paul penned this letter before 50 C.E.

3. All of these authors and texts are referenced and documented in the book, and while some offer only passing reference to virginity, others write letters, epistles, and polemics devoted entirely to virginity.

4. Throughout this book the term "catholic" is to be understood as those writers and documents which either were or have been generally accepted as "orthodox" by contemporary or later Christian writers.

*Part One*

# VIRGINITY
# IN THE ANCIENT WORLD

## Chapter One

# Views of Virgins and Virginity in the Ancient Greek and Roman Writings

## THE GREEK WRITINGS

Peter Brown tells us that "virgin women . . . [were] part of the timeless religious landscape of the classical world,"[2] and it was in the context of the religious or the sacred that virgins most appear in the ancient Greek writings. While some Greek gods were sexually profligate (e.g. Aphrodite) and even sexually violent (e.g. Zeus), there existed goddesses who were virgins; (e.g., Athena, Artemis, Hestia, Atalanta, and Astraea). To serve these goddesses, virgin priestesses were selected for the shrines and temples dedicated to these virgin goddesses.[3] Their terms of service varied from place to place. The priestesses of Artimis Hymnia in Arcadia and the priestesses of Heracles at Thespiae in Boeotia were to remain virgins throughout their lives, while the priestesses of Artimis Triclaria at Patrae and the priestesses of Poseidon at Calaria were to remain virgins only until the age of marriage. While these women were, indeed, part of the "religious landscape," we must ask the question—what did these virgin women represent?

Giulia Sissa says that the priestess of Apollo "is not simply a case of Greek virginity; she discreetly fills a leading role."[4] While Sissa does not explain what this role is, Brown comments that "the message conveyed . . . was that their state [of virginity] was of crucial importance for the community precisely because it was anomalous. They fitted into a clearly demarcated space in civic society."[5] In a culture where there was a convergence of civic responsibility and religious observance, virgin priestesses filled both a civic and religious role. The priestesses acted as the mediators between the society and the goddesses. Mary Beard writes that that demarcated space was between the pure and the profane.[6] The everyday activities of the populace, even

3

the leaders of the communities, in some way(s), disqualified them from service in the presence of the goddesses. Louise Zaidman says that "purity, associated with chastity, was required of both priests and priestesses."[7] Evidence provided by the ancients strongly suggests that the activity which made the people unfit to come before the goddesses was sexual. Plutarch admonished the populace that the Pythia at Delphi must be a woman "pure of any carnal union and completely isolated throughout her life from all contact and relations with strangers."[8]

Friedich Hauck writes that in the early stages of the development of Greek religion the "system of purification was 'purely cultic' and not moral," and this "demand for cultic purity is dominant. The [person] who dares to approach deity must be careful not to violate it by anything contradictory," and that "only in a state of cleanliness can a [person] draw near to the deity"[9] However, "even in the cultic sphere the demand for moral purity is finally recognized as a presupposition for drawing near to deity."[10] Beard also notes that these priestesses needed to be perceived as holy, and that holiness was "directly related to their virginity and purity."[11] She goes on to say that in the ancient world "it is well known that [there existed a] popular belief that sexual activity was polluting and thus disqualified a person from close contact with the deity."[12] The sexual act was viewed as inherently polluting, even when it was practiced between a husband and wife. Therefore, since the various temples dedicated to the goddesses needed either priests or priestesses, and since contact with these gods required holiness and purity, and since sexual activity negated a persons holiness and purity, the priestesses, who were in constant contact with the gods, needed to be virginal as long as they served in their presence.[13] This virginity was practiced in the collective public eye and the anomalous nature of virginity being practiced by young women was never fully removed from the Greek consciousness. Therefore, "the presence in some cities of a handful of young girls, chosen by others, to forgo marriage, heightened an awareness of contemporaries that *marriage and childbirth were the unquestioned destiny of all other women*"[14] (emphasis mine). That which disqualified all other women from serving in the temples was their civic and moral duty—to both society and to family—to conceive and bear children. All respectable women filled some moral role. The virgin priestesses served a moral purpose for society by remaining sexually pure, and although the marital act was polluting vis-à-vis service to the goddesses, that same act was the moral responsibility of the married women.

However, the Greek religious pantheon was not populated only with virginal gods and goddesses. The creators of the Greek gods and goddesses were poets and storytellers whose lives extended over hundreds of miles, and hundreds of years. The myths concerning the gods, repeated orally in different dialects, in different places and in different times, expanded and contracted with each new generation of storytellers. These stories changed to meet the political and cultural needs or demands of the recipients and helped explain their present existence. The gods and goddesses were bigger than life and were able to be and do things that were beyond the pale of mere human existence. In spite of this, these stories echo the experiences of the Greek populace. Stories of uncontrollable lust, greed, rape, violence, abuse of power; arbitrary, erratic and even inconceivable decisions; revenge for slights real or imagined. These were stories that the people would understand, because they were stories that either they themselves or someone they knew had experienced. Many of the stories of the gods and goddesses were their own stories writ large.[25]

If the stories of the gods and goddesses reflect the Greek culture as it developed through the centuries and through contraction and growth, then one can assume that the stories concerning the gods and goddesses sexual activities, to some degree, reflect the sexual mores of the Greek populace. Greek writers from the creators of the *Iliad* and *Odyssey* to Hesiod, to the philosophers, poets, and historians of the classical age, to the Greek writers in the Hellenistic age, tell us stories that either reflect of the dreams and fantasies of the Greek people, or express their actual experiences. And woven through many of these stories are the dangers of giving over to sexual lust.

Therefore the state of virginity was "an elaborately contrived suspension of the normal process."[15] This point cannot be overstated. Throughout the history of Greece, from the heroic age through the age of Hellenism, young Greek women were expected to marry and bear children.[16] Virginity was "an eminently divine luxury that no mortal, male or female, can choose."[17] "Heroic Greek society demanded that all mature women be married and destined all young women for that end."[18] This story is reinforced by the story in the *Odyssey* of Odysseus urging Nausica to find a husband and enjoy a harmonious marriage. Gail Corrington says that "for women . . . marriage was not even a burden that might be assumed out of Stoic duty, but a necessity that was social, familial, and legal."[19] She argues that "responsible fathers in classical Athens did not raise female babies unless they foresaw a proper marriage for them at maturity,"[20] and gives as an example the funeral oration of Pericles where he "exhorted married women to bear more children."[21] Corrington even argues that "celibacy was an affront to the Greco-Roman social order."[22] When discussing the sexual regulations and laws attributed to Solon, Sarah Pomoroy notes that the "aim of marriage between citizens was the production of legitimate children," and that "the main purpose of their union was to produce an heir."[23]

Less traditional voices concerning marriage were heard from the philosophers. While "neither Epicurus nor Diogenes . . . favored conventional marriage

. . . Epicurus admitted that marriage could occur in special circumstances," and Diogenes begrudgingly "advocated a community of wives."[24]

Therefore, while it was always considered dangerous to give oneself over to any sort of lust, that belief did not translate into a cultural fearful of sexual activity. This was especially true of the upper classes. Brown writes that "Pagan and Christian alike, the upper classes of the Roman Empire in its last centuries lived by codes of sexual restraint and public decorum."[26] For these men, within the walls of their own homes, "fidelity to one's wife remained a personal option," [and] infidelity with servants was 'a thing which some people consider quite without blame, since every master is held to have it in his own power to use his slave as he wishes.'"[27]

Hippocrates, the ancient western world's earliest authority on medicine and health, encourages young women, after marriage, to engage in regular intercourse both for social and health reasons. Jody Rubin Pinault notes that, "Such Hippocratic treatises as *Diseases of Young Girls* were instruments of . . . socialization insofar as they encouraged young girls to marry at the proper time, that is, at menarche, by threatening them with the physical dangers they would risk if they did not."[28] Hippocrates in his work *On Virgins* says that "virgins who do not take a husband at the appropriate time for marriage . . . at the time of their first monthly period . . . [become] sluggish, and then, because of the sluggishness, numb, and then, because of the numbness, insanity takes hold of the woman."[29] These girls are warned of hallucinations and "these visions order her to jump up and throw herself into a well and drown, as if this were good for her and served some useful purpose."[30] The cure? "My prescription is that when virgins experience this trouble, they should cohabit with a man as quickly as possible. If they become pregnant, they will be cured."[31] In I.M. Lonie's translation and commentary on Hippocrates' treatises he notes that women who "have intercourse with men" experience better health "than if they do not."[32] The same was true for men. Brown writes that "at times, doctors might even council ejaculation, so as to relieve the body of the excessive deposits of seed that caused headaches and torpor. Health-conscious gentlemen made love, wrote Galen, even when the act gave them no particular pleasure."[33]

Soranus of Ephesus in *Gynecology*, wrote the first important Greek treatise challenging the views of Hippocrates on the advisability of sexual activity. However, unlike the Christian and gnostic writers who were beginning to advocate lifelong virginity for believers for moral, soteriological and spiritual reasons, Soranus' advise was for health reasons. Pinault tells us that Soranus "wrote that lifelong virginity was more healthful for women than childbearing, and that intercourse was harmful for both men and women."[34] That Soranus' views found later audiences is evidenced by three later Latin paraphrases in the fifth century by Theodorus Priscianus, Caelius Aurelianus and an author named Muscio,[35] the Greek medical compilers Oribasius (fourth century), Aetius (sixth century), and Paul of Aegina (seventh century), and "through Paul, in turn, Soranus' teaching passed into Islamic medicine."[36]

Although Soranus' work proved to be the standard for later writings on the health benefits of virginity, he was not the only Greek writer to praise abstinence. Other Greek writers praised virginity for reasons other than physical health. The fourth century Christian Jerome, in an attempt to prove that virginity is morally superior to marriage, says in his first letter against Jovinianus, that his position is not new to him or to Christianity. He states, "I will quickly run through Greek and Roman and foreign history, and will show that virginity ever took the lead of chastity."[37] Jerome then lists ancient women who heroically defended their virginity. Pinault reminds us that both Celsus (1st c. C.E.) in his *De Medicina* and Aretaeus praise continence.[38] Rufus of Ephesus, earlier in the second century, and Galen, later in the same century, wrote on the dangers of intercourse.[39] However, none of the pagan writers called for lifelong virginity as Soranus did. They simply warned of the deleterious effects of intercourse on the body. Further, we have no evidence that these warnings had any significant impact on the sexual practices of the Greek populace. We do not have in our possessions any evidence that groups of men or women, large or small, voluntarily turned away from marriage and intercourse.

There is evidence, however, which does speak to the growing asceticism of the second century C.E. practiced to one degree or another by Stoics, Neo-platonists, Neo-pythagoreans, and Epicureans. Corrington notes that "a third-century B.C.E. Pythagorean treatise enjoins chastity on married women . . . 'with respect to the marriage-bed.'" Brown notes that even for the married couple, "frequent sexual activity was frowned upon."[40] He points to Quintillion who insisted that "busy lawyers must practice, among other things, 'abstinence from sex.'"[41] Pinault quotes the Stoic Musonius Rufus who "justified intercourse only when it was used in marriage for the purpose of procreation."[42] The Stoic Seneca said that "although he had not broken off complete sexual abstinence, he observed a limit that was almost as strict as complete abstinence."[43] Corrington quotes the warning of Epicurus to his followers of the dangers of "sexual indulgence."[44] The Stoic attitude toward sexual activity is summed up by Brown in the following manner:

> The notion of eugenic sex committed both the man and the woman to
> codes of decorum in bed that were continuous with the public self. The Stoic

insistence that intercourse should happen only "according to nature" converged on this potent fantasy. For the Stoics intercourse was supposed to take place only so as to produce children. The couple must not make love for the sake of pleasure alone; even the positions that they adopted should only be those that enabled the seed to be "sown" to best effect. All other forms of lovemaking were a *tolmema*: they were "gratuitous acts." . . . The adoption of a variety of sexual positions was a form of playing around in the face of mankind's great Mother, "Nature": men invented other positions as a result of wantonness, licentiousness and intoxication.[45]

Matthew Black notes that for Pythagoreans celibacy "if not required, was at least highly esteemed."[46] Although Brown claims that there were philosophers who were "allowed" to practice "life-long celibacy," their numbers must have been small.[47] What one does not hear from these philosophers is a call for complete and total lifelong virginity.What we do hear from the literate representatives of these Hellenic philosophies is a call for a life that is not ruled by passions and sexual lust. Even Marcus Aurelius "a paragon of public sobriety, had 'given way to amatory passions' for a requisite, short time. Though a man of great austerity, he by no means considered himself to be bound to perpetual sexual abstinence."[48]

We can conclude from this evidence that the Greek populace, both men and women, simply did not choose lifelong virginity as a life style.They were expected to remain virginal only until their marriage. The evidence that women were expected to marry and bare legitimate children, for her husband, for her family, and for the state is abundant. We have also discovered, however, that these voices were not unanimous. The growing asceticism among the different philosophies urging chastity as a virtue, and the writings of Soranus of Ephesus testify to a changing political, philosophical and social ethos. How these views of virginity in the pagan Greek culture either resonated or differed with the emerging views of Christianity over the first five centuries will be discussed in later chapters.

## VIEWS OF VIRGINS AND VIRGINITY IN THE ANCIENT LATIN WRITINGS

In the ancient Roman culture, as in the ancient Greek culture, very few women had any degree of control over their lives, including their bodies. Aline Rousselle states unequivocally that "in the ancient Mediterranean world there was no room for choice [for women]: a woman did not choose celibacy, she did not choose marriage, and she did not choose remarriage after widowhood."[49] Roman women who married went directly from the control of their fathers to the control of their husbands. For women living in the Roman Empire this lack of self control extended, very often, from the cradle to the grave. As a point of fact "few women remained unmarried. Further, women did not choose when to marry" nor whom to marry.[50] "Marriage contracts were concluded between the bride's father and her future husband, and originally did not require her consent."[51] This is not to say that virginity was not valued in Roman society. But like the Greeks, outside of the virgins serving in the temples of the gods, virginity was valued only for newlywed brides. Rousselle states that "in late antiquity virginity was such an important aspect of a bride's character that it figured as a key element in various pagan romances."[52] It was understood that a woman's virginity ended on the wedding night.

It cannot be forgotten that "Roman law defined the purpose of marriage as procreation."[53] Both Tacitus[54] and Dio Cassius[55] both speak of marriage and the procreation . . . of children with little distinction. The Emperor Augustus, in 18 BCE, alarmed at the falling marriage rate, the growing number of divorces, and the increasing number of childless marriages, enacted laws to encourage marriage and the production of children.[56] Corrington says that marriage [in this period] became an issue which, according to Paul Veyne, "created the illusion of a marriage crisis, and a spread of [male celibacy]."[57] This illusory "crisis" was addressed by the Augustinian marriage-legislation which was "intended to direct the attention of good citizens toward their minimal obligation to the Roman state; producing children."[58] Suetonius in his *Life of Augustus* writes that Augustus reformed or overhauled laws dealing with "adultery and chastity, . . . and marriage of the various classes."[59] What is surprising about this passage from Suetonius is the reference to "chastity." If laws were passed to deal with real or perceived problems, then we can assume that Augustus was aware of a group of people (men and/or women?) who had chosen a chaste lifestyle. However, without further evidence that people choose to live chaste (virginal?) lives, we cannot say more.[60]

The populace's resistance to these laws is evidenced by Suetonius writing, "when [Augustus] found out that the law was being sidestepped through engagements to young girls and frequent divorces, he put a time limit on engagement."[61] Dio Cassius writes that Augustus "assessed heavier taxes on unmarried men and women, . . . and by contrast offered rewards for marriage and childbearing."[62] This penchant of the Romans to legislate peoples everyday lives extended to widows and divorcees.[63] Simply put, adult women were not just morally expected, but legally required to remain married and to produce children. Yan Thomas says that "in Rome men looked at women essentially as mothers."[64] This was not a mean title for "it carried with it honor, dignity, and even majesty appropriate to the civic, if not political, virtue of the function."[65] Whether the women of Rome felt honored is open to question. What they undoubtedly felt was the pressure to produce children.

The insistence on virginity for newlywed brides when coupled with the Roman's belief that "there was a scientific reason for girls to marry before puberty, namely, that early sexual relations facilitated the onset of menstruation" presents us with at least one picture of Roman sexual practices.[66] Emil Eyben states that according to ancient physicians, girls reached puberty at age fourteen,[67] and Rousselle notes that "women were expected to marry and have at least one child by the time they were twenty."[68] But they could not stop at one child, and three children, "for the census," by the time she was twenty was better. Rousselle tells us that "wives became anxious if children were slow in coming" and "sterile couples . . . visited temples and prayed to the gods for help."[69] When all of these pressures; legal, civic and familial, are brought together one hears of brides as young as ten and eleven, under the control of their husbands, wishing to fulfill their appointed role for god and country, dying, while giving birth, as young as thirteen.[70] The entire weight of Roman culture, then, mitigated against women choosing a life of perpetual virginity. Steve Mason notes that "the celibate life was too extreme for ordinary living, [and] it was a common assumption among Romans that marriage was unavoidable, though exclusively or mainly for the purpose of procreation."[71] Corrington reminds us that "Life-long celibacy was not an option in the social sphere from Solonic Greece to fourth-century Rome, since the woman's duty—indeed, a daughter's very reason for existence—was to marry and have children, thus assuring the preservation and proper transfer of private property."[72] Virginity, then, was not a choice that would have even occurred to most non-Christian women even well into the Christian era.

The Romans were not unlike the Greeks in demanding sexual purity of the priestesses that served in the temples. And it is an examination of the rituals and practices of the Vestal Virgins and the laws and traditions surrounding them that does give us an insight into Roman understandings of the intersection of the ideas of sexual purity and the gods.

Plutarch in his *Life of Numa Pompilius* gives the following account of both the institution of the Vestal Virgins, and the punishment for the virgins who break their vow of virginity.

10.1 At first they say that Gegania and Verenia were made priestesses by Numa, and next Canuleia and Tarpeia. Later Servius added two more, to bring the number up to what has been since that time. The king set the term of service for the holy virgins at thirty years; in the first decade they learn their duties, in the middle decade they do what they have learned, and in the third they teach others.

10.2 After that a virgin is free to marry if she wishes to or to adopt another style of life, once her term of service has been completed. But few are said to have welcomed this opportunity, and that matters did not go well for those who did, but rather because they were afflicted by regret and depression for the rest of their lives they inspired pious reverence in the others, so that they remained constant in their virginity until old age and death.

10.4 The Virgins' minor offences are punished by beating, which is administered by the Pontifex, with the offender naked, and in a dark place with a curtain set up between them. A Virgin who is seduced is buried alive near what is known as the Colline gate. At this place in the city there is a little ridge of land that extends for some distance, which is called a 'mound' in the Latin language.

10.5 Here they prepare a small room, with an entrance from above. In it there is a bed with a cover, a lighted lamp, and some of the basic necessities of life, such as bread, water in a bucket, milk, oil, because they consider it impious to allow a body that is consecrated to the most holy rites to die of starvation.

They put the woman who is being punished on a litter, which they cover over from outside and bind down with straps, so that not even her voice can be heard, and they take her through the Forum. Everyone there stands aside silently and follows the litter without a word, in serious dejection. There is no other sight so terrifying.

10.7 and the city finds no day more distasteful than that day. When the litter is borne to the special place, the attendants unfasten her chains and the chief priest says certain secret prayers and lifts his hands to the gods in prayer because of he is required to carry out the execution, and he leads the victim out veiled and settlers her on the ladder that carries her down to the room. Then he, along with the other priests, turns away. The ladder is removed from the entrance and a great pile of earth is placed over the room to hide it, so that the place is on a level with the rest of the mound. That is how those who abandon their sacred virginity are punished.[73]

We also have a description of the punishment of Vestal Virgins who have fallen in Sophocles' *Antigone*.

I will take her where the path is deserted, unvisited by men, and entomb her alive in a rocky vault, setting out a ration of food, but only as much as piety requires so that all the city may escape defilement. And praying there to Hades, the only god she worships, perhaps she will obtain immunity from death, or else will learn, at last, even this late, that it is fruitless labor to revere the dead.[74]

The actual rituals that were followed, the language to describe this punishment, and the uniqueness of the rituals that were scrupulously followed in carrying out the punishment reveal the importance of the Vestal Virgins maintaining their virginity and the sacredness of their virginity.

The first signal of the seriousness of this offense—engaging in sexual intercourse—is that it was in fact punishable by death. Ariadne Staples reminds us that "in no other instance that we know of was the transgression of a ritual injunction ever punishable by death."[75] Staples goes on to note that in a culture where "public, often gory, often lingering death, in battles, executions, or in the arena" stands in stark contrast to the manner of the death of the guilty Vestal Virgin.[76] In fact, she says that the entire spectacle is a construction of "an elaborate fiction—the fiction that the unchaste Vestal, who was killed for the loss of virginity, was not really killed at all."[77] The suspected Vestal was not executed in any traditional or expected manner. She was led to the underground chamber where she, alone, unaided, descended into the chamber, a chamber described as a habitable room, never to be seen again.

The uniqueness of the death of the suspected Vestal is further testified to by the fact that she was buried inside the walls of the city. This was an act specifically forbidden by Roman law, for it was believed that burials inside the walls of the city was polluting.[78] The Roman's belief that ritual pollution would bring the displeasure of the gods, which would bring disaster to the city, caused them to be meticulous about sacred rituals, which if not done correctly would cause the gods to remove their protection. Defeats of Roman armies and periods of political instability were often followed by suspicions that at least one of the Vestal Virgins had polluted herself and the State by engaging in sexual intercourse. Therefore, the "virginity of the Vestal was a powerful force," both politically and militarily.[79]

It can be argued, then, that upon the actual continuing virginity of these twelve women rested the continued existence of one of the most powerful empires of the ancient world. Rome must be right with its gods to continue to expand and dominate her world, and "the loss of a Vestal's virginity was a sign that all was not well with the state's relationship with its gods."[80] If Staples is correct in assuming that "in a ritual sense the Vestals were Rome,"[81] then she is also correct in stating that "a single lapse by a single priestess threatened the very existence of the state."[82]

This ritual and mystical relationship with the gods that these virgins possessed could only be maintained as long as they remained true to their vows of virginity. This is all the more remarkable when we understand that the virginity that the virgin priestesses who served in the Greek temples, and the Vestal Virgins who served in Rome, stood out, over against, in bold relief, the expected role of women, "in a [society] where procreation was of fundamental importance."[83] These women were in fact "defined by their virginity,"[84] and it was "on the[se] foundations of physical virginity [that there was] constructed an ideology of a unique religious function."[85] Beard agrees stating "great stress is laid on the physical virginity of the women and their total abstinence from sexual intercourse during their thirty or more years in the college."[86]

## NOTES

1. My intent, here is not to provide a full examination of virginity in these ancient cultures; it is to discover what roles virginity played in the societies in which Christianity developed its own views on virginity.

2. Peter Brown, *The Body and Society: Men, Women and Sexual Renunciation in Early Christianity* (New York: Columbia University Press, 1988), 8.

3. For an excellent discussion of the role of women in Greek cultic practices see Ruth Padel, "Women: Model for Possession by Greek Daemons," in *Images of Women in Antiquity*, ed. Averil Cameron and Amelie Kuhrt (Detroit: Wayne State University Press, 1983), 3-19.

4. Giulia Sissa, *Greek Virginity*, trans. Arthur Goldhammer (Cambridge, MA: Harvard University Press, 1990), 2-3.

5. Brown, *Body and Society*, 8.

6. Mary Beard, "The Sexual Status of Vestal Virgins," *The Journal of Roman Studies* 70 (1980): 12.

7. Louise Bruit Zaidman, "Pandora's Daughters and Rituals in Grecian Cities," in *A History of Women in the West*, vol. 1, *From Ancient Goddesses to Christian Saints*, ed. Pauline Schmitt Pantel, trans. Arthur Goldhammer (Cambridge, MA: The Belknap Press of Harvard University Press, 1992), 373.

8. Plutarch *On the Disappearance of Oracles* 438c.1-2.

9. Friedrich Hauck, "Katharos," in *Theological Dictionary of the New Testament*, vol.3, ed. Gerhard Kittle (Grand Rapids: Wm. B. Eerdmans, 1964), 415. He points to Hesiod's *Opera et Dies* 336f, and Homer's *Odyssey* as examples to support his argument.

10. ibid., 413-417. Hauck says, "moral purity seems not to have been demanded until a later period," and he cites Origen *Contra Celsum* 3.59. Hauck, "Katharos," 416, n.10.

11. Beard, "The Sexual Status of Vestal Virgins," 12.

12. ibid.

13. While daily worshippers were not required to be virgins, still the polluting effect of sex needed a few days to be removed. "Entry into a temple . . . might be forbidden to a person for two or three days after intercourse." Beard, "The Sexual Status of Virgins," 13.

14. Sissa, *Greek Virginity*, 9.

15. Brown, *Body and Society*, 9.

16. Sarah B. Pomoroy, *Goddesses, Whores, Wives and Slaves: Women in Classical Antiquity* (New York: Schocken Books, 1975), 18.

17. Nicole Loraux, "What is a Goddess?," in *A History of Women in the West*, vol. 1, *From Ancient Goddesses to Christian Saints* ed. Pauline Schmitt Pantel, trans. Arthur Goldhammer (Cambridge, MA: The Belknap Press of Harvard University Press, 1992), 22.

18. Pomoroy, *Women in Classical Antiquity*, 18.

19. Gail Corrington, "The "Divine Woman:" Propaganda and the Power of Celibacy in the New Testament Apocrypha: A Reconsideration," *Anglican Theological Review* 70 (July 1988): 214.

20. ibid.

21. ibid.

22. Pomoroy, *Women in Classical Antiquity*, 86-87.

23. ibid., 136.

24. ibid.

25. "Socrates and Plato had talked sublimely four hundred years before; but Lust and Murder were yet the gods of Greece, and men and women were like what they worshipped." From *Ante-Nicene Fathers*, vol. 2. cf. Clement of Alexandria *Exhortation to the Heathen* 2.

26. Brown, *Body and Society*, 22.

27. ibid., 23. From Musonius Rufus *Fragment* 12. Brown goes on to write that "in the pagan world of the second century A.D., a marked degree of tolerance was accorded to men, both on the matter of homosexuality and in their love affairs before and outside marriage." 29.

28. Jody Pinault, "The Medical Case for Virginity in the Early Second Century C.E.: Soranus of Ephesus, *Gynecology* 1.32," *Helios* 19 (1992): 129.

29. Hippocrates *On Virginity* 8.466-470.

30. ibid.

31. ibid.

32. I.M. Lonie, *The Hippocratic Treatises, "On Generation," "On the Nature of the Child," "Diseases IV": A Commentary* (New York: Walter De Gruyter, 1981), 13.

33. Brown, *Body and Society*, 20; from Galen *de locis affectis* 6.5.

34. Pinault, "The Medical Case for Virginity," 123.

35. ibid. Theodorus Priscianus' paraphrase is found in bk.3 of his *Euporista*. Pinault says that "Muscio's compendium of Soranus was widely read in the Middle Ages and was used in turn by later writers." 123.

36. ibid.

37. Jerome *Against Jovinianus* 1.41. Jerome does not ask his readers to take his word alone, and draws on the non-Christian writers Virgil, Seneca, and others to buttress his case. None of the other early Christian authors writing on virginity followed Jerome's lead in pointing to pagan experiences of virginity.

38. Pinault, "The Medical Case for Virginity," 127.

39. ibid.

40. ibid., 19; From Quintillian *Institutio oratoria* 11.3.19.4.

41. ibid., 23. From Musonius Rufus 12.

42. ibid. From Seneca *Epistle 108* to Lucilius.

43. Brown, *Body and Society*, 18.

44. ibid. From Diogenes Laetius 10.118.

45. ibid., 21.

46. Matthew Black, *The Scrolls and Christian Origins: Studies in the Jewish Background of the New Testament* (New York: Thomas Nelson and Sons Ltd, 1961), 29.

47. Brown, *The Body and Society* 7.

48. ibid., 29.

49. Aline Rouselle, "Body Politics in Ancient Rome," in *A History of Women in the West*, vol. 1, *From Ancient Goddesses to Christian Saints*, ed. Pauline Schmitt Pantel, trans. Arthur Goldhammer (Cambridge, Ma: The Belknap Press of Harvard University Press, 1992), 302.

50. ibid.

51. ibid.

52. ibid., 306.

53. ibid., 315.

54. Tacitus *Annals* 3.25.

55. Dio Cassius 54.16.1-2.

56. The *lex Julia de maritandis ordinibus*. These laws, including the ones spelling out the rather harsh punishments for adultery were later modified in the *lex Papia Poppaea.*

57. Paul Veyne, "The Roman Empire," in *A History of Private Life I: From Pagan Rome to Byzantium*, ed. Paul Veyne (Cambridge, MA: Harvard University Press, 1987), 38.

58. Corrington, "The "Divine Woman,"" 214.

59. Suetonius *Life of Augustus* 34.

60. The Roman rulers finally gave up on enforcing these laws, for Tertullian, tells us that "Severus, that most resolute of rulers, but yesterday repealed the ridiculous Papian laws which compelled people to have children." Tertullian *The Apology* 4.

61. ibid. One can only assume that the engagement to young girls was to postpone marriage and the birth of children.

62. Dio Cassius *History of Rome* 54.16.1. Dio Cassius understands that it is not just any children that Augustus wants, but legitimate children. Dio writes that Augustus "permitted anyone who wished (except for Senators) to marry freedwomen, and decreed that children of such marriages be legitimate." ibid. That Augustus was interested in legitimate children is also reflected in the fact that The *lex Julia* spent as much time on adultery as it did on marriage.

63. The Roman's inability to allow adult women who were not either slaves or prostitutes to remain unmarried is seen by their insistence that widows were to remarry within a year; divorcees within six months.

64. Yan Thomas, "The Division of the Sexes in Roman Law," in *A History of Women in the* West, vol. 1, *From Ancient Goddesses to Christian Saints*, ed. Pauline Schmitt Pantel, trans. Arthur Goldhammer (Cambridge, Ma: The Belknap Press of Harvard University Press, 1992), 117.

65. ibid., 88.

66. ibid., 304.

67. Emil Eyben, "Antiquity's View of Puberty," *Latomus* 31 (1972): 678-679.

68. Rousselle, ""Body Politics in Ancient Rome," 316.

69. ibid.

70. cf. Rousselle pp. 316-317.

71. Steve Mason, "What Josephus Says About the Essenes in his *Judean War*, " in *Text and Artifact in the Religions of Mediterranean Antiquity: Essays in Honor of*

*Peter Richardson*, ed. Stephen G. Wilson and Michel Desjardins (Waterloo: IA: Wil-frid Laurier University Press, 2000), 434-467.

72. Corrington, "The Divine Woman," 212.

73. Plutarch *Life of Numa Pompilius* 10.1-7.

74. Sophocles *Antigone* 774-780.

75. Ariadne Staples, *From Good Goddess to Vestal Virgins* (New York, NY: Rout-ledge Publishing, 1998), 132.

76. ibid., 131.

77. ibid., 133.

78. *The Twelve Tables* 10.1

79. Staples, "From Good Goddess to Vestal Virgins," 135.

80. ibid., 129.

81. ibid., 130

82. ibid., 135.

83. ibid., 130.

84. ibid., 132.

85. ibid., 135.

86. Mary Beard, "The Sexual Status of Vestal Virgins," *The Journal of Roman Studies* 70 (1980): 15-16. It is interesting that earlier in the same article Beard notes that some "argue that the type of virginity represented by the Vestals is not virginity in the sense of total abstinence from sexual intercourse, but rather chastity of a iniver-ate Roman matron, a quality defined by her fidelity to a single husband and by sober-ness of conduct and dress." ibid., 14. However, the weight of the evidence for total abstinence does not allow this argument to stand.

*Chapter Two*

# Views of Virgins and Virginity in the Ancient Jewish Writings

An understanding of virgins and virginity in the Jewish culture comes from an analysis of five primary sources, i.e., the Hebrew Scriptures, rabbinic literature, the *Testaments of the Twelve Patriarchs*, the literature produced by the Essene communities, and Josephus and Philo. As we work through these sources we will discover that throughout the history of the ancient Jewish culture, young Jewish men and women (post-mense) were expected to marry and produce children. In the *Interpreter's Dictionary of the Bible* we read the following:

> Sons are needed in order to preserve the father's name and personality. Thus sex relations are important to the family or clan group, even as the birth of a child is hailed by the entire community (Ruth 4.14, 17). One finds no condemnation of sex in the sources, for it is viewed as fundamentally good in serving an essential societal purpose which is at the same time deeply personal. The function of sex in preserving the perpetuating the family name motivates a vigorous biblical reaction to its abuse and perversions.[1]

What is of interest is that unlike the Greek and Roman literature on virginity, the Jewish writings on virginity are not always directed toward women, nor are they even primarily directed toward women, but often are directed toward men.

## VIRGINITY IN THE HEBREW SCRIPTURES

Although the Hebrew word *betulot* literally means " a young woman of marriageable age," the context of its appearances in the Hebrew Scriptures strongly suggest a translation of "virgin." The authors of the Pentateuch use the words "virgin" and "virginity" to refer to physical virginity, and the prophetic writings use these same terms metaphorically to refer to either entire nations or peoples. The authors of Isaiah speak of the "virgin daughter of Sidon" (23.12), the "virgin daughter of Zion" (37.22), and the "virgin daughter of Babylon" (47.1). These collective nouns were used to speak of peoples or nations who had fallen, and were in danger of divine judgment. These virgin daughters are described as oppressed (23.12), who have no rest (23.12), who sit in the dust and on the ground without a throne (37.22), who are despised and scorned (47.1), and who shall no more be called tender and delicate (47.1). It is curious that these fallen nations and peoples were called "virgin daughters." One might suspect that these peoples who had fallen under judgment would have earned the name "prostitute" as the fallen people of God did in Hosea. (see Hos 1.2; 4.12-19).

The author of Jeremiah and Lamentations repeatedly mourns the fate of "the virgin daughter of my people" (14.17), "virgin Israel" (18.13), and the "virgin daughter of Zion" (Lam 2.13). He calls on "virgin Israel" (31.4,21) to return to God so that He may "build you" (31.4). He urges "virgin Israel" to adorn herself with timbrels (31.4), to go forth in the dance of the merrymakers (31.4), and return to her cities (31.21). He even calls on the "virgin daughter of Egypt" to "go up to Gilead and take balm" (46.11).[2]

A number of interpretations are possible for this use of the term "virgin" to describe nations during the time of the prophets (ca. 800-600 B.C.E.); for these authors the idea of virginity is no longer just an ideal for individual unmarried maidens. In these passages from Isaiah, Jeremiah, and Lamentations, Israel and other nations (e.g., Egypt and Babylon) have been raised up by God, and are to be, in some sense, like virgin daughters; pure and undefiled. It is in this state of virginity—in this state of purity—that these nations find God's favor. These nations, when in a state of virginity, are virginal for God. These verses in the Hebrew Scriptures are a coupling of the idea of virginity and the divine; a coupling that we have already seen in both the Greek and Roman cultures.

However the majority of the authors of the Hebrew Scriptures who speak of virginity speak of it in a literal, physical sense. The importance of young women remaining virginal until marriage is found in several passages in the Pentateuch. In these passages it becomes clear that pre-marital virginity is important not just for the individual woman, but for her family and for the community. G. Ernest Wright writes that "chastity is stressed more strongly than might have been expected at the time. The standards of physical purity were much higher in Israel than among the neighboring peoples."[3] Tikva Frymer-Kensky argues that "at all periods, girls living in their father's house were expected to be chaste."[4] For the young girls of Israel this was a state of being that was to be valued and protected, and those who would assume to violate that virginity were severely punished. The authors of Exodus, Leviticus, and Deuteronomy speak of the punishment of those who "seduce" (Ex 22.16-17), "defile" (Lev 21.13-14), or "violate" (Dt 22.23-24, 28-29) virgins. In some cases the violators were to compensate the father of the girl who had been violated. In other cases he was to be stoned. If the girl was an unwilling participant in this act she was forced to marry the man who defiled her, and he was to pay an unspecified amount of money called the "bride price" for the use/abuse of the young woman. Walter Brueggeman notes that "the law pays no attention to the violated woman herself, and in that regard, the settlement with the father is not unlike the other cases of retribution for 'the owner.'"[5] If, however, the girl was a willing participant she was to be stoned, publicly, by the elders of the city, at the door of her father's house. Baab says that "because of her sexual function in a patriarchal society, a women's violation of law and custom received harsher treatment than that of her male counterpart who might be involved in the same situation."[6] The reason the young woman was publicly stoned by the men of the city was because "she has wrought folly in Israel by playing the harlot in her father's house; so you shall purge the evil from the midst of you" (Dt 22.21).

While it was possible for the men of Israel to marry widows, divorcees, women who had been defiled or were even harlots, this was expressly forbidden for priests. The priests of Israel, the men who handled the things of God, i.e., sacrifices, incense, blood, showbread, etc., and who daily entered into the Holy Place of the Sanctuary, were instructed to "take a wife in her virginity." (Lev 21.13-14). The priests of God could not allow themselves to be "one" sexually with a woman who had previously been "one," sexually, with another man. From this perspective sexual activity was not polluting, but sacred. Sexual activity, in marriage, with a virgin, was acceptable. Any other sexual arrangements were not acceptable, and disqualified the priests from ministering before God.

While it is tempting to make some comparisons between the demands for sexual purity between the priestesses of the Greek and Roman temples, and the priests of Israel, there are major differences that must be kept in mind. First, the priests of Israel were priests and not priestesses. Women were forbidden to represent the Hebrew God, cultically, to His people. Secondly, priests were not demanded nor encouraged to be virginal. Leviticus 21 urged priests to marry. They only needed to be careful about whom they married, because the office of the priesthood was inherited from one generation to the next, and the priests were expected to produce legitimate, male heirs with their wives. If the wives were not virginal before marriage, there was always the possibility that the fist child was not the husband's. And if the first child was a male, the possibility existed that an illegitimate heir could be mediating between God and God's people. That would have been unacceptable.

All of the political and religious leaders of the Jews—prophets, priests, and kings—were eligible to be married and had children. There are no texts in the Hebrew Scriptures which call for a life of virginity. Babb tells us that while "sexual intercourse took place principally for the procreation of children," it was also practiced for "mutual pleasure."[7] Even the Nazarites, who were set apart for service to God, were not required to be celibate.

Just as the leaders of the Jewish people were not expected to remain unmarried or celibate, neither was the general populace. The command to "be fruitful and multiply" was never rescinded. Even when God "repented" from creating humankind and reduced the number of humans to eight, they were not instructed to become virginal and cease procreation. Marriage and procreation were the expected norms for the Jewish people. Ronald Ecker says that "since Hebrew men and women were expected to get married and have children, and since the enjoyment of sex was encouraged with the confines of marriage . . . the idea of lifelong virginity as a virtue was foreign to the biblical Hebrews."[8] Gordon Fee notes that in the Jewish culture "marriage was not only normal but in some cases viewed as next to obligatory."[9] H.M. Orlinsky argues that "the concept of virginity is not as significant in ancient Israel (or in the ancient Near East generally, including Greece and Rome) as it became in the post-biblical period and in Christian thought in particular."[10] Black writes that "sexual relations (by which is clearly meant marriage) are assumed to be the norm at the time of full moral maturity when the young 'Israelite' is admitted as a full member of the community."[11] He goes on to say that for Judaism postponement of marriage "was . . . most irregular, if not totally unheard of."[12] O.J. Baab writes that for the Israelites, God "is the source of sexuality and demands its use for the perpetuation of his people and the glory of his name."[13] Frymer-Kensky sums up this argument as follows:

> The Bible considers a strong marital unit essential to societal well-being, with sex cementing the marital bond . . . Intact families demand sexual fidelity, and the best way to ensure this is to find sexual satisfaction in marriage: "Find joy in the wife of your youth . . . let her breasts satisfy you at all times, be infatuated with love of her always." (Prov 5.18-19).[14]

## VIRGINITY IN EXTRA-BIBLICAL LITERATURE

### Rabbinic literature

The evidence from Rabbinic literature suggests that not only is marriage the norm for both man and women, but that the act of marriage has both salvific and gender identity implications. We find the author of *b. yeb* in 63b saying that,

"R. Hama b. Hanina stated: As soon as a man takes a wife his sins are buried; for it is said: 'Whoso finds a wife finds a great good and obtains favor of the Lord.'"[15] In 63a he says, "R. Eleazar said: Any man who has no wife is no proper man; for it is said, 'Male and female created he them and called their name Adam.'"[16] *Midrash Rabba: Genesis* 21.1 goes even further. It declares:

> He who does not engage in procreation of the race is as though he sheds human blood. When Adam saw his offspring were fated to be consigned to Gehenna, he refrained from procreation. But when he saw that . . . Israel would escape the Law, he applied himself to producing descendants.[17]

The *Babylonian Talmud: Baba Bathra* 60b reads:

> Concerning the man who loves his wife as himself, who honors her more than himself, who guides his sons and daughters in the right way, and arranged for them to be married around the period of puberty, of him it is written: "You will know that your tent is at peace.[18]

## The Testaments of the Twelve Patriarchs

Although there are calls for asceticism found in the *Testimonies of the Twelve Patriarchs*, they have no basis in the Torah and may be later Christian glosses. The call for self-control and self-discipline in the *Testament of Naphtali* was not a call for a life of virginity.[19]

## Essene Literature

The only exception to this weight of evidence is found in the writings concerning the Essene communities. No one doubts that the Essenes were ascetics. But the question of virginity among the Essenes rests on seemingly contradictory evidence. Josephus writes, "[The Essenes] shun pleasures as a vice and regard temperance and the control of passions as a special virtue."[20] Because Josephus says that the Essenes "do not conclude marriages,"[21] and Philo insists that "no Essene takes a woman,"[22] and Pliny the Elder writes that the Essenes have "no women and [have] renounced all sexual desire,"[23] it is not surprising to hear some modern scholars, including Emil Schurer, say that the Essenes "entirely condemned marriage."[24] Schurer goes on to say that "[The Essene's] repudiation of marriage is indeed a matter quite heterogeneous to genuine Judaism,"[25] and sums up his argument as follows:

> For since the act of marriage as such made an individual unclean and necessitated a Levitical bath of purification, the effort to attain to the highest degree of purity might well lead to the entire repudiation of marriage. In all these points a

surpassing of ordinary Judaism is apparent, and this is also the case in the strongly puritanical trait, by which the Essenian mode of life is characterized.[26]

Further, Steve Mason reads Josephus as saying that the Essenes are a "very impressive *celibate* group, whose special virtue springs precisely from their *celibate* communities." (emphasis mine).[27]

The claim that the Essenes were celibate is further supported by Ita Sheres and Anne Blau who suggest that the immaculate conception of Aseneth in the Egyptian pseudopigraphic romance of *Joseph and Aseneth* has its origin in the fragmentary *Marriage Ritual* from Qumran. They argue that "the roots of this creative tale go back to Qumran and the sectarians who were searching for a way to wipe out 'pollution' and 'iniquity' . . . and that [the legend] was constructed as a poplar gloss on exotic, secret practices a Qumran."[28]

Tales of immaculate conceptions are found in many of the religious myths of the ancient world. This is especially true of the mystery religions, many of which found homes in Egypt. Sheres and Blau admit to calling "on some particulars in Egyptian mythology from the era to help uncover the true meaning of *Joseph and Aseneth*."[29] However, they do not explain how a piece of fragmentary literature from an obscure Jewish sect in Palestine found its way to Egypt and was used to construct a story concerning immaculate conception. They also admit that "no scroll of *Joseph and Aseneth* has yet been identified among the Dead Sea Scrolls."[30] They could also say that no Essene documents have yet to turn up in Egypt.

Despite the efforts of Josephus, Philo, and modern scholars' attempts to place the Essenes in the camp of celibate ascetics, Helmer Ringgren points out the following:

> The *Rule of Congregation* speaks of women and children and gives instructions concerning the age one should have reached before having sexual intercourse. *The Damascus Document* also assumes communities of families with women and legislates concerning the cases in which "they take wives according to the law and beget children."[31]

Black, in agreeing with Ringgren , says that "in the Appendix to the *Manual [of Discipline]*, in the so-called *Rule of the Congregation*, marriage and family life are contemplated as the norm, as in every other Jewish community."[32] Further, while Mason dismisses Josephus' category of marrying Essenes out-of-hand, Ringgren proposes that there were "different groups within the community which had different attitudes toward [the question of marriage.]"[33] Jane Simpson, while noting that "the majority of Essenes shunned marriage" she does not rule it out.[34] Finally Millar Burrows proposes that "the sect included both communities of celibates and settlements of families,"[35] and adds *"The Rule of Congregation* assumes that there will be families in the community of 'the last days.'"[36]

## NOTES

1. O.J. Baab, "Sex," in *The Interpreter's Dictionary of the Bible*, vol. 4 (New York: Abingdon Press, 1962), 297.

2. We also hear of virgins being defiled in the later writings of Judith (9.2, 27), Sirach (42.10.3), and 2 Esdras (10.22.72).

3. G. Ernest Wright, "Deuteronomy," in *The Interpreter's Bible* (Nashville: Abingdon Press, 1953), 464.

4. Tikva Frymer-Kensky, "Sex and Sexuality," in *The Anchor Bible Dictionary* (New York: Doubleday Publishing, 1944), 1145.

5. Walter Brueggeman, "Exodus," in *The New Interpreter's Bible* (Nashville: Abingdon Press, 1994), 867.

6. Babb, "Sex," 299.

7. ibid., 300.

8. Ronald Ecker, *And Adam Knew Eve: A Dictionary of Sex in the Bible*, Nov 2001, <http://www.hobrad.com/and.htm>.

9. Gordon Fee, *The First Epistle to the Corinthians* (Grand Rapids: William B. Eerdmans Publishing, 1987), 332.

10. H.M. Orlinsky, "Virgin," in *The Interpreter's Dictionary of the Bible* (Nashville: Abingdon Press, 1976), 939.

11. Black, *The Scrolls and Christian Origins*, 28-29.

12. ibid., 29.

13. Baab, "Sex," 300.

14. Frymer-Kensky, "Sex and Sexuality," 1144.

15. Fee, *The First Epistle to the Corinthians*, 332, n.43.

16. ibid.

17. *Midrash Rabba: Genesis* 21.1; quoted in Brown, *Body and Society*, 63.

18. *Babylonian Talmud: Baba Bathra* 60b. Quoted in Brown, *Body and Society*, 63.

19. *Testament of Naphtali* 8.8.

20. Josephus *Bellum Judaicum* 2.8.2.

21. Josephus *Antiquities* 18.21.

22. Philo *Apologia* 14.

23. Pliny the Elder *Natural History* 5.15.73.

24. Emil Schurer, *The History of the Jewish People in the Age of Jesus Christ (175 BC–AD 135)*, trans. T.A. Burkhill (Edinburgh: Clark, 1973), 211.

25. Schurer, *The History of the Jewish People*, 211.

26. ibid.

27. Steve Mason, "What Josephus Says About the Essenes in His *Judean War*," in *Text and Artifact in the Religions of Mediterranean Antiquity: Essays in Honor of*

*Peter Richardson*, ed. Stephen G. Wilson and Michel Desjardins (Waterloo, IA: Wilfrid Laurier University Press, 2000) 434.

28. Ita Sheres and Anne Blau, *The Truth About the Virgin: Sex and Ritual in the Dead Sea Scrolls* (New York: Continuum Publishing, 1995), 94.

29. ibid., 95.

30. ibid., 94.

31. Helmer Ringgren, *The Faith of Qumran: Theology of the Dead Sea Scrolls*, ed. James H. Charlesworth, trans. Emilie T. Sander (New York: Crossroad Publishing, 1995), 140.

32. Black, *The Scrolls and Christian Origins*, 28.

33. Ringgren, *The Faith of Qumran*, 140.

34. Jane Simpson, "Women and Asceticism in the Fourth Century: A Question of Interpretation," *The Journal of Religious History* 15 (June 1988): 40.

35. Millar Burrows, *The Dead Sea Scrolls* (New York: Viking Press, 1955), 233.

36. Millar Burrows, *More Light on the Dead Sea Scrolls* (New York: Viking Press, 1958), 383.

## Chapter Three

# Christian Virginity
# and Its Interpretations

### THE NEW TESTAMENT

The Greek word *parthenos* is found fourteen times in the New Testament; four times in the Gospel of Matthew, three times in the Gospel of Luke, once in Acts, four times in I Corinthians, once in II Corinthians, and once in Revelation. The only virgins in the New Testament that are named are Mary, the mother of Jesus, who is identified as a virgin in Mt 1.23, and twice in Lk 1.27, and the prophetess Anna in Lk 2.36 who is said to have "lived with her husband seven years after her marriage."[1] The four virgin daughters of Philip the Evangelist are mentioned, almost in passing, in Acts 21.9, but not named.

There are a number of texts in the New Testament where a virgin or virgins are used in parables or as metaphors. In Mt. 25 Jesus says that "the kingdom of heaven will be comparable to ten virgins, who took their lamps, and went out to meet the bridegroom." In this parable, as in all of the parables of Jesus, the characters are not meant to be actual persons, but are used as metaphors for pedagogical purposes. In II Cor 11.2 a "chaste virgin" is used as a metaphor for the church whom Paul will present to the Bridegroom Christ. And in Rev 14.1-4 there are 144,000 men who the author of Revelation, in vision, describes as standing on Mt. Zion with Christ, the name of Christ and His Father on their foreheads, singing a new song before the throne of God. Further, these men do not lie, are blameless, and have not defiled themselves with women, for they are virgins. These men, in this apocalyptic vision, are the redeemed for they "are purchased from the earth."

What can be learned from these various passages concerning the understanding of virginity in New Testament Christianity? Let us begin with the Virgin Mary.

Stephen Benko, in his article "Second Century References to the Mother of Jesus" says that "it is well known that none of the Mary doctrines of the Roman Catholic Church can be documented from this early period."[2] Wolfgang A. Bienert agrees, and sums up the problems the modern researcher faces in any attempts to reconstruct the importance of the mother of Jesus in early Christianity, and in particular early Christian views of her virginity.

> The number of contributions to research on Mary and the beginnings of Mariology stands in inverse relationship to what we possess in the way of historically reliable tradition[s] about the mother of Jesus. Later dogmatic decisions about the mother of God and the 'perpetual virgin'—the terms are attested from the 4th century on—have overlaid the original picture and made it almost unrecognizable. In any attempt to recover this original picture—at least in its basic features—it must here also be noted, as recent research has strongly emphasized, that even our oldest sources already reflect the theological interests of their respective authors.[3]

This assessment would, of course, include those early Christian writers who were interested in using the virginity of Mary to buttress their arguments for virginity in the early Christian communities. This is in contrast to the New Testament authors who are almost completely silent about the mother of Jesus, and are only slightly interested in her virginity. Beinert points out that while the oldest documents from the New Testament, the letters of the Apostle Paul, do not even mention the name of Mary, the earliest reference in the Gospel of Mark (6.3) only mentions her in passing, and her virginity is not mentioned at all.

It is in the Gospel of Luke that we find the virginity of Mary being integral to the story of the miracle of the virgin birth of Jesus. But Benko argues that even in two of the earliest commentaries on the incarnation (from Irenaeus and Origen) "the Incarnation [itself] is the significant event. Everything around it has peripheral importance only. The person of Mary is important only so far as she is that 'human womb' through which the incarnation took place. The virginity of Mary is important only so far as it is the *sign* of the Messiahship of Jesus."[4]

Two other second century fathers, Tertullian and Hilarius, in commenting on the encounter of Jesus with his mother and siblings as he was teaching, say that Mary, in this story, represents the synagogue, and her virginity is not mentioned at all. Therefore, it is "later traditions, . . . above all . . . the addition of the infancy narratives, in which Mary emerges from this shadow and gains a positive significance, while at the same time her importance for the history of salvation is given a stronger emphasis."[5] The other second century Christian writers who do mention Mary (Ignatius, Justin, and Irenaeus)[6] do so in connection with the incarnation. Benko concludes, then, that "the second century Fathers " were interested in [Mary] merely as the mother of Jesus . . . [and] all references to Mary were made only in connection with Jesus."[7]

## THE QUESTION OF MARRIAGE

Although this book is principally about the views of virginity in the early church, much of the early Christian literature that discusses virginity does so in the context of virginity *vs.* marriage. We have discovered in our analysis of virginity in the Greek and Roman literature that, outside of virgins dedicated to the temples of the gods, young men and women married at an early age, and began to raise a family. We have no literary evidence from these cultures that the general populace was ever asked to make a choice between marriage or life-long virginity. Likewise, in the Hebrew Scriptures all young men and women were expected to marry and raise families. And while Matthew Black and Emil Schurer have chosen to believe Philo and Josephus's argument that the Essenes were celibate, the evidence from the Essene literature itself proves that, while the Essenes practiced an ascetic lifestyle, married couples with children were part of the community.[8]

In the New Testament marriage is often used as part of a parable (Mt 22.1-14), to help illustrate a particular teaching (Rom 7.1-6), or to symbolize the union between Christ and His people (Eph 5.22-33;[9] Rev 19-7-9). In other places Jesus teaches about divorce and adultery (Mt 5.31-32; 19.1-9 (cf. also Mk 10.1-16; Lk 16.18). In Eph 5.22, Col 3.18, and 1 Pet 3.1 wives are counseled to be submissive to their husbands. In all of these texts, written by Christians to other Christians, marriage is not seen as something that needs to be avoided or shunned. Marriage is part of the landscape of which all the readers of the New Testament would recognize, and although the teachings about divorce and how husbands and wives are to treat each other may sound somewhat different to some, these teachings are certainly not completely foreign to the general populace.

## THE CASE FOR VIRGINITY IN 1 CORINTHIANS 7

The other New Testament text that speak of virginity, marriage and/or wives — 1 Cor 7—however, merits more than a cursory notice, and is perhaps the most significant for our purposes. Brown asserts that "the forty highly condensed verses that made up the seventh chapter of [Paul's] First Letter to the Corinthians have been justly acclaimed as 'the most important in the entire Bible for the question of marriage and related subjects.'"[10]

What we find in I Cor are the earliest Christian discussions concerning virginity and its relative merits vis-à-vis marriage and salvation.

That there were Christian virgins in Corinth is obvious from the text, and that these virgins, both male and female, were the subject of a letter received by Paul is also clear by part of Paul's response in ch.7. We cannot assume from this letter, being written no more than 20-25 years following the death of Jesus, that there was a recognized community of virgins, the likes of which we hear of in later documents on virginity. It is far more probable that there were simply individual virgins who were part of the Corinthian congregation. It also seems unlikely that any of the new Christian congregations would have had the time or luxury to organize themselves or develop a sophisticated theology which dictated the sexual morality of the believers. Still, there certainly were ascetics in Corinth. Ross Kraemer says that "the rise of asceticism in early Christianity apparently dates from the earliest communities, but the degree to which it prevailed, either in theory or practice, varied from community to community, from region to region, and from time to time."[11] It also appears that these ascetics seemingly were already attempting to impose their understanding of Christian sexual ethics on the rest of the community. Working from Paul's response to the letter he received, it can be suggested that these ascetics were demanding unmarried Christians to remain unmarried and virginal, and that married couples were to refrain from future sexual contact.

What we do not know is to what or to whom these ascetics were pointing to to support their views. The canonical gospels were not yet written, and most New Testament scholars agree that the only genuine Pauline epistle written before 1 Corinthians was 1 Thessalonians, where the believers are given the general caution to "abstain from sexual immorality." (1 Thess 4.2). Even if the Corinthian ascetics appealed to the Hebrew Scriptures, a favorite tool of early Christian writers, to find support for a commitment to lifelong virginity and marital celibacy based on religious beliefs, they would have found no resonance there. It is also too early to talk about an ascetic Christian gnostic influence.

What the Corinthian ascetics were attempting to create was a culture completely foreign to the social and religious cultures in which early Christianity grew. And even if the ascetics in Corinth were calling for this lifestyle based on their belief that the return of Jesus Christ was eminent, it does not explain why Christians from the second century on continue to call for a life of lifelong virginity, when it was clear that the expected second coming of Christ was not close at hand. And yet it is interpretations of Paul's response to the questions of the Corinthians in the first century that later supporters of lifelong virginity base their arguments.

Therefore, either the ascetics are looking to Paul to support their views on celibacy and virginity, or others in Corinth, who were opposing the ascetics, were seeking answers from Paul on these teachings. The more likely scenario is that some of the Corinthian Christians were demanding an asceticism which was so severe that it was causing anxiety and strife in the church.[12] Paul attempts to respond to these concerns, and, as we will later discover, his responses are interpreted and used by later Christian authors to construct a soteriological paradigm centered on the practice of virginity.

1 Corinthians 7 reads:

> Now concerning the things of which you wrote to me: It is good for a man not to touch a woman. Nevertheless, because of sexual immorality, let each man have his own wife, and let each woman have her own husband. Let the husband render to his wife the affection due her, and likewise also the wife to her husband. The wife does not have authority over her own body, but the husband does. And likewise the husband does not have authority over his own body, but the wife does. Do not deprive one another except with consent for a time, that you may give yourselves to fasting and prayer; and come together again so that Satan does not tempt you because of your lack of self-control. But I say this as a concession, not as a commandment. For I wish that all men were even as I myself. But each one has his own gift from God, one in this manner and another in that. But I say to the unmarried and to the widows: It is good for them if they remain even as I am; But if they cannot exercise self-control, let them marry. For it is better to marry than to burn with passion.
>
> Now to the married I command, yet not I but the Lord: A wife is not to depart from her husband. But even if she does depart, let her remain unmarried or be reconciled to her husband. And a husband is not to divorce his wife. But to the rest I, not the Lord, say: If any brother has a wife who does not believe, and she is willing to live with him, let him not divorce her. And a woman who has a husband who does not believe, if he is willing to live with her, let her not divorce him. For the unbelieving husband is sanctified by the wife, and the unbelieving wife is sanctified by the husband; otherwise your children would be unclean, but now they are holy. But if the unbeliever departs, let him depart; a brother or a sister is not under bondage in such cases. But God has called us to peace. For how do you know, O wife, whether you will save your husband? Or how do you know, O husband, whether you will save your wife?
>
> But as God has distributed to each one, as the Lord has called each one, so let him walk. And so I ordain in all the churches. Was anyone called while circumcised? Let him not become uncircumcised. Was anyone called while uncircumcised? Let him not be circumcised. Circumcision is nothing and uncircumcision is nothing, but keeping the commandments of God is what matters. Let each one remain in the same calling in which he was called. Were you called while a slave? Do not be concerned about it; but if you can be made free, rather use it. For he who is called in the Lord while a slave is the Lord's freedman. Likewise he who is called while free is Christ's slave. You were bought at a price; do not become slaves of men. Brethren, let each one remain with God in that state in which he was called.

Now concerning virgins I have no command of the Lord, but I give an opinion as one who by the mercy of the Lord is trustworthy. I think then that this is
good in view of the present distress, that it is good for man to remain as he is.
Are you bound to a wife? Do not seek to be released. Are you released from a
wife? Do not seek a wife. But if you should marry, you have not sinned; and if
a virgin should marry, she has not sinned. Yet such will have trouble in this life,
and I am trying to spare you. But this I say, brethren, the time has been shortened, so that from now on those who have wives should be as though they had
none; and those who weep, as though they did not weep; and those who rejoice,
as though they did not rejoice; and those who buy, as though they did not possess; and those who use the world, as though they did not make full use of it; for
the form of this world is passing away. But I want you to be free from concern.
One who is unmarried is concerned about the things of the Lord, how he may
please the Lord; but one who is married is concerned about the things of the
world, how he may please his wife, and his interests are divided. And the
woman who is unmarried, and a virgin, is concerned about the things of the
Lord, that she may be holy both in body and spirit; but one who is married is
concerned about the things of the world, how she may please her husband. And
this I say for your own benefit; not to put a restraint upon you, but to promote
what is seemly, and to secure undistracted devotion to the Lord.

But if any man is acting unbecomingly toward his virgin daughter, if she
should be of full age, and if it must be so, let him do what he wishes, he does
not sin; let her marry. So then both he who gives his own virgin daughter in
marriage does well, and he does not give her in marriage will do better.

A wife is bound as long as her husband lives; but if her husband is dead she
is free to be married to whom she wishes, only in the Lord. but in my opinion
she is happier if she remains as she is; and I think that I also have the spirit of
God.

Let us first consider vv.1-9. In verse 1 Paul makes it clear that what follows
is a response to a matter to which the Corinthians had written him; "Now concerning the things of which you wrote, it is good for a man not to touch a
woman." It seems that someone had convinced some of the Corinthian believers that, as Christians, they must practice complete and total celibacy. Married
believers were being urged to practice abstinence, the unmarried were to remain virgins, and the widows were to remain celibate widows. The authors of
the *New Jerome Biblical Commentary* reading this verse in its context argues
that "This [saying: 'It is good for a man not to touch a woman'] is not Paul's
opinion, but that of certain Corinthians who idealistically believed that married couples should abstain from sexual relations, but Paul's argument is that
abstention can only be by mutual agreement and for a limited time."[13]

In an effort to not drive a wedge between factions in the Corinthian church
Paul agrees that it is good for the unmarried and widows to "remain even as

I am (v.8), i.e., unmarried.[14] However, Paul makes it clear that his words are only a "concession, and not . . . a commandment" (v.6). Gordon Fee points out that, for Paul, "marriage or singleness lies totally outside the category of 'commandments' to be obeyed or 'sin' if one indulges."[15] Paul's use of the words "nevertheless" and "but" allows the Corinthians to live as Christians without committing to celibacy. Not only are men and women given permission to marry, but they are not to withhold sexual relations from each other except by mutual consent for fasting and prayer, and then only for a period. Even John Chrysostom, who was never a fan of marriage, asks, "What is the meaning of 'due honor?' 'The wife has not power over her own body;' but is both the slave and the mistress of the husband. And if you decline the service which is due, you have offended God."[16] This is over against "the strongly ascetic element" in Corinth which had "taken the form of criticism and avoidance of the intimate sex relationship in married life; indeed, it seems to have looked askance on marriage itself."[17]

In vv.1-9 Paul, recognizes that the sexual drive in both men and women, including Christian men and women, is so overpowering that, for many believers, attempts to completely abstain from further sexual contact would make shipwreck of their faith. Paul views the practice of virginity and/or celibacy as a gift from God; a gift which not all have; "Each man has his own gift from God, one in this manner and another in that." (v.7). *The Abingdon Bible Commentary* says that Paul "recognizes differences of temperament as varied gifts from God, refusing to impose his advise as an injunction."[18] Paul uses the phrases "because immoralities;" "come together again lest Satan does not tempt you because of your lack of self-control;" "if they do not have self-control, let them marry;" and "it is better to marry then to burn" to say that he sees singleness and/or abstinence as preferable. However, those who choose to marry are not in any spiritual danger is they choose to marry. Likewise, those who are married, are not in any spiritual danger by engaging in sexual intercourse. John Chrysostom asks, "Do you see the strong sense of Paul how he both signifies that continence is better, and yet puts no force on the person who cannot attain to it; fearing lest some offence arise?"[19] Brown says that "Paul was . . . determined that his own state of celibacy should not be adopted by the church of Corinth as a whole."[20] *The Interpreters Bible* understands Paul to be saying that "if it is too difficult for them to maintain the celibate vow, it is not sin for them to marry."[21]

Paul understands that his words to the Corinthians will be taken seriously, otherwise they would not have written to him with these questions. We do not know if this is Paul's first response to Christian asceticism, but we do not find him demanding or resonating with a sexual morality that is found in Christianity as early as the second half of the first century. Brown writes that "in coming down firmly on the side of allowing marriages to continue within the Church, Paul acted as he usually did whenever his converts were tempted to erect excessively rigid barriers between themselves and the outside world."[22] What can be said about Paul's council here is that the believers should remain as they are; "Brethren, let each one remain with God in that state in which he was called." (cf. vv.17-24). Let the married remain married, and in that marriage it is expected that most will continue to have sexual relations. It is a good idea for the unmarried and the widows to remain unmarried, but if that is not possible it is better to marry than to commit some form of sexual fornication because of the lust that is part of human existence. Paul certainly does not believe, that God automatically removes from Christians their sexual desires. That is a belief that we hear from some of the later gnostics.

In v.17 Paul says, "as God has called each [one], in this manner let him walk." And in v.20 he writes, "Let each man remain in the condition in which he was called." In v.24 he says, "Brethren, let each man remain with God in that condition in which he is called." The repetition of this council seems to be directed at those in Corinth who are trying to create a sexless community, and if Paul is responding to the things "concerning the things about which [the Corinthians] wrote," we have, in ch.7, evidence for this conclusion. To the married believers in Corinth who are being urged to stop having sexual relations, Paul says, "Let the husband fulfill his duty to his wife, and likewise also the wife to her husband." To the unmarried (ἀγάμοις)[23] and widows who are being urged to remain unmarried and widows, Paul says, "it is better to marry than to burn." Further, believers married to unbelievers are being told that they should leave their unbelieving spouses, thereby insuring the cessation of sexual relations in those marriages. To this Paul's response is even more pointed. "Now to the married I command, yet not I but the Lord: A wife is not to depart from her husband." He repeats this command in v.39; "A wife is bound [to her husband] as long as her husband lives."

The great prize for the Corinthian ascetics would be to convince the young virgins to remain virginal. The married and widows had already sacrificed their virginity. They had succumbed to their lust. But there was a chance to save the virgins from the pollution of sexual intercourse. However, if they were looking to Paul to support their position regarding Christian virginity, they received a less-than-hoped-for response. In *The Interpreters Bible* we read that "it is possible that since the apostle was unmarried the ascetic element in the [Corinthian] church was making a bid for his support of their views."[24] But as Fee observes "much of Paul's answer is less than certain."[25] Verses 25-40 of ch.7 begins with the words, "Now concerning virgins I have no command of the Lord." This is the second time in this chapter that Paul says that what he is saying is not a command. In v.6 he says that what he has said in vv.1-5 is a concession, not a command (οὐ κατ᾽ ἐπιταγήν), and in v.25 he says that concerning virgins he has no command of the Lord (ἐπιταγὴν κυρίυ οὐκ ἔξω). Hans Conzelmann says that what Paul is doing here is "not *commanding,* but *advising*: to adopt a different mode of conduct is not a sin."[26] What he does offer the Corinthians is "an opinion" which begins in v.26.

Verse 26 can read, "I think then that this (τοῦτο) is good in view of the present distress, that it is good for a man so to be (οὕτως ειναι)." Determining the antecedent to "this" (τοῦτο) will help the reader to decide if the intent of Paul's words are; "this, *my opinion,* is good," or "this, *the idea of virginity,* is good?" However, Paul continues, in the same verse, "it is good for a man so to be?" This does not seem to be a commentary on his own opinion, but a commentary on the idea of virginity. Most standard English translations of "οὕτως ειναι" read "remain as he is."[27] However, in vv.20 and 24 Paul uses the word "μενέτω" (lit. "let him remain") not "οὕτως ειναι" to convey his thoughts about people remaining where they are. Therefore, if we use the more literal translation "it is good for a man so to be," the more obvious intent of Paul's words in v.26 is, "I think then that virginity is good in view of the present distress, and it is good for a man to be virginal." If this is a better translation, the most, then, that can be said about Paul's words to the Corinthians in vv.25-26 concerning their questions about virginity is that it is a good thing. In vv. 20 and 24 Paul argues that people should remain in whatever state they are in vis-à-vis marriage. But his endorsement is not unequivocal, and he seem reluctant to even suggest it. His words "I suppose" cannot be confused with "I suggest" or "I urge." And it is only because of the "present distress" that he even considers the option of virginity for the believers at Corinth. He seems to be saying, "I suppose virginity is a good thing, and it is good for believers to be virginal, but only because of the present distress."

Therefore, it seems fairly clear that much of Paul's comments on virginity and marriage in vv.27-40 are contextualized by his eschatological perspective. F.F. Bruce argues that "the whole discussion of marriage in this chapter is influenced by Paul's eschatological awareness in addition to his pastoral concern."[28] At least Paul, if not the rest of the Apostles, believed that the return of Jesus was eminent. He speaks of "the present distress" (v.26), warns that "the time has been shortened" (v.29), and that "the form of this world is passing away." (v.31).

However, even with the introduction of the eschatological element, Paul's council remains constant. Even though it is good for the believer to be virginal, yet "Are you bound to a wife? Do not seek to be released. Are you released from a wife? Do not seek a wife." (v.27). Be content in the state you are in. The shortness of time is not a reason to alter your married/single status. Fee writes that for Paul "celibacy is not the only existence, nor is it to be preferred on moral grounds, only eschatological."[29]

Hard upon Paul's words, "do not seek a wife" comes, "But if you should marry, you have not sinned." (v.28a). It is possible that single believers in Corinth were being told by the ascetics that if they married they would be guilty of sin. The *Women's Bible Commentary* argues that "Paul is obviously concerned to reassure the Corinthians that marrying a "virgin" is no sin. This means that someone in the community is suggesting it is a sin to marry a virgin."[30] Paul tells them they have not sinned, and that there is no soteriological merit in their singleness.

What is more important for our purposes are Paul's words in 28b; "And if a virgin marry, she has not sinned." So neither the male nor the female virgins are committing an act of sin if they marry. Fee points out that, for Paul, "marriage is a perfectly valid alternative; and whatever else, it is no sin."[31] Paul repeats this in vv.36-38. However, translators of v.36 do not seem to be able to determine who the virgin(s) is/are; "him" (LB), "them" (KJV, NKJV, MLB, RSV), or "her" (NASB). The Greek is "γαμείτωσαν" (lit. "let *them* marry"). Nor are they unanimous in deciding whether "his virgin" (v.36— "παρθένον αὐτοῦ"; v.37—"ἑαυτοῦ παρθένον") is a daughter or a betrothed. "Betrothed" seems the more natural translation.[32] However, neither "daughter" nor "betrothed" nor "gives" appear in the Greek text.[33] Therefore, Paul's words are, "let him do what he wishes, he does not sin; let them marry." Further, "He who marries does well, and he who refrains from marriage does better." It seems fairly clear, then, from a straight-forward reading of the text that, for Paul, Christians considering the question of marriage have options, and they are not damning themselves if they choose marriage. Paul has just finished telling the Corinthians in ch.6 that there are sins of the flesh, and there are profound consequences of sinning against the flesh. Chapter 6.15-20 reads;

> Do you not know that your bodies are members of Christ" Shall I then take away the members of Christ and make them members of a harlot? May is never be! Or do you not know that the one who joins himself to a harlot is one body with her? For he says, "The two will become one flesh." But the one who joins himself to the Lord is one spirit with Him. Flee immorality. Every other sin that a man commits is outside the body, but the immoral man sins against his own body. Or do you not know that your body is a temple of the Holy Spirit who is in you, whom you have from God, and that you are not your own? For you have been bought with a price: therefore glorify God in your body.

Therefore, if husbands and wives are to fulfill their marital duties to each other, and if they are not to sexually deprive each other except by agreement for a season, and if Christians who decide to get married are not sinning, and if Christians are to glorify Christ in their bodies, then, for Paul, sexual intercourse between husbands and wives is neither polluting nor sinful. Paul tells the Corinthians in ch.8. that when you sin, "you sin against Christ." Therefore, married couples engaging in sexual intercourse, and Christians who decide to marry are not sinning against Christ.[34] They are not separating themselves from the Lord. Their salvation has not been sacrificed, nor are they in need of forgiveness. Their status in Christ has remain unchanged.

## NOTES

1. Unless otherwise noted all translations are from the NASB

2. Stephen Benko, "Second Century References to the Mother of Jesus," in *Women in Early Christianity* vol.14, ed. David M. Scholer (New York: Garland Publishing, 1993), 103.

3. Wolfgang A. Beinert, "The Relatives of Jesus," in *New Testament Apocrypha* vol. 1, ed. and trans. R. McWilson (Louisville, KY: Westminster/John Knox Press, 1990), 479-480.

4. Benko, "Second Century References to the Mother of Jesus," 102.

5. Beinart, "The Relatives of Jesus," 480.

6. For Ignatius see his letters to the Trallians 9; to the Smyrnians 1.1-2; and to the Magnesians 11. For Justin Martyr see *1Dialogue* 44,49, 66,67. And for Irenaeus see *Adversus Haersus* 3.22.2; 4.33.2; 5.12.4-5.

7. Benko, "Second Century References to the Mother of Jesus," 11, 33.

8. See earlier discussion of virginity in Jewish literature.

9. Eph 5.22-33 serves a dual purpose. Not only does the author of Ephesians speak of marriage as a model of the relationship between Christ and His people, but husbands and wives are to look to the idealized relationship between Christ and the church as the model for their marriage.

10. Brown, *Body and Society*, 53. Quote from J. Hering, *The First Epistle of Saint Paul to the Corinthians*, 147.

11. Ross S. Kraemer, "The Conversion of Women to Ascetic Forms of Christianity," *Signs* (Winter 1980), 1.

12. cf. Fee, *The First Epistle to the Corinthians*, 323f.

13. Raymond E. Brown, Joseph A. Fitzmyer, and Roland E. Murphy, eds., *The New Jerome Biblical Commentary* (Upper Saddle River, NJ: Prentice-Hall, Inc.:, 1990), 804.

14. ibid.

15. Fee, *The First Epistle to the Corinthians* 334.

16. John Chrysostom *Homily 19 on 1 Corinthians* 2.

17. George Arthur Buttrick, ed., *The Interpreters Bible*, vol. 10, *I and II Corinthians* (Nashville: Abingdon Press, 1981), 87.

18. Frederick Carl Eiselen, Edwin Lewis, and David Downey, eds., *The Abingdon Bible Commentary* ( New York: Abingdon-Cokesbury Press, 1929), 1182

19. Chrysostom *Homily 19* 3.

20. Brown, *Body and Society*, 54,

21. Buttrick, *The Interpreter's Bible* 88.

22. Brown, *Body and Society*, 54.

23. All Greek texts are taken from *The Interlinear Greek—English New Testament*, 2nd ed., edited by Alfred Marshall (Grand Rapids: Zondervan Publishing, 1959).

24. Buttrick, *The Interpreters Bible* 88.

25. Fee, *The First Epistle to the Corinthians* 322.

26. Hans Conzelmann, *A Commentary on the First Epistle to the Corinthians*, trans. James W. Leitch (Philadelphia, PA: Fortress Press, 1975), 132. cf. William F. Orr and James Arthur Walther, *The Anchor Bible: I Corinthians, A New Translation* (Garden City, NY: Doubleday & Company, Inc., 1976), 220.

27. Curiously, the KJV gives the phrase its more literal translation.

28. F.F. Bruce, ed., *New Century Bible: 1 and 2 Corinthians* (Greenwood, SC: The Attic Press, Inc., 1971), 74. cf. William R. Farmer, ed., *The International Bible Commentary* (Collegeville, MN: The Liturgical Press, 1988), 1614.

29. Fee, *The First Epistle to the Corinthians* 348.

30. Carol A. Newsom, and Sharon H. Ringe, eds., *Women's Bible Commentary: Expanded Edition* (Louisville, KY: Westminster John Knox Press, 1992), 415.

31. Fee, *The First Epistle to the Corinthians* 324.

32. In *The International Bible Commentary* we read that for vv.36-38 "No agreement exists about the identity of the two persons spoken of in this case. Four proposals can be listed: father and daughter, master and female slave, a man and a 'spiritual' sister, engaged man and 'virgin.' It would seem that the last proposal is the most probable." William R. Farmer, ed., *The International Bible Commentary: A Catholic and Ecumenical Commentary for the Twenty-First Century* (Collegeville, MN: The Liturgical Press, 1998), 1615.

33. Fee points out that "the terms father, guardship, daughter, etc. never appear in the text; furthermore, there is no known evidence for one's speaking of a father-daughter relationship in terms of her being 'his virgin.'" 326. Also cf. *The Abingdon Bible Commentary* 1181

34. Fee suggests that the Corinthian ascetics message to the betrothed was that they "would sin against the Spirit if they consummated their marriages. 328. cf. Buttrick, *The Interpreters Bible* 88.

*Chapter Four*

# The Church Fathers
# on 1 Corinthians 7.25–39

The early, extant, Christian documents dealing specifically with virginity, beginning with the earliest, are as follows:

Tertullian (ca.150-ca.225) *On the Veiling of Virgins*
Pseudo-Clement. (Late 2nd century)—*Two Epistles Concerning Virginity*
Cyprian of Carthage (ca.200-258) *Of the Discipline and Advantage of Chastity*
—— *The Dress of Virgins*
Methodius of Olympus (?—ca.311). *On Virginity: Discourse 1 To Marcella*
—— *Discourse 6 To Agathe*
Basil of Caesarea (ca.330-379) *To a Fallen Virgin*
Gregory of Nyssa (ca.330-395) *On Virginity*
Ambrose (ca.339-397) *Concerning Virgins: To His Sister Marcellina*. 3 bks.
Jerome (ca.342-420) *To the Virgins of Aemona* (Letter 11)
—— *Against Helvidius*
—— *To Eustocium* (Letter 22)
—— *Against Jovinianus*
—— *To Pammachius* (Letter 48)
—— *To Demetrias* (Letter 130)
Chrysostom, John (ca.347-407) *On the Necessity of Guarding Virginity*
—— *On Virginity*
—— *Homilies on First Corinthians (Homily XIX)*
Augustine (354-430) *Of Holy Virginity*
Sulpitius Severus (ca.360-ca.435) *Concerning Virginity: To His Sister Claudia* (Letter 2)
Anonymous (5th century) *The Epistle of Titus, the Disciple of Paul, on the State of Chastity*

Pseudo-Athanasius (5th century) *On Virginity*
Leander of Seville (540-600) *On the Training of Nuns and the Contempt of the World*

All of these authors buttress their arguments in support of virginity through the use of what they considered the word of God, using both the Hebrew Scriptures and the emerging, and later fixed, New Testament. However, the only portion of Scripture that all of the writers quote is 1 Corinthians 7, and it is vv.25-39 that they spill the most ink.

First, it should be noted that those Fathers who do comment on v.25 understand the word "command" to be read as a command *to* virginity, not as a command *concerning* virginity. They also are reading Paul's word "virgins" as "virginity." They understand Paul to be talking primarily about the practice of virginity in the ontological sense, without reference to time or place, rather than Paul talking to virgins in Corinth in the first century.

Ambrose, Jerome, and Sulpitius Severus read v.25a to mean that virginity is not subject to a command as other duties that Christians are to do or not to do. Virginity is above the mundane concerns of "dos" and "don'ts." Commands to be obeyed are for mere mortals. Ambrose, after quoting v.25a, writes, "If the teacher of the Gentiles had none [commands], who could have one? And in truth he had no commandment, but he had an example. For virginity cannot be commanded, but must be wished for, for things which are above us are matters for prayer rather than under mastery."[1]

Jerome offers a number of interpretations to v.25a, and in each of them he gives a different reason why virginity is above a commandment. In his epistle *To Eustochium* he describes virginity as a "free choice,"[2] and in his epistle *Against Jovinianus* he claims that virginity is both "a favor" from God and a gift from God "to whom it is given."[3] Therefore, there was no need for God to give a command to live a life of virginity. Virginity is a gift which, when recognized as a gift from God, is freely chosen, and when one freely chooses the life of the virgin, God honors that choice by giving that believer the strength to maintain the life that he/she has chosen.[4]

While Jerome, in *Against Jovinianus* 12, talked about virginity being a "favor" and a "gift", and talked about believers tasting "the sweets of virginity," he also spoke of the "burden of perpetual virginity." Virginity was both a free choice and a gift that was both sweet and a burden.

Sulpitius Severus agrees that virginity is above commandments. However, he understands Paul in v.25a to be talking not about adopting a life of virginity, but of "maintaining virginity," and of "preserving virginity."[5] He says, "When, therefore, [Paul] simply gives advise about maintaining virginity, and lays down no precept, he acknowledges that it is above the commandment.

Those, therefore, who preserve virginity, do more than the commandment requires."[6] The context of Severus' passage is full of language of obedience and disobedience and the consequences of each. The practice and maintaining or preserving of virginity is interwoven into his council on obedience to all of the commandments of the law. Following the above quote he writes:

> But it will then only profit you to have done more than was commanded, if you also do that which is commanded. For how can you boast that you have done more, if, in respect to some point, you do less? Desiring to fulfill the Divine counsel, see that, above all things, you keep the commandment: wishing to attain to the reward such as can receive a recompense . . . See that you keep fast hold of what is necessary to merit life, that your chastity may be such as can receive a recompense. For as the observance of the commandments ensures life, so, on the other hand, does the violation give rise to death. And he who through disobedience has been doomed to death cannot hope for the crown pertaining to virginity; nor, when really handed over to punishment, can he expect the reward promised to chastity.[7]

Severus has taken Paul's few words in v.25 and couched them in language about a person's salvation. He seems to be saying that Paul is talking about (or to) Christians who have already made a commitment to lifelong virginity who need to remain faithful to that "vow" of virginity for the sake of their own souls.

Chrysostom, Jerome, and Augustine take pains to explain that the reason God had not given a command to His church to adopt a virginal life, was because it would be tantamount to condemning marriage. However, Chrysostom puts a qualifier on Paul's statement by arguing that Paul "is not speaking about her who has made the choice of virginity, for if it comes to that, she has sinned."[8] And although the Fathers who write about virginity can never see marriage as anything more than a second choice for the weak, they cannot afford to be seen as condemning marriage. One can only suppose that they found no way of getting around Hebrews 13.4, "Let marriage be held in honor among all," or Paul's own words earlier in ch.7 concerning marriage. Therefore, we hear Jerome saying, "If the Lord had commanded virginity he would have seemed to condemn marriage, and to do away with the seed-plot of mankind, of which virginity itself is a growth."[9]

Augustine, after quoting v.25a says, "Wherefore, because it is not sin to marry a wife or to be married, but if it were a sin, it would be forbidden by a "command;" on this account there is no 'command' of the Lord concerning virgins."[10]

The net effect of these various interpretations is to make Paul speak to the issue of virginity rather than individual virgins in Corinth. However, the most obvious meaning of v.25a is that Paul has no commandment from the Lord, because he has no commandment from the Lord. There is already a degree of anxiety over the issues of virginity and marriage, and Paul has no desire to add to it. "I have no command from the Lord concerning the virgins in Corinth, because it matters little if they remain virgins or if they marry. Both are acceptable, and neither is bad."

Moving on to v.26, we begin with the observation that the overwhelming majority of biblical commentators, both ancient and modern, understand v.26 to be eschatological in nature. Ambrosiaster, writing in the fourth century, says, "Here Paul teaches that virginity is better, not just because it is more pleasing to God, but also because it is the more sensible course to follow in the present [end-time] circumstances."[11] For Jerome, this "present distress" is not the troublous and exciting times preceding the return of Jesus Christ, but is both the impregnation of women, and the raising of children. In *Against Jovinianus* Jerome, after quoting v.26, asks:

> What is this distress which, in contempt of the marriage tie, longs for the liberty of virginity? 'Woe unto them that are with child and to them that give suck in those days.' We have not here a condemnation of harlots and brothels, of whose damnation there is not doubt, but of the swelling womb, and wailing infancy, the fruit as well as the work of marriage.[12]

Jerome repeats this in *Against Helvidius* where he again asks, "What is meant by present distress? 'Woe unto them that are with child and to them that give suck in those days?'"[13] In *To Eustochium*, Jerome asks, "What is this distress which does away with the joys of wedlock? The apostle tells us, in a later verse: 'The time is short: it remaineth that those who have wives be as though they had none.' Nebuchadnezzar is at hand."[14] Who the fourth century Nebuchadnezzar is is not discussed, but in all three mentions of v.26 the term "present distress" is associated with the trouble, and even condemnation, of pregnancy and child birth." As we will see later, Jerome can never quite bring himself to totally and completely condemn marriage, but Jerome takes Paul's words about what is "good" and what is "better", and changes them into "good" and "bad." Where Paul says, "For it is good for a man so to be," Jerome interprets as "it is bad for a man not to be." In other words, it is bad for a man to not be virginal, i.e. married. Christians have a choice between what is "good" and what is "better." Jerome implies that Christians *must* choose what is better, i.e. virginity, whereas Paul says that Christians *should* choose what is better. While Paul places no soteriological significance to the choice between the two states, Jerome does. Therefore, for Jerome, Paul is not just talking to first century believers in Corinth, expressing his belief that, because of the immanent parousia, people should not bother themselves with the anxiety that accompanies a change in their status as singles or marrieds. It is good for a man to be unattached ("so to be"), but if "you are bound to a wife . . . do not seek to be released."

Augustine, in *Of Holy Virginity*, in what seems to be a very convoluted argument, uses v.26 as part of a discussion to argue against those who apparently were suggesting that not only does marriage have equal value with virginity in this age, but that the rewards of virgins and non-virgins will be equal in heaven "as though in that eternal life, they, who had chosen this better part, would have nothing more than the rest of men."[15]

Ambrose takes up this argument in his comments on v.27, and he makes it clear that that which is good is far inferior to that which is better. Notice his words in *Concerning Virginity*:

> I am not indeed discouraging marriage, but am enlarging upon the benefits of virginity. "He who is weak," says the Apostle, "eats herbs." I consider one thing necessary, I admire another. "Are you bound to a wife? Seek not to be loosed. Are you free from a wife? Seek not a wife." This is the command to those who are [see v.26b]. But what does he say concerning virgins" "He who gives his virgin in marriage does well, and he who gives her not does better." The one sins not if she marries, the other, if she marries not, it is for eternity. In the former is the remedy for weakness, in the latter the glory of chastity. The former is not reproved, the latter is praised.[16]

While Ambrose is careful not to condemn marriage or those who choose marriage over virginity, his language is very telling. Those who choose marriage are weak, and as such eat herbs rather than meat. Marriage, unfortunately, is necessary, and the remedy for weakness (cf. Paul's words in ch.7.1-9). Those who marry do not sin, and are not reproved. However, those who choose virginity (or receive the gift of virginity) are admired, and their choice stands for eternity. Therefore, although this argument is based on the words of Paul, there is a glory and praise of virginity here that simply cannot be found in the writings of Paul.

If we can group vv.28-31 together, we discover that (of our authors) vv.28 and 29 receive the most attention, v.30 is not mentioned at all, and only Leander of Seville comments on v.31.

Jerome and Augustine are the authors who, in their writings on virginity, reference 1 Corinthians 7.28. Jerome's analysis of v.28, found in *Against Jovinianus*, reads as follows:

> "But and if you marry, you have not sinned." It is one thing not to sin, another to do good. "And if a virgin marry, she has not sinned." Not that a virgin who has once for all dedicated herself to the service of God: for, should one of these

marry, she will have damnation, because she has made of no account her first
faith . . . For virgins who marry after consecration are rather incestuous than
adulterous. And, for fear [Paul] should by saying, "And if a virgin marry, she has
not sinned," again stimulate the unmarried to be married, he immediately checks
himself, and by introducing another consideration, invalidates his previous concession. "Yet," he says, "such shall have tribulation in the flesh."[17]

Jerome's deliberations on 7.28 are some of the most interesting of his readings of 1 Corinthians. In these few lines Jerome does three things.

1) He demonstrates his disappointment with Paul's lack of censure for
those who do marry. Paul said to the Corinthian believers that if they decided
to marry they were not committing a sin, and while Jerome agrees with Paul,
he argues that what Paul did not say is that not sinning is not the same as doing good. Therefore, whenever a comparison is made between marriage and
virginity, it matters little what language is used, marriage always stands in an
inferior position to virginity. Jerome says, " The difference, then, between
marriage and virginity is as great as . . . between good and better."[18] Jerome
is setting up a hierarchy of commitment to Christ, and those who, because of
their weakness, do marry, are obviously not as committed to the cause of
Christ as those who choose a life of virginity. Jerome's interpretation of v.28
almost sounds like an attempt to persuade his readers to disregard what Paul
said, because Paul clearly did not say enough. If Christians are to do what is
good (and in v.38 what is "better") then simply not sinning reveals a rather
weak commitment to the cause of Christ.

2) The next phrase in v.28 reads, "And if a virgin marry, she hath not
sinned." These words of Paul's are entirely unacceptable to Jerome. However,
since he can neither overtly dispute Paul nor condemn marriage, he again explains what Paul really meant. But his explanation, makes Paul say the very
opposite of what he (Paul) just said. For Jerome the only virgins who do not
sin by marrying are those young girls who have not yet committed themselves
to a life of virginity. Once that commitment to virginity has been made, marriage not only becomes a sin, but a damnable sin; a damnable sin equal to that
of incest. Jerome says, "Not that virgin who has once for all dedicated herself
to the service of God: for, should one of these marry, she will have damnation, because she has made of no account her first faith . . . For virgins who
marry after consecration are rather incestuous than adulterous."[19] John
Chrysostom agrees with Jerome, and says, "Paul is not speaking about the
woman who has chosen virginity, for if such a woman decides to marry, she
has indeed sinned."[20]

The first thing that needs to be noticed here is that Paul knew of Christians
who, because of their own understanding of how best to serve Jesus Christ,
had either taken a vow of celibacy or virginity. Some of those believers were

in the Corinthian church. However, in none of the extant epistles of Paul do we hear him even hint that those who have chosen that life are forever tied to it. If he wanted to say that, he had the perfect opportunity to say it in this letter to Corinth. It is hard to imagine that Paul would even think of damning someone who had taken a vow of virginity and later made the decision to marry. The only sexual sins damned in 1 Corinthians are incest (5.1) and other generalized fornications (6.9ff). We have no evidence that the "virgins" in Corinth had been placed into categories determined by age. Nor do we have any evidence that there were, in the middle of the first century, Christians who were taking formal, public vows of virginity. There were young girls and boys who were virgins, and there were young men and women who were also virgins. Paul's words to them is that if they decide to marry they have not sinned. What they will have is trouble, and Paul, being pastoral, is trying to spare them.

3) In Jerome's final words of commentary on v.28 he essentially says that some of what Paul said, he (Paul) really didn't mean to say, and instead of simply erasing these words from his epistle, Paul realizes he has made a mistake, and corrects himself. Jerome says that Paul immediately realizes he may be giving license to those who are championing marriage, corrects himself, and even "invalidates his previous concession."[21] He goes on to say that Paul had mistakenly been "indulgent" with them. However, warning those who are contemplating marriage that they may experience trouble is a long way from damning them from the presence of Christ, and accusing them of the incest Paul himself condemns in ch.5. Further, Paul does not mention that those who marry have "made of no account [their] first faith." And saying to those contemplating marriage that they will experience trouble in the flesh is not contradicting the statement, "If a virgin marry, she has not sinned." Contradicting this statement would sound something like, "If a virgin marries, she has sinned." Jerome makes Paul's council in v.28 say what he, Jerome, wants to say, and is using Paul's (now canonical) words as a validation or justification for his own views.

Augustine is far more magnanimous to both Paul and those who are contemplating marriage. Augustine, after quoting v.28 in *Of Holy Virginity* says, "in this manner [Paul is] exhorting unto virginity, and continual continence, so as some little to alarm also from marriage, with all modesty, not as from a matter evil and unlawful, but as from one burdensome and troublesome."[22] Origen, earlier, had written, "The virgin is spared earthly troubles and set free by her purity, as she awaits the blessed Bridegroom."[23] Augustine, in his commentary on this text, feels no need to qualify Paul's words, and says that what Paul is saying is that marriage is neither evil nor unlawful, but is burdensome and troublesome. Quoting v.28b in ch.19 of his epistle Augustine says that there are "disputants" who have used this verse to "altogether condemn [marriage]." However, while Augustine does not condemn marriage, he is still of the opinion that virginity is in some sense better than marriage. But he warns in ch.18 those who have chosen virginity that they "judge not marriage an evil: and that they understand that is was in no way of deceit, but of plain truth that it was said by the apostle, (he here quotes sections of vv.38, 28, 40)."[24] Augustine is saying that there is no reason to question Paul's words. Marriage is not en evil, but virginity is an obviously better choice. Following Augustine's reasoning Ambrosiaster states, "The man who marries does not sin because he is doing something which is permitted. But is he refuses to do it, he earns merit and a crown in heaven."[25]

Jerome's quotes of v.29 are parts of longer arguments in favor of marital chastity. In *To Eustochium* he points to the prophets Elijah, Elisha and Jeremiah as examples of virginity in the Hebrew Scriptures, and says that Jeremiah remained a virgin because of the times in which he lived ("Nebuchadnezzar is hard at hand."). Jerome argues that Christians are living in similar times, and because "the time is short . . . it remains that those who have wives be as though they had none."[26] Likewise in *Against Helvidius* he says that it is upon Christians, "whom the ends of the world have come," to avoid marriage. And now "in tones of thunder the words were heard, 'the time is shortened, that henceforth those what have wives may be as though they had none.'"[27] Severian of Gabala picks up the same theme, and says, "If married people are supposed to live as if they were single, how is it possible not to prefer virginity."[28]

This call to chastity is also heard in Leander of Seville—the lone commenter on v.31[29]—who says in *The Training of Nuns and the Contempt of the World* that gold and silver of the earth . . . return to the earth; estates, inheritances, and incomes are worthless and transitory, "for this world, as we see it, is passing away."[30] Therefore, "it is above the skies that we must seek, whence you received the gift of virginity, that you may also find there the reward and inheritance of that virginity."[31]

It is from 1 Cor 7. 32-34 that the greatest number of writers quote to support their arguments for virginity. And although each author's contribution will be looked at individually (as well as chronologically), of interest will be any comments or understandings of these verses that keep reappearing.

Tertullian in *On the Veiling of Virgins* is intent on dividing the female sex between virgins and "not-virgins," and in a rather odd translation of 1 Cor 7.34 he says that Paul wrote, "Divided is the woman and the virgin."[32] In other words each woman's persona, her essence as a human being, has been reduced to the status of her hymen. If she has or currently is engaging in sexual activity, she has become a woman. She is not considered as a person in her own right. She is either a wife/mother or a virgin. The point Tertullian is endeavoring to make is clear.Virgins are not women in the way women were normally perceived, and their non-woman status should be reflected in their public persona, i.e., veiled, which in ancient Mediterranean cultures meant she was unapproachable.

Cyprian of Carthage, in his *On the Dress of Virgins*, is also interested in the appearance of virgins, and in ch.5 uses 7.32-34 to remind virgins that "virginity is destined for the kingdom of God," and as such, then, "what have they to do with earthly dress, and with ornaments." He says that "A virgin ought not only to be so, but also to be perceived and believed to be so: no one on seeing a virgin should be in any doubt as to whether she is one." But the stakes are much higher than just appearances. Those virgins who do concern themselves with "earthly dress, and with ornaments, are striving to please men." And, for Cyprian, those who are striving to please men, have, by definition, "offend[ed] God." Not only does God not "wink" at such behavior, He is positively offended by it. Not only that, but because "they who please men are put to confusion . . . God hath despised them." And finally, men pleasers have failed "to be the servent[s] of Christ." He then quotes vv.32-34 of 1 Cor 7.

For Cyprian, then, the married person, and in this case the married woman, in fact does care for the things of this world, and because she care for the things of this world she is offending God, God despises her, and she has been unfaithful to her calling as a servant of the Lord. If Cyprian had not included vv.32-34 the stakes might not be so high, but he did. And in using vv.32-34 he seems to be saying that married persons, because they are married, have cut themselves off from God and His graces. It is not possible for married persons to care for the things of God, nor is it possible for a married person to seek to please both God and their spouse. John Chrysostom argues that "the evil is not in the cohabitation, but in the impediment to the strictness of life."[33] A Christians affections cannot be divided between God and a spouse. Ambrosiaster adds, "Looking after a wife and family is a worldly thing. Sometimes, just to keep them happy, it even leads to doing things which ought to be punished."[34]

On the surface, Paul does seem to be drawing a dichotomy in these verses. The unmarried care for the things of God, but (and) the married person cares for and seeks to please his/her spouse. However, these verses in 1 Corinthians cannot be read out of context. Paul just finished telling the Corinthians in v.28 that "if you should marry you have not sinned' and if a virgin should marry, she has not sinned." Nor does Paul's language in the first part of ch.7 indicate that he has written off married believers.

Therefore, Cyprian, in his attempts to win undivided devotion to the practice of virginity, has lifted biblical verses out of their context to create an argument, which if not followed, has extremely severe, and even eternal, consequences.

The Pseudo-Clement documents *Concerning Virginity* uses v.32 twice, but the interpretation is much more serene than Cyprian of Carthage. In Book 1 the author, coupling together phrases from vv.32 and 34, says that, "true virginity . . . is anxious how it may please its Lord with a holy body, and with its spirit," and that "every virgin . . . [is] solicitous how she may please her Lord."[35]

Scholars do not know who wrote these two books on virginity or where they originate, and even the date is uncertain. However, if the author is quoting from a manuscript in front of him it is a manuscript which has variants from the manuscripts used by other authors who quote these verses. Also, if the estimation of a late first century to early second century authorship is correct, then it makes his use of these texts even more curious, for the majority of the other authors who use these verses are from a much later date (fourth century), and are in much greater agreement with extant Greek manuscripts. It would be difficult to attribute this seemingly anomalous translation to one being used widely in either Asia, Europe, or Africa, for the later authors represent all of these areas. The possibilities left to us are that the author simply paraphrased these verses to suit his purposes, or this translation of 1 Corinthians was being used at least locally in the home of Pseudo-Clement at the time of his writing, and did not survive into later manuscripts. However, since the phrase "how *he* may please the Lord" (πῶς ἀρέσῃ τῷ κυρίῳ) in v.32 has been changed to "it" in Bk 1.5, and to "she" in Bk1.7, it seems that Pseudo-Clement is paraphrasing this verse to fit the needs of his argument. Therefore, Pseudo-Clement had something in mind that he wanted to say, and the words of Paul in 1 Corinthians did not say it in exactly the way he wanted it said.

Methodius quotes v.34 as part of a call for virgins to separate themselves from the world. In *Concerning Virginity* he says that virgins will be "addicted to nothing slothful," and they will put away from themselves "the foulness of luxury, lest in any way some slight hidden corruption should breed the worm of incontinence."[36] Methodius, throughout this discourse, reveals his belief that human nature is being constantly tugged at, and very readily and easily responds to the things this world has to offer. Virgins have not been put in a place where they are free from these distractions, so the "irrational desires of virgins" must be kept in check. Virgins have the advantage, though, for "the unmarried woman careth for the things of the Lord," how she may please the Lord, "that she may be holy both in body and in spirit."[37]

Basil of Caesarea, in *To A Fallen Virgin*, finds it necessary to write to a virgin who has succumbed to the call of the world, and it seems that he was fearful that this might happen. In ch.3 He quotes Job 3.25, "The thing which I greatly feared is come upon me, and that which I was afraid of is come unto me." He was "ever afraid 'lest by any means as the serpent beguiled Eve through his subtlety, so your mind should be corrupted.'" (2 Cor 11.3). He talks about striving to "control the agitation of your senses," and "lifting you to Jesus. Yet through fear of evil I helped you not to fall." Finally he stresses that it is the unmarried *alone* that "careth for the things of the Lord, that she may be holy both in body and spirit."[38] The implication here is one that we have already heard, i.e., that the married, because they are married, cannot care for the things of the Lord. Married women, therefore, have sacrificed the opportunity to serve the Lord with undivided devotion.

Both Basil and Methodius use language which suggests an inherent distrust of the ability of female virgins to remain faithful to their vows. What is difficult to determine is whether this betrays a distrust of the spiritual stability of female Christians or a recognition of the strength of the pull of sexual lust; or both. It would be easy to lump these two writers in with other early Christians who have been accused of, and have demonstrated clear evidence of, either misogyny, or a general distrust of women.[39] James Goehring reminds us that Epiphanius, a contemporary of Basil, viewed all women "as sexual beings whose lust led them even to attempt to seduce the 'righteous' Epiphanius himself."[40] The language of contemporaries that the best and most secure females are the ones who are no longer women, but have become men, cannot be dismissed.

In Gregory of Nyssa we again hear the language heard in Cyprian of Carthage and in Basil of Caesarea that Christians must have completely undivided devotion to the Lord. You either care for the things of this world or you care for the Lord and are anxious to serve Him. These are opposing camps at war with each other. To try to serve the Lord while married is almost tantamount to treason. It is spiritually, emotionally, and physically impossible to serve God while "caring for the things of this world." Why these writers have been driven to this extreme antipathy towards marriage is unrevealed, but to conceive of a married woman serving God, and God lovingly accepting that service and devotion is not even considered. Tertullian went so far as to say that marriage is the essence of fornication.[41] Simpson tells us that "Chrysostom once likened marriage to two fugitive slaves whose legs are bound together."[42] This is excessive "black and white" thinking, and it has caused these men to stake out a theological position which most Christians, both in the fourth century and today, would find impossible to follow, or even understand.

Gregory of Nyssa, like his brother Basil, uses language that suggests that a repudiation of an earlier vow to virginity is a personal affront to God. Basil quotes Jeremiah 18.13, "Hast thou seen what the virgin of Israel has done to me?"[43]

Calling on the experience of Hosea he has God saying, "I betrothed her to me in trust, in purity, in righteousness, in judgment, in pity, and in mercy . . . but she loved strangers, and while I, her husband, was yet alive, she is called adulteress, and is not afraid to belong to another husband."[44] Gregory, in *On Virginity* 9 says that it is impossible to "fulfill that first and great commandment of the Master, 'Thou shall love God with all thy heart and with all thy strength'" if one has "turned to the world" and "engages his heart in the wish to please men." Those who have done that have "exhaust[ed] the love which he owes to Him alone in human affections."[45] Here he quotes v.32, and again in ch.20 of his own epistle, after reflecting that no man can serve two masters, goes on to say that "he who is wise will choose the one most useful to himself, so, when two marriages are before us to choose between . . . we cannot contract both, for 'he that is unmarried cares for the things of the Lord, but he that is married careth for the things of the world.'"[46] We will discover that for all of these authors, it is these verses in 1 Corinthians 7 that allows them to draw a line in the sand. It is always "either . . . or." It is never "both . . . and."

Jerome, twice, in the immediate context of vv.32-34, declares that not only is virginity preferable to marriage, but that virgins are a completely different sex. There are of the human race men, women (wives/mothers), and virgins. In *Against Helvidius*, after quoting vv.32-34 he asks, "Why do you cavil? Why do you resist? The vessel of election says this; he tells us that there is a difference between the wife and the virgin. Observe what happiness of that state must be in which even the distinction of sex is lost. The *virgin is no longer called a woman*." (emphasis mine).[47] He then quotes v.34. In the next chapter he says, "I do not deny that holy women are found both among widows and those who have husbands; *but they are such as have ceased to be wives*, or such as, even in the close bond of marriage, imitate virgin chastity." (emphasis mine).[48] He then quotes v.34.

The language here suggests that virgins, and wives who have made a decision to live chastely with their husbands, have escaped the burden of being female. His words are, "Observe what happiness of that state must be . . ." The only way women can escape the curse of "femaleness" is to deny the sexual part of their "womanness." In other words women who engage in sexual intercourse are acting like women; this is what women do. In their weakness, they give into that thing that all women are born with; their sexual lusts and desires. A women is defined as a female that willingly and repeatedly engages in sexual intercourse. However, women who either never have sexual intercourse or cease to have sexual intercourse have transcended their sex. They have become another sex.

John Chrysostom uses v.34 in ways that earlier and contemporary writers have. In *On Virginity*, Chrysostom, referring to Paul's analogy in ch.9.24-27, says that Christians are athletes, and "if one takes part in an athletic contest, he cannot receive the winner's crown unless he has kept the rules. What, then, are the laws of this contest? Hear again his words, or rather Christ Himself . . . 'The virgin is concerned with the things of the Lord, in pursuit of holiness in body and spirit.'"[49] Chrysostom uses the image of the "winner's crown"— a very powerful image in the early church when speaking of those who have gained salvation—to argue for virginity. The virgin is the one who "has kept the rules." The virgin is the one who has followed the "laws of the contest." And because the virgin has denied himself/herself, and has concerned himself/herself with the things of the Lord, he/she receives the "winner's crown." This argument becomes a very profound and powerful soteriological paradigm for early and medieval Christians. Only by sacrificing your sexual self; only by maintaining sexual discipline, will you be eligible for salvation.

Chrysostom uses the same language of competition in ch.34.5 where he asks, "will someone still dare to compete marriage with virginity? Or look marriage in the face at all? Saint Paul does not permit it. He puts much distance between each of these states. 'The virgin is concerned with the things of the Lord, in pursuit of holiness in body and spirit.'"[50] Chrysostom, like many of his contemporaries who argue for the superiority of virginity over marriage, continues to quote only those words in 1 Corinthians that can support his argument, ignoring the rest.

Augustine, in *Of Holy Virginity*, uses v.34 to also argue for the superiority of virginity over marriage. In concluding an argument begun earlier he says, "Therefore, that virgin is with good reason set before a married women" for the married woman takes "thought of the things of the world, 'how to please her husband.'"[51] This text, along with others which we will examine later, is testimony to what can be called a "hierarchy of sex" that had developed by the fourth and fifth century. And in that hierarchy, virgins were, with the exception of a few dissenting voices, always painted with the brighter colors. Virginity was always the first choice, and marriage a distant second or even third. What Augustine does not tell us in this text is who sets virgins "before a married woman." Is it the church who sets virgins before married women, or is it God? Or is it both? We will answer that question when we examine the dozens of texts taken from the early church Fathers on the relative merits of virginity vs. marriage.

In ch.22 of Augustine's work he draws a straight line between virginity and heaven with 1 Cor 7.32-34 as the justification for that connection. He says, "And now by plainest witness of divine Scriptures . . . let it more clearly appear that not on account of the present life of this world, but on account of that future life which is promised in the kingdom of heaven, we are to choose perpetual continence.."[52] He then quotes vv.32-34. What we do not know is if

Augustine is arguing that perpetual continence will bring assurance of the "future life" or whether he is saying since chastity will be practiced in heaven, it should be practiced in the "present life." Either scenario can be argued, but he seems to be saying the latter, and vv.32-34, words from the Apostle Paul, are the justification for a call to a life of virginity.

Leander of Seville muses about the virgin who cares for the things of this world rather than the things of God and asks, "Shall not the married woman, in such a case, be preferred to [the virgin]? Yes, since she by caring for the things of the world pleases at least her husband, but the other neither pleases her husband, since she does not have one, nor can she please God." This seems to be the only possible scenario in which a married woman can be preferred to a virgin; one who is spiritually conflicted. But it still denies that a married woman can care for the things of God. By becoming married she automatically cares only for the things of this world or her husband. If she cared for the things of God before marriage, she now ceases, and cares for the things of the world. The married woman, then, has made a conscious decision to abandon a life devoted to caring for the things of God, and will now only care for the things of this world..

In all of these quotes and uses of vv.32-34 only two of the Fathers, Jerome and Augustine bother with the first two words in the Greek text of v.34. those words are "καί μεμέρισται" which literally translates "and has been divided." Jerome, in *Against Helvidius* 22, translates this as "And there is a difference also between the wife and the virgin." Augustine, in *Of Holy Virginity* 22, translates the phrase, "and a woman unmarried and a virgin is divided." However, "καί μεμέρισται" seems to be completing a thought begun in v.33, and at least the LB, the RSV, and the NASB translate it that way. To use the translation of the NASB as an example, v. 33 with the addition of "καί μεμέρισται" reads, "But one who is married is concerned about the things of the world, how he may please his wife, and his interests are divided." These translators, then, are understanding Paul to be saying that the married man, as a married man has divided interests. He has concerns for both the Lord and his wife. And although Paul's language suggests that this new state of divided interests is detrimental to the spirituality of the person, it at least allows him to still care for the things of God. This translation also seems to make more sense than those suggested by both Jerome and Augustine. If these modern translators are correct, then, virgins are not abandoning a life solely devoted to God for a life solely devoted to their spouse, but they now simply have divided interests which does not automatically consign them to the flames of Hell.

Finally, Ambrose, Jerome, and Augustine in quoting vv.37-38 spend the most time on v.38, and while not being able to dismiss v.38a ("So then both he who gives his own virgin in marriage does well . . .) place the heaviest emphasis on v.38b ("and he who does not give her in marriage does better.). Notice the language of Jerome in *Against Jovinianus*. After quoting vv.37-38 he says:

> With marked propriety [Paul] had previously said, "He who marries a wife does not sin": here he tells us, "He that keepeth his own virgin does well." but it is one thing not to sin, another to do well. "Depart from evil," he says, "and do good." The former we forsake, the latter we follow. In the last lies perfection . . . [Paul] forthwith detracts from this seeming good and puts it in the shade by comparing it with another, and saying, "and he that gives her not in marriage shall do better.[53]

Jerome's argument is that while marriage is tolerated, virginity is clearly preferred, for in it "lies perfection." Augustine is much more circumspect in his language in the context of his quotes of vv.37-38 and says, in effect, that marriage is not an evil (ch.18), that the good of marriage is only surmounted by virginity (ch.21), and that it is not a crime to wed (v.21). However, Augustine argues in *Of Holy Virginity* 21 that virginity, when compared to marriage, is the "greater good."

## NOTES

1. Ambrose *Concerning Virginity* 1.5.23.
2. Jerome *To Eustochium* 20.
3. Jerome *Against Jovinianus* 12.
4. Feminist scholars Elizabeth Clark and Rosemary Ruether are adamant that female virgins chose virginity as a way of throwing off male domination. Simpson notes that Ruether says that this was a "liberating choice as 'the sense of taking charge of one's own life; of rejecting a state of being governed and defined by others' and of having the 'sense of moving from being an object to becoming a subject.'" Simpson, *Women and Asceticism* 46.
5. Sulpitius Severus *Concerning Virginity* 4.
6. ibid.
7. ibid.
8. John Chrysostom *Homily 19 on 1 Corinthians* 27.
9. Jerome *Against Jovinianus* 1.12
10. Augustine *Of Holy Virginity* 14
11. Ambrosiaster *Commentary on Paul's Epistles,* in *Ancient Christian Commentary on Scripture,* vol. 7, *1-2 Corinthians,* ed. Gerald Bray (Downers Grove, IL: Intervarsity Press, 1998), 69. All the quotes in this section from Ambroaster, Origen, Severian of Gabala, and Caesarius of Arles are taken from vol. 7 pages 69-72 of this series edited by Bray.

12. Jerome *Against Jovinianus* 12.

13. Jerome *Against Helvidius* 23

14. Jerome *To Eustochium* 21.

15. Augustine *Of Holy Virginity* 19.

16. Ambrose *Concerning Virginity* 1.6.24.

17. Jerome *Against Jovinianus* 13

18. ibid.

19. ibid., 13.

20. Chrysostom *Homily 19* 7.

21. ibid.

22. Augustine *Of Holy Virginity* 15.

23. Origen *Commentary on 1 Corinthians 3.39*. From Bray, 70.

24. Augustine *Of Holy Virginity* 18.

25. Ambrosiaster *Commentary on Paul's Epistles*. From Bray, 70.

26. Jerome *To Eustochium* 21.

27. Jerome *Against Helvidius* 22.

28. Severian of Gabala *Pauline Commentary from the Greek Church*. From Bray, 70.

29. None of the Fathers quote or reference v.30 which together with v.29-31 speaks of Paul's concern that Christians not allow the cares of this world to consume them, but to live lives above these cares.

30. Leander of Seville *The Training of Nuns and the Contempt of the World* 1.

31. ibid., 4.

32. Tertullian *On the Veiling of Virgins* 4.

33. Chrysostom *Homily 19* 35.

34. Ambrosiaster *Commentary on Paul's Epistles*. From Bray, 72.

35. Pseudo-Clement *Concerning Virginity* 1.5.

36. Methodius *Concerning Virginity* 1.1.

37. ibid., 1.4.

38. Basil of Caesarea *To A Fallen Virgin* 3.

39. However, Jane Simpson warns us that "this emphasis on the misogynism of the Church Fathers, to the exclusion of a systematic study of contextuality, has created a portrayal of fourth-century ascetics as victims of male theology, who were de-sexed with the tools of theological argument." 39.

40. Goehring, "Libertine or Liberated: Women in the So-called Libertine Gnostic Communities," 338.

41. Tertullian *De Exhortatione Castitatis* 9, in *The Anti-Nicene Fathers* vol.4, ed. Alexander Roberts and James Donaldson. (Edinburgh, 1864-72), 55.

42. Simpson, *Women and Asceticism*, 45.

43. Basil of Caesarea *To a Fallen Virgin* (Letter 46) 3.

44. ibid.

45. Gregory of Nyssa *On Virginity* 9.

46. ibid., 20.

47. Jerome *Against Helvidius* 22.
48. ibid., 23.
49. Chrysostom *On Virginity* 7.2.
50. ibid., 34.5.
51. Augustine *Of Holy Virginity* 11.
52. ibid., 22.
53. Jerome *Against Jovinianus* 1.13.

# Chapter Five

# Views of Virgins and Virginity in the Ancient Gnostic and New Testament Apocrypha Writings

The expected "normal" life of the people who lived in the ancient Greek, Roman, and Jewish cultures, i.e., marrying, begetting and raising children, finds no resonance in Christian gnostic literature. The importance of this cannot be overstated. And while there is ample evidence that there were pagan as well as Jewish gnostics[1], it is clear from the extant evidence from both the gnostic and Christian anti-gnostic writers that most of the gnostics identified themselves as Christian, and it is the Christian gnostics that will be of interest here.

Modern scholars have often defined ancient gnosticism in sociosexual terms. Anne McGuire writes that "the texts of Nag Hammadi demonstrate clearly that gnostic literature abounds in images of sexuality and gender."[2] Richard Smith agrees, and notes that "language about the sex act and organs pervades those texts which we call gnostic."[3] Gnostics, based on their sexual orientation, were described as either ascetic or libertine. The asceticism practiced by these gnostics most often focused on their abstinence and even abhorrence of sexual contact of any sort. Libertine gnostics, on the other hand, not only participated in sexual acts with many partners, but encouraged it in others as well. Also, working with texts from the *Apocryphon of John,*[4] the *Trimorphic Protennoia,*[5] and the Valentinian *Tripartite Tractate,*[6] Smith proposes a gnostic soteriological paradigm, and argues that for some gnostics "salvation comes to this world as a penis enters a women."[7]

Representatives of libertine gnosticism were the Phibionites. In writing about female Phibionites McGuire says that "it is fair to say that there were Phibionite women who were instrumental in the group's development, and that they found in the group an avenue to express their release from the societal constraints imposed upon them by their sex."[8] And if the reports of the heresiologists are to be believed, "the participation of women in these so-called libertine communities was as extensive as in the ascetic branches."[9] For the libertine gnostics, since the physical or carnal part of their being was of no eternal consequence, indulging the appetites of the body was also of no eternal consequence.

However, the surviving gnostic literature is overwhelmingly supportive of an ascetic lifestyle. We find in these writings Gnostics who not only disdained the physical part of their being, but the urges which drove the physical needs of the body; most specifically the sexual urges. Daniel Hoffman points out that "the birth process, physical bodies, and sexual relations in many cases were considered evil by gnostics."[10] Jane Simpson points out that Marcion, who came under the influence of Cerdo, a gnostic teacher, "demanded absolute continence within marriage, and Marcionite communities in Syria admitted to their congregation as full members only celibates and continent married persons."[11] Goehring notes that "the practice of *coitus interruptus* and the use of abortion suggest [a] theology centered on the avoidance of procreation," because " procreation was the demiurge's device to effect" the unnatural division between women and men.[12]

It should also be noted that the asceticism practiced by the Christian gnostics of the first few centuries of the common era was, in some very important ways, dissimilar to the pagans who practiced asceticism. For the Christian gnostics an ascetic lifestyle was not just an attempt to live a virtuous life free from the pull of the desires of the flesh, it was an attempt to identify, sometimes in a very personal way, with the one true God, and to gain salvation from that God. It was about a purity and perfection which would make them "savable" to God. In effect asceticism was an important element in the Christian gnostic soteriological economy. The One True God conveyed his truth and will through a Divine Holy Word in the person of the Divine Holy *Logos*, the incorporeal Jesus Christ. And since the physical world, including human bodies, were the creation of either a false god or false gods, and the true God was incorporeal, and had nothing to do with the creation of the physical world, an ascetic lifestyle, a denial of all physical urges, would bring the gnostic believers in harmony with the incorporeal Savior God that they worshiped. The gnostics believed that the true God of heaven demanded an asceticism that included a life of virginity, or at least chastity. And those few gnostic believers who were called by the true God, understood the true esoteric *gnosis* from the true God, and followed the demands of the true God, would find favor in the eyes of that God. Brown writes that the gnostics believed that "those who indulged in sexual passion show they are assisting the world. No process could be more antithetical to the ethereal bonds that linked spirit to spirit than was physical procreation: sex was 'the unclean rubbing that is from the fearful fire that came from the fleshly part.'"[13] The Christian gnostics, who were attempting to identify with their God, found the stories surrounding the virginal *Logos*, Jesus Christ, who was conceived by God, sans sexual intercourse, with the virgin Mary, models for their own commitment to virginity. We will see, in the gnostic writings, a coupling of divinity and virginity in various ways. We begin with the gnostic gospels.

In the *Gospel of the Nativity of Mary* the angel Gabriel, after greeting Mary with the salutation, "Hail Mary! O virgin highly favoured by the Lord, virgin full of grace," tells her that "in choosing chastity, you have found favor with the Lord; and therefore you, a virgin, *will conceive without sin*, and will bring forth a son."[14] (emphasis mine). This retelling of the story of the conception of the *Logos* highlights the virginity of Mary far more than the canonical gospels. In conceiving while a virgin, and by remaining a virgin, she has not fallen into sin, and because she has maintained her virginity she has "found favor with the Lord." We can assume, then, that, according to this author, had Mary conceived through intercourse, she would have conceived with sin. It is worth noting that the virginity of Mary is something that she has chosen rather than something that God has required, and this "choosing [of] virginity" has brought "favor [from] the Lord."

That the Gnostic writers understood the abnormality of a woman refusing a life of marriage and procreation is witnessed to in the *Gospel of Pseudo-Matthew*. In this story Abiathar the priest offers bribes to the High Priest to obtain Mary for his wife and to bear him a son. The priests and all of Mary's relations keep saying to her "God is worshiped in children and adored in posterity, *as has always happened among the [children] of Israel*."[15] (emphasis mine). The full response of Mary bears repeating.

> It cannot be that I should know a man, or that a man should know me . . . God is worshiped in chastity, as is proved first of all. For before Abel there was none righteous among men, and he by his offerings pleased God, and was without mercy slain by him who displeased Him. Two crowns, therefore, he received — of oblation and of virginity, because in his flesh there was no pollution. Elias also, when he was in the flesh, was taken up in the flesh, because he kept his flesh unspotted. Now I, from my infancy in the temple of God, have learned that virginity can be sufficiently dear to God. And so, because I can offer what is dear to God, I have resolved in my heart that I should not know a man at all."[16]

Mary is horrified by the prospect of marrying for the purpose of procreation. Then using an exegetical devise used often by early Christian writers, she points to examples from the Hebrew Scriptures to buttress her argument. And the language she uses here needs attention.

Abel, she says, received two crowns; one because of his virginity which allowed him to escape "pollution" of his flesh, and Elias (Elijah), because he kept his flesh "unspotted," "was taken up [into heaven]." By inference, then, for this Gnostic writer, polluted and spotted flesh, which becomes polluted and spotted through sexual intercourse, disallows one to enter into God's presence.[17] It is possible that the use of the term "unspotted flesh" is a reference to the sacrificial lamb without spot or blemish offered to God in Num 19.2ff for the purpose of "purifying from sin." This imagery is also heard in Heb 9.12-14 where the sacrificial Lamb "without spot" is Jesus Christ. And just as the sacrificial lamb in Num 19 removed sin from the congregation, so the ante-typical sacrificial Lamb of Heb 9, Jesus Christ, also removes sin from the congregation.

> Not with the blood of goats and calves, but with His own blood He entered the Most Holy Place one for all, having obtained eternal redemption. For if the blood of bulls and goats and the ashes of a heifer, sprinkling the unclean, sanctifies for the purifying of the flesh, how much more shall the blood of Christ, who through the eternal Spirit offered Himself without spot to God, purge your conscience from dead works to serve the living God?[18]

Mary was horrified at the prospect of becoming polluted or spotted through sexual intercourse, even if it was with a husband. This understanding of sexual intercourse as being inherently polluting is also a reflection of the belief in the Greek and Roman cultures concerning sexual pollution, i.e., people who are considered polluted cannot enter into the presence of god. Mary believes that if she looses her virginity she has nothing of value to offer to God, and, therefore, she must maintain her virginity, and all of the urgings of religious leaders and family fall on deaf ears, for she will listen only to God, as she has from her infancy in the temple. Mary even believes, in this passage, that engaging in sexual intercourse disqualifies her to worship God. God is not "worshiped in children;" He is "worshiped in chastity."

Mary reminds the religious leaders and her family that Abel and Elias were not only blessed by God for their virginity, but they were saved by their virginity. Abel received his crown after death, and it was specifically Elias's virginity, according to the understanding of Mary, that kept him from even tasting death. Brown writes about "the Gnostic tendency to link redemption with nothing less than a definitive modification of the sexual drive. The men and women who had been redeemed by Valentinian teaching and initiation looked toward the stilling of sexual feeling as the outward visible sign of a mighty subsidence that had first taken place in the spiritual reaches of the universe."[19] It is possible, then, to extrapolate from this conclusion, that redemption came to those gnostic believers who not only refrained from sexual activity, but who had so disciplined themselves that they no longer even heard the calls of the "flesh."

This, then, is a quite new interpretation of the stories of these two men. There is nothing in the passages where these stories are found in the Hebrew Scriptures to even hint that it was their virginity that pleased God so much that it moved Him to reward them with crowns and eternal life. Nor do we find this interpretation suggested in any rabbinic or early Christian commentaries on these texts which suggests that their virginity was salvific. Indeed, the greatest Jewish heroes, Abraham, Moses, and David were married and had children. Prophets, judges, priests, kings; men whom God called to lead His people, some of which, like Joseph, who were saviors of His people, were married and had children. Therefore, a C.E. text calling on stories from the Hebrew Scriptures to support an argument for lifelong virginity which brings salvific rewards from God is not supported by the Hebrew Scriptures.

The call to virginity in chapter 6 of the *Gospel of Bartholomew* is less rigorous, but still present. In ch. 6.7-8 Bartholomew is receiving instructions from Jesus, and he asks a question which reveals that, for this writer, there is an expected divine reward for living a life of chastity. Bartholomew asks Jesus, "O Lord, and if any sin with sin of the body, what is their reward?" Jesus, in response, begins to talk about first, second, and third marriages. All the baptized should be blameless, but if a man cannot control his lust he should marry, and if he and his wife "are good and pay tithes, [they] will receive a hundredfold." A second marriage is lawful, but only under certain restrictions, "but a third marriage is reprobated: and virginity is best."[20]

Jesus, according to this gnostic text, allows marriage, even two marriages. And there is no indication that these marriages are to be ones in which the husband and wife are to live as "brothers and sisters" that other Christian authors (both catholic and gnostic) write about. Indeed, it is because of the "lust of the flesh" that these people are marrying. This, then , is an asceticism and view of virginity which is less extreme than that seen in the *Gospel of Pseudo-Matthew*. But "virginity is best." We will discover later that catholic, Christian writers spend a great deal of time comparing the relative virtues of marriage vs. virginity, with virginity always the victor.

The belief that virgins are assured of salvation is heard again in vv.73 and 76 of *The Gospel of Philip*. In this gospel a dichotomy is presented concerning those who are allowed into "the bridal chamber," and those who are not. The author says that the "bridal chamber is not . . . for the slaves or for defiled women; but it is (only) for free men and virgins." If free men are the opposite of slaves, then we can assume that virgins are the opposite of defiled women, and if virgins are defined by their physical virginity, then the defiled women would be those who no longer are virgins, and have, therefore, become defiled. And it is only these free men and virgins who are allowed into the bridal chamber where "redemption is." Defiled women, those who are no longer virgins, cannot enter into the "holy of holies," the "bridal chamber." These women, who are numbered with slaves and animals, no longer have access to that redemption

Drawing on Hebrew Scripture imagery, the author of this gospel says that "the Holy of Holies is the bridal chamber." In the Hebrew Scriptures it is God's presence, revealed in His Shekinah glory, that dwells in the "Holy of Holies." This place is, for the Jewish believers, the most sacred place on earth. No one enters into the Holy of Holies except the High Priest, and that only on the Day of Atonement, for the purpose of cleansing the Temple from the accumulated pollution of a full year of sacrifices brought to the Temple. In this Day of Atonement ritual, "lots" are cast over two goats. One is sacrificed, the blood taken into the Holy of Holies, and sprinkled over the Mercy Seat, symbolically cleansing the Temple from the sin offerings. These sins then are (again symbolically) placed on the head of the other goat, the "scapegoat," who is removed far from the camp and left in the wilderness, thereby removing sin from the nation.[21]

In the *Gospel of Philip*, however, what is taken into the Holy of Holies, to relieve God's people from the burden of the stain and guilt of sin, is not sacrificial blood but virginity. These women have specifically not shed their blood through the breaking of the hymen through sexual intercourse. For the gnostics blood is foul and polluting, and only those who have not shed their blood are eligible for entrance into the presence of God. If the Day of Atonement analogy can be carried further, then, virginity is not just salvific for individual virgins, but for the rest of God's people, and Christians very early on understood that they, in fact, were God's people; the "new Israel."[22]

The idea that virgins, by their virginity, are saviors is not limited to this solitary gnostic writer. Earlier and later catholic Christian writers also believed that a woman's virginity was not just salvific for herself, but for others. In *Adversus Haersus* Irenaeus, caught up in his own rhetoric, and using the imagery and language of Paul in Romans 5.14-19, but substituting Adam and Jesus with Eve and Mary, says, "and thus, as the human race fell into bondage to death by means of a virgin, so it is rescued by a virgin; virginal disobedience having been balanced in the opposite scale by virginal obedience."[23] Whereas Paul points to "the obedience of the One [that] the many will be made righteous" (Rom 5.19), Irenaeus says that is "by virginal obedience" that the human race is rescued. Further, Leander of Seville, a catholic Christian, writing in the 6th century, explicitly tells his sister that her virginity is the only hope for his salvation.

In the *Acts of Thomas* the belief that sexual intercourse is essentially foul and polluting, and divine rewards await those who abstain from intercourse is seen again. Notice the language used to describe sexual intercourse in the following passages.

12. . . . Remember, my children, what my brother spake unto you and what he delivered before you: and know this, that if you abstain from this foul intercourse, you become holy temples, pure, quit of impulses and pains.

12. . . . But if you be persuaded and keep your souls chaste before God, there will come unto living children whom these blemishes touch not.

14. . . . it is because I am joined in another marriage; and . . . I have had no intercourse with a husband that is temporal . . . I am yoked unto a true husband.

28. . . . For fornication blinds the mind and darkens the eyes of the soul.

31. . . . and he had intercourse with her and did other shameful acts with her.

43. . . . He came, therefore, in that night and was joined unto me in his foul intercourse . . . and on the night following that he came and abused me.

51. . . . Whosoever shall partake in the polluted union, and especially in adultery, he shall not have life with God whom I preach. Whereas therefore I loved her much, I entreated her and would have persuaded her to become my consort in chastity.

Sexual intercourse in these passages is described as "foul intercourse" twice, as well as "the polluted union," and "fornication." It is abusive to women, and it is coupled with "other shameful acts," and "lasciviousness and bitterness." These words come from a "bride" who is explaining to her father why she cannot marry. She explains to him that she is "in great love," and that she will ask for "that husband of whom I have learned today." In the same passage she says that marriage to "this [present] husband . . . [has] passed away from before mine eyes . . . [for] I am joined in another marriage; and that I have had no intercourse with a husband that is temporal. . . [for] I am yoked unto a true husband."

The writer of the *Acts of Thomas* again using Hebrew Scripture imagery says that not only do the chaste have access to God in His Temple, but they themselves, through their virginity, become "holy temples, [and] pure . . ." In the Hebrew Scriptures God communicated to His people, and His people found release from sin at the temple. The virgins, then, symbolically, by becoming pure, holy temples have become the conduits of God's will and word, and the mediators of His salvation. Similar language is found in 1 Cor 3.16-17 where Paul asks the Corinthian believers, "Do you not know that you are the temple of God and that the Spirit of God dwells in you? If anyone defiles this temple of God, God will destroy him. For the temple of God is holy, which temple you are." Paul does not here explain how someone would "defile this temple." But whoever is guilty of that particular sin "God will destroy." Paul returns to this language in ch.6 where, following a lengthy warning about sexual immorality, says, "Or do you not know that your body is the temple of the Holy Spirit who is in you, whom you have from God, and you are not your own?" The converts to Pauline Christianity are being told that their bodies are the temple of God, and the severest divine punishment will follow those who engage in "sexual immorality."

Gnostic Christians are also being told in the *Acts of Thomas* that they have become "holy temples, [and] pure," and to remain in that state of purity, they are to refrain from "foul intercourse." There is, however, not a straight theological line from 1 Corinthians to the *Acts of Thomas*. Although similar language is used, it is not identical, and the differences are more than just theological "hair splitting." First, the author of the *Acts of Thomas*, being true to gnostic theology, does not say that it is the believers "bodies" that have become holy and pure. He simply says that they (spiritually?) have become holy and pure. Paul explicitly, in both ch.3 and ch. 6, says that it is the believers "bodies" that are the temple of God. Gnostic writers could never, given their theological positioning vis-à-vis the carnality of the body, write that the believer's bodies represent the very Temple of God.

Further, while the gnostic believers reading the *Acts of Thomas* are warned about engaging in *sexual intercourse*, the believers reading 1 Corinthians are warned about engaging in *sexual immorality*. Paul makes it abundantly clear in the very next chapter of 1 Cor that sexual intercourse between husbands and wives is not only not sinful, but encouraged. (see ch. 7.2-5). We see here, then, a divergence in the theology of sex between those who eventually followed the teachings of Paul, and those who followed the teachings of the gnostics. However, what we will discover later, is that by the time we get to the fourth century, catholic Christians writing on virginity, sound very much more theologically like the author of the *Acts of Thomas* than the author of 1 Corinthians.

Complicating this discussion are the words found in *The Acts of Paul and Thecla* 5, where we read, "Blessed are they that have kept the flesh chaste, for they shall become a temple of God." This, of course, comes closer to the council of Paul, but there is still an important difference. For Paul Christians have become Christians because of the grace of God, and because they are Christians, they have metaphorically become the temple of God, and now that they are the temple of God, that temple is not to be defiled by engaging in sexual immorality. In *The Acts of Paul and Thecla* the believers do not become the temple of God unless they keep their flesh chaste. For Paul becoming the temple of God is a gift. For this gnostic author becoming the temple of God is earned.

This is illustrated in v.101 of the *Acts of Thomas* where a man named Charisius tells the king of India that a "certain Hebrew, a sorcerer" was gathering people to him and he was teaching them of a new God, and was laying on them "new laws such as never yet were heard, saying: 'It is impossible for you to enter into that eternal live which I proclaim unto you, unless you rid you of your wives, and likewise the wives of their husbands.'" This writer is not only calling for the unmarried to remain unmarried, and to abstain from what is described in vv.12 and 13 as "foul intercourse," and "foul desire," but he/she is also telling husbands and wives to "rid" themselves of their spouses.

This writer understands that this teaching is going against what was perceived as the natural order of life, i.e. marriage and the bearing of children. The writer has Charisius saying that this teaching is a "desolation," and that Thomas must be stopped before "our nation perish." The teachings of Thomas are "such as never yet were heard." According to this writer all sexual intercourse must cease, and husbands and wives must part from each other. Corrington points out that the stories in the *Acts of Thomas*, the *Acts of Andrew, Acts of Paul and Thecla,* and *Acts of John* not only "function as propaganda for female conversion, . . . but to the celibate life [and] its inevitable consequences."[24] She goes on to say that "in each of these stories, despite resistance to the adoption of celibacy by the woman's family, husband (or fiancé), male civic authority, or even a male apostle, the woman, with the help of divine power, wins approval of her choice."[25] This is no longer just a call for virginity, nor is it a call for a selected few. It is a call for a new social order. It is a call, not from men, but from God, especially for women, to abandon a social order which had been in place for centuries. Kraemer reminds us that "to be a woman [was] to be a wife [and] she who refuses has committed sacrilege—she is *anomos*."[26] It might not even be a stretch to say that these women became *persona non grata* to their families. Centuries long traditions and understandings of the defined role of a woman was being rejected outright. In the *Acts of Paul and Thecla* we hear Thecla's mother, at Thecla's trial cry out, "Burn the lawless one! Burn her that is no bride in the midst of the theater, that all women who have been taught by this man may be afraid."[27] Kraemer, commenting on this mother's hostility, draws a rather odd conclusion, when he says that, "the fact remains that the woman who renounces acceptable forms of sexual behavior in favor of celibacy is doomed to the most degrading form of the very sociosexual identity she has rejected—prostitution."[28] On the contrary; these women were not doomed to prostitution, for they had chosen a life of celibacy. If their families never even considered celibacy as a life choice, then they might conclude that their female relative might be doomed to prostitution. But they now had another choice. One that, though unheard of before, was in the second century beginning to gain numbers and popularity.

It is precisely because of these radical teachings which are entirely hostile to marriage, that catholic Christians Jerome, Augustine and other later catholic

Christian writers had to spend time explaining that while virginity was the preferable life, marriage was not an unforgivable sin. When word came to Jerome that he was being accused of condemning marriage, and thus falling into various heretical camps who, in fact did condemn marriage, he had to start back-peddling, and telling his readers that marriage was a forgivable sin.

This hostility towards marriage is further seen in a story from the *Acts of Philip*. Philip assures a widow who is about to bury her son that he will raise him "in the name of Jesus. She said: It seems it were better for me not to marry, and to eat nothing but bread and water. Philip [said]: you are right. Chastity is especially dear to God." If she had not married; if she had re-mained chaste; she would not have to go through the suffering that she now must bear. Indeed, "Chastity is especially dear to God."

It was only as the gnostic believers became aware of how damaging and polluting sexual activity was to themselves and their relationship to God that they appreciated the urging of God to refrain from sexual contact, including that of the wedding bed. In the *Acts of John the Evangelist* we hear John of-fering up a prayer of thanksgiving to God "who has kept me also till this pres-ent hour pure for Yourself and untouched by union with a woman; Who, when I wished to marry in my youth did appear to me and say: . . . "John, if you were not mine, I should have allowed you to marry."[29] he implication here is that those who God does allow to marry are not his. Allowing oneself to en-gage in a union with a woman; more specifically a sexual union with a woman, brings with it a price too high to pay.

This insistence on abstinence from sexual intercourse, and the language de-scribing sexual intercourse as "polluting" is heard in further gnostic texts. The author of the *Book of Thomas the Contender* pronounces a woe "to you who love intimacy with womankind and polluted intercourse with them."[30] In the *Exegesis on the Soul* the soul who has a female name and an androgynous form falls (into sin?) and takes on a female body. She is immediately set upon and "some made use of her by force, while others did so by seducing her with a gift. In short, they defiled her and she [lost] her virginity."[31] In the *Hypostasis of the Archons* Norea is "the virgin whom the Forces did not defile."[32]

It appears from these texts that of all the cravings of the body, of all the lusts that must be kept in subjection, sexual lust is the one that the gnostics were the most fearful of, and, therefore, the one that received the most atten-tion. They saw a capitulation to sexual lust as an act which completely dis-qualified them for the intimate fellowship with the *Logos* which they all de-sired. All intercourse is polluting, and a person who is polluted cannot enter into the presence of God.

While in many gnostic texts engaging in sexual intercourse disqualifies a person for communion with God, in the *Acts of Paul and Thecla* there is a return to the idea that virginity brings rewards from God. Three of the beatitudes pronounced on the believers are specifically for those who are virgins.

> 5. Blessed are they that have kept the flesh chaste, for they shall become a temple of God.
>
> 5. Blessed are they that have wives as not having them, for they shall receive God for their portion.
>
> 6. Blessed are the bodies of the virgins, for they shall be well pleasing to God, and shall not lose the reward of their chastity; for the word of the Father shall become to them a work of salvation against the day of His Son, and they shall have rest for ever and ever.

The bounties from God for the persons who maintain their virginity for life are multitudinous. First, in v.5 those who keep their "flesh chaste" will become the temple of God.[33] Verse 5 also says that those men who "have wives as not having them . . . shall receive God as their portion." While "living with wives as not having them" includes more than just a celibate marriage, we can assume that it at least includes celibacy in the marriage. The implication, then, is that only those married people who are celibate in their marriage will receive God as their portion, while those who do not live in a celibate marriage will not receive God as their portion. What "receiving God as their portion" means is not explained, but the language suggests that this is something that all Christians desire. Kraemer argues that the "women who do not fulfill their traditional sociosexual roles can find in ascetic Christianity a new standard of worth by which they are superior to all other sexual bound women."[34]

In v.6 we read that the "bodies of the virgins . . . [are] well pleasing to God," and they will not "lose the reward of their chastity; for the word of the Father shall become to them a work of salvation against the day of His Son, and they shall have rest for ever and ever." The reward promised to the chaste is the "word" (*Logos*) of the Father, and that "word" becomes to them a work of salvation." Therefore, the *Logos*, which in gnostic soteriology is centrally important, is promised to those who keep their bodies chaste. Also, in a glimpse of gnostic eschatology, the reward is not just for the present, but it is a "work of salvation against the day of His Son" which is most likely a reference to the second coming of Christ that most Christians expected. And the reward, taking the virgins through that "day of His Son," carried them into an eternal rest. Corrington observes that this teaching "certainly sheds light upon the reasons why the celibate life is represented as having appealed so readily to the female Christian converts of the [Apocryphal Acts of the Apostles]."[35] Females living in the ancient world were promised very little, and hoped for less. For a religion to promise rewards in both this life and the next would have a strong pull.

Not only are the virgin gnostics recipients of God's special favors, including salvation, in the *Hypostasis of the Archons* the virgin/mother Norea is cast in the role of savior. McGuire argues that the virgin Norea "is involved in the salvation history of the gnostic race," and that she plays the "role as a savior, [or] more specifically that of a 'saved savior.'"[36] Not only will Norea abide "in Incorruptibility, where the virgin spirit dwells, who is superior to the Authorities of chaos,"[37] but, according to her mother Eve, God "has begotten on me a virgin as an assistance for many generations of humanity."[38] McGuire concludes by saying that "Norea is not merely [a] 'female counterpart' to her brother Seth in this 'variant' of the 'Sethian' system but a female figure of greater significance and power then her male counterpart Seth."[39]

Since gnostic Christians were not the only Christians writing on the various aspects of virginity, the questions about influence must be addressed. For instance, by the time the Manicheans, who flourished in the Empire in the fourth and fifth centuries began to make their presence felt, not only gnostic Christians, but catholic Christians had produced a great deal of literature supporting the practice of virginity. Brown says that the Manicheans also believed that "sexual desire and procreation stood for the horrendous opposite of true creation."[40] The Manicheans, like the gnostics "believed that the sexual urge could be totally transcended: it could be banished forever from the self."[41] But to whom do we assign influence for the Manichean understandings of sexuality; catholic Christians or gnostic Christians? Or do we allow the Manicheans to develop these ideas independent of both gnostic and catholic Christians? Brown states that "by the year 300, Christian asceticism, invariably associated with some form or other of perpetual sexual renunciation, was a well-established feature of most regions of [what was rapidly becoming] the Christian world."[42] But Brown's further assertion that "the heroes and heroines of the *Apocryphal Acts* were the heroes and heroines also the Manichean church"[43] is an extremely important piece of information, for many of the heroes and heroines in the *Apocryphal Acts* were heroes and heroines because of their sexual renunciation. Therefore, a shared belief that the sexual urge could be excised from the human psyche, along with a shared set of heroes who have gained victory over a culture antithetical to a life devoted to virginity, allows us to tentatively conclude that the gnostic beliefs resonated more deeply with the Manichean beliefs than those of the catholic Christians, at least on issues concerning sexuality.

However, since we have not yet discussed other Christian views of virginity stronger conclusions must await. What can be said here is that while the first extant gnostic texts appear c. 150 C.E., some 120 years following the birth of Christianity, the majority, though not all, of early catholic Christian texts on virginity appear even later than many of the gnostic texts. It must also be remembered that even though the earliest evidence for Christian gnosticism dates to the middle of the second century, we cannot conclude that gnostic groups and ideas did not exist before then. In other words, Christian gnosticism may have roots in the first century C.E. Simpson argues that Christian "asceticism had its roots in Jewish desert spirituality and found expression in certain ascetic tendencies in the gospels and in the Pauline epistles."[44] Indeed, if the Gospel of John, which some scholars believe to be antignostic, can be dated at the end of the first century or the beginning of the second century, we have further evidence for the existence of first century Christian gnosticism. Therefore, did gnostic views on virginity influence catholic Christian writers views on virginity? Or were the theologically synchronistic gnostics borrowers of early catholic Christian texts on virginity that we are not aware of? These questions cannot be answered here, but if it can be demonstrated that catholic Christianity's views on virginity are reworkings of gnostic views, traditional understandings of the growing interest of ancient catholic Christians concerning their virgins and virginity needs to be revisited.

## NOTES

1. The *Nag Hammadi* Library contains Jewish and Pagan as well as Christian Gnostic texts.
2. Anne McGuire, "Virginity and Subversion: Norea Against the Powers in the Hypostasis of the Archons," in *Images of the Feminine in Gnosticism*, ed. Karen L. King (Harrisburg, PA: Trinity Press International, 1988), 239.
3. Richard Smith, "Sex Education in Gnostic Schools," in *Images of the Feminine in Gnosticism*, ed. Karen L. King (Harrisburg, PA: Trinity Press International, 1988), 345.
4. *Apocryphon of John* 26.13-17
5. *Trimorphic Protennoia* 40.29-34
6. *Tripartite Tractate* 60.34-61; 94.16-18
7. Smith, "Sex Education in Gnostic Schools," 356. Smith points out, apparently as a buttress to his argument, that "another gnostic group, the Essenes, virtually deifies the penis and the semen. The origin of everything, yet shaping all things. It is the mystical word." 357.
8. McGuire, "Virginity and Subversion," 344.
9. James E. Goehring, "Libertine or Liberated" 338.
10. Daniel Hoffman, *The Status of Women and Gnosticism in Irenaeus and Tertullian*, (Lewiston, NY: The Edwin Mellen Press, 1995), 86.
11. Simpson, "Women and Asceticism," 40.
12. Goehring, "Libertine or Liberated," 340.
13. Brown, *Body and Society*, 116. First quote from the *Testimony of Truth* and the second from the *Sophia of Jesus Christ*.

14. *The Gospel of the Nativity of Mary* 9.

15. *The Gospel of Pseudo-Matthew* 7.3.

16. ibid., 7.3-4.

17. cf. ritual laws in Leviticus.

18. Heb 9.12-14. Of course the whole idea of the blood of Jesus being the source or means of salvation is foreign to gnostic soteriology. The purpose of the incarnation of the *Logos* was not to shed His blood as a sacrifice to God, but to reveal the true God and the true *gnosis* to the true believers.

19. Brown, *Body and Society*, 111.

20. *The Gospel of Bartholomew* 7-8.

21. see Lev 16.

22. see Gal 3.7-9.

23. Irenaeus *Adversus Haersus* 5.19.1.

24. Corrington, "The "Divine Woman" 208

25. ibid.

26. Kraemer, "The Conversion of Women to Ascetic Forms of Christianity, " 302.

27. *Acts of Paul and Thecla*, 20.

28. Kraemer, "The Conversion off Women to Ascetic Forms of Christianity," 306.

29. *Acts of John the Evangelist* 113.

30. *The Book of Thomas the Contender*

31. *The Exegesis of the Soul*

32. *Hypostasis of the Archons* 91.30 - 92.4.

33. cf. discussion on the *Acts of Thomas*.

34. Kraemer, "The Conversion of Women to Ascetic Forms of Christianity," 306.

35. Corrington, "Propaganda and the Power of Celibacy," 214.

36. McGuire, "Virginity and Subversion," 273, 274.

37. *Hypostasis of the Archons* 93.30-32

38. ibid., 99.1-3.

39. McGuire, "Virginity and Subversion," 274.

40. Brown, *Body and Society*, 200.

41. ibid.

42. ibid., 202.

43. ibid.

44. Simpson, "Women and Asceticism," 40.

*Chapter Six*

# The Gendering of Virginity: "Who Gets to Call Whom What?"

## ESCAPING FEMALENESS = BECOMING MEN

The early church Fathers who wrote their letters, epistles, and tracts in support of virginity reveal not only their attitudes about virginity, but about women and sex as well. And although these documents cover half a millennium, we will discover that the attitudes towards women, sex, and virginity remain fairly constant.

For many of these Fathers the unregenerated female mind was naturally given to lust and hysteria. Women's thinking was suspect and unreliable. Even the regenerated female spirit was weak and unable to reach the heights of male Christians. The only release from this state that all women found themselves in was to somehow become male, and the most obvious solution was to abandon those things which made women women; sexual activity and child bearing. Whereas male Christians were required to overcome their bodily lusts, and bring them under subjection to the will of Christ, female Christians had to go further. Not only did they also need to overcome their natural bodily lusts, which were stronger in females than in males, but they had to overcome a much more basic and profound nature; being female. This is why women who were able to remain completely virginal over the span of their lives were regarded as superior Christians. Their overcoming was miraculous. Late in his career Jerome writing to the virgin Demetrias says about her, "How high an esteem I entertain for this virgin, nay more what a miracle of virtue I think her."[1]

This also helps explain why female Christians were warned in the most graphic language of the consequences of turning away from a life devoted to virginity. They had been given a gift, and had reached spiritual heights that other Christians could only imagine. Falling from virginity, after a commitment to virginity, was a rejection of a divine gift that was close to unforgivable. However to receive and remain faithful to this divine gift, female Christians needed to become "other" than what they were; females. Jerome writes to Demetrias that "[you] must act against nature or rather above nature if you are to forswear your natural function, to cut off your own root, to cull no fruit but that of virginity, to abjure the marriage-bed, to shun intercourse with men, and while in the body to live as though out of it."[2]

While the most virulent verbal attacks against the female sex are found in the writings of Jerome, he certainly has a chorus of supporters. And it is in these attacks against "femaleness" that we are exposed to the raw, unapologetic misogyny of the early Fathers. Tertullian, in his work urging all women to veil themselves, says that the virgin who obeys this wish "conceals her virginity . . . [and] denies even her womanhood."[3] We hear Jerome saying, "as long as woman is for birth and children, she is different from man as body is from soul. But when she wishes to serve Christ more than the world, she will cease to be a woman and will be called man."[4] We hear this same language from Ambrose when he writes, "She who does not believe is a woman, and should be designated by the name of her sex, whereas she who believes progresses to perfect manhood, to the measure of the adulthood of Christ. She then dispenses with the name of her sex, the seductiveness of youth, [and] the garrulousness of old age."[5] Jo Ann McNamara writes that "Melania the Younger's biographer noted that male monks received her into their monasteries as though she were a man, 'for she had gone beyond the limits of her sex and acquired a virile mentality."[6] Susanna Elm says that many of the early Church Fathers argued that it was only through "asceticism [that] a woman achieves 'male' virtue, and is thereby transformed into a 'manly woman,'" and it is through this practice of the ascetic life that "she has not only achieved true equality with her male counterparts, but has been transformed into an ideal, complete human being."[7] McNamara, reflecting on statements by Gregory of Nazianzus[8] and Gregory of Nyssa[9] says that "such language betrays a deep-seated tendency to despise the [very] nature of women."[10] However, it needs to be noted that this attitude toward women was not uniquely Christian, nor even first heard among Christians. Brown reminds us that according to the ancients "women . . . were failed males."[11] Brown writes that "Plutarch warned Pollianus that women were intractable creatures. Left to themselves they 'conceive many untoward ideas, low designs and emotions.'"[12]

It is interesting, but hardly surprising, that we also hear this dismissing of the femaleness of women in the writings of the Gnostics. In *The Gospel of Mary* 5 we read this account.

But [the Apostles] were grieved. They wept greatly, saying, "How shall we go to the Gentiles and preach the gospel of the Kingdom of the Son of Man? If they did not spare Him, how will they spare us?" Then Mary stood up, greeted them all, and said to her brethren, "Do not weep and do not grieve nor be irresolute, for His grace will be entirely with you and will protect you. But rather, let us praise His greatness, for He has prepared us and made us into men."[13]

Daniel Hoffman, in his work on gnostic attitudes toward women, notes that the *"Gos. Phil.,* like *Gos. Thom.,* sees in the division between male and female the symbolic origin of the evil human condition. n some fashion and/or through some ritual, the woman must again be reunified with the man to destroy death."[14] Brown, in his discussion of gnostic, Valentinian cosmology, sums up God's plan to restore the cosmos to this pre-fall purity:

Valentinus drew upon the polarity of male and female so as to preach a process of redemption that took place in two stages. The spiritual principles whose confusion had brought about all that was unnecessary in the universe would regain their stability. They were the fluid female that would be given form by the dominant male. But this was not all. All that was other to the spirit must be absorbed back into it: the polarity of male and female itself would be abolished. The female would become male. Hence the distinctive manner in which Valentinus adapted the conjugal imagery current in his age.[15]

Brown goes on to say that for Valentinus, "the female would be swallowed up in the male. It would not simply be disciplined by the male; it would become male."[16] Hoffman notes that Patricia Wilson-Kastner supports this conclusion, and says that in the "Gnostic *Gospel of Mary* and *Pistis Sophia, . . .* women must become male in some fashion and follow an encriatic lifestyle to be leading Christians."[17]

Of the scholars who have written about this gendering of virginity, Rosemary Ruether has done some of the most extensive work. In *Religion and Sexism* she argues that women, because they were females, were viewed as being, by themselves, incomplete, both essentially and spiritually. She claims that Augustine in *On the Trinity* 7.7.10 is saying that "woman is not really seen as a self-sufficient, whole person with equal honor, as the image of God in her own right, but is seen, ethically, as dangerous to the male."[18] She points out that Leander of Seville speaks of "all the weak traits of mind and body, which are contrary to salvation, as feminine by nature."[19] Joyce Salisbury writes that "the early Fathers understood men to be primarily spiritual and women carnal."[20] She further states that "since by nature women were primarily carnal, in order to achieve spirituality they had to renounce those things that defined them as women."[21] Therefore, "by choosing a spiritual life women had to reject or transcend their gender, which was by definition sexual and reproductive."[22] Corrington, in an argument concerning the power that celibacy gave to women, states, "Therefore, if a woman is not to be 'mastered' by a male, she must become a male or adopt a male paradigm of empowerment."[23]

Ruether concludes that these views of women manifested themselves in an early Christian soteriological paradigm. She argues that, based on the writings of the early Fathers who wrote on virginity, women, as women, do not have access to the kingdom of God.

> [The] slippage between woman's nature as a consequence of sin and the characterizing of these lower traits of mind and body as feminine by nature caused a confusion in patristic thought over the sexual nature of the risen body. If woman was essentially body and had sensual and depraved characteristics of mind, then it followed (according to a dualistic view of redemption) that either she was irredeemable or else she was redeemed only by transcending the female nature and having become "male," [and] in the Resurrection there would be only male bodies, all females having been changed into males.[24]

## ESCAPING FEMALENESS = ESCAPING SEX

The only escape, then, for women, from a life doomed to domination and damnation, was to spiritually become male, and many of these early Christians writers believed that the only way for females to become spiritual males was through a commitment to life-long virginity. And this devotion to virginity, which carried with it gifts from God to maintain that commitment, had consequences for both this life and the next.

First, it required a complete self and sexual re-orientation. Brown notes that "the girl who found herself among the 'brides of Christ' was spoken of by the clergy as a human *ex voto*. She was no longer a woman; she had become 'a sacred vessel dedicated to the Lord.'"[25] Virgins were to assume an entirely new identity; an identity that had no resemblance to their former identity.

The church Fathers sought to convince women who chose a life of virginity that their own body was their worst enemy. They were attempting to save these women from themselves; from their femaleness. Ruether says that "sexual relations [were seen as] intrinsically debasing to the mind . . . [and] the marital act as intrinsically debasing to a woman."[26] However, the sexual act was not dangerous just to women, but to men as well.

> It is common for the Fathers to regard the sexual act as so inherently "polluting" that even the married who have recently indulged in it are advised not to

approach the church or the sacraments. For Jerome and others it is axiomatic that one cannot pray if one is living in carnal union. Either temporary or permanent vows of continence are the prerequisite for prayer, and so the priest, who must pray constantly, should be wholly continent.

Not only were sexual relations to be avoided, but women are constantly reminded of the laborious and burdensome life brought about by childbirth and children. These men viewed women's bodies, and the sexual lust that their bodies aroused in both them and in other males, with horror and disgust. And they sought to impose this view on women as well. They were teaching women to hate their bodies.

Salisbury reminds us that "according to the Fathers, [women] were carnal and sexual by nature."[27] Therefore, we are not surprised to hear Tertullian urge women to "renounce the carnality of [their] sexuality."[28] Jerome argued that when "the distinction of sex is lost" that it brings a state of happiness that is observable.[29] He goes on to say that "the virgin is no longer called a woman . . . [and] the virgin's aim is to appear less comely; she will wrong herself so as to hide her natural attractions."[30] Jerome not only rails against make-up, jewelry, coiffed hair, and fine clothes, but virgin women were urged to not even bother with bathing. Ruether tells us that with the Fathers there was an "obsession with blotting out the female bodily image," and it is in that obsession "that we find that peculiar involvement in the Fathers with questions of female dress, adornment and physical appearance. The woman must be stripped of all adornment. She must wear unshapely dress and a veil that conceals her face and limbs. Finally, she must virtually destroy her physical appearance so that she becomes unsightly."[31] All of these adornments and activities belied an interest in how one looked, which was a sure sign of spiritual weakness. And the only reason a woman would want to draw attention to herself would be to sexually seduce the men who would see her. Salisbury says "it was felt that if it were not for the temptations of women, men would be more able to avoid the sins of the flesh."[32] She adds that "it is important to note that women were not temptresses out of a desire to be so; it was just part of their nature."[33] Finally, she says that this perceived power in women to corrupt not only men, but almost everything else, is remarkable and must have been quite threatening to the principle that defined maleness—that is, power. Therefore, the most effective way to strip women of this power that they held over men was to call them to virginity; to make the vocation of virginity so much more appealing than a life of marriage and motherhood, that women would forget about their sexuality. And if they listened to the Fathers, they understood that not only were they to forget about their own sexuality, but they must never be guilty of the sin of tempting men to fall from the commitment they had made to Christ. If women would follow this wise council, men could retain their power over these women, and these women would then be safe.

Jerome says that to guard against becoming a temptor some virgins "change their garb and assume the mien of men, being ashamed of being what they were born to be—women. They cut off their hair, and are not ashamed to look like eunuchs."[34] This language finds echoes in the early Middle Ages, for Ruether tells us that in the sixth century Leander of Seville "speaks of virginity as freeing woman from the sexual oppression of male domination of the curse of Eve, yet nevertheless speaks of all the weak traits of mind and body, which are contrary to salvation, as feminine by *nature*."[35] Therefore, a woman, because she is a woman, finds it difficult, if not impossible, to respond to the call of God. "The virgin, by contrast, 'forgetful of her natural feminine weakness,' . . . lives in manly vigor and has used virtue to give strength to her weak sex, nor has she become a slave to her body, which, by natural law should have been subservient to a man."[36]

J.T. Schulenburg writes that the "Church Fathers, as ascetics, and in some cases fanatical celibates, shared an uneasiness and fundamental suspicion toward women: they feared and also abhorred female sexuality," and they "described the female body in abusive and disdainful terms. Although deceptively attractive, a woman's body was to be shunned as an inherently ugly, repulsive receptacle."[37] She goes on to say that in the Latin West Tertullian, Cyprian, Ambrose, Jerome, and Augustine "established the notion of a hierarchy of sexual perfection with distinct grades measured in terms of the degree of a person's denial of or withdrawal from sexual activity."[38] This "sexual hierarchy," in descending order is as follows:

Virginity
Celibacy (either for marrieds or widows)
Sexual intercourse only for marrieds, and only for the purpose of procreation
Sexual intercourse for marrieds who cannot control themselves
Fornication in all of its forms, i.e., adultery, homosexuality, bestiality, masturbation, etc.

Eusebius, in *Proof of the Gospel*, distills this hierarchy down to two ways of life:

Two ways of life were thus given by the Lord to His church. The one is above nature, and beyond common human living; it admits not marriage, childbearing, property nor the possession of wealth . . . Like some celestial beings, these gaze down upon human life, performing the duty of a priesthood to Almighty God for the whole race . . . And the more humble, more human way prompts men to join in pure nuptials, and to produce children, to undertake government, to give orders to soldiers fighting for right; it allows them to have minds for farming, for trade and for the other more secular interests as well as for religion.[39]

Tertullian argues that virgins must at all times be modest in their dress and deportment, and goes on to describe those "who have fallen into wedlock" as "women of the second degree of modesty."[40] Cyprian writes that virginity "maintains the first rank . . . the second in those who are continent, the third in the case of wedlock."[41] Methodius argues that the lessons of the history of marriage in the Hebrew Scriptures lead God's people to the perfection of virginity.

> First they should abandon the intermarriage of brothers and sisters, and marry wives from other families; and then that they should no longer have many wives, like brute beasts, as though born for the mere propagation of the species; then that they should not be adulterers; and then again that they should go on to continence, and from continence to virginity, when, having trained themselves to despise the flesh, they sail fearlessly into the peaceful haven of immortality.[42]

Jerome argues that "just as widows receive a greater reward from God than wives obedient to their husbands, they, too, must be content to see virgins preferred before themselves."[43] Ruether says that for Gregory of Nyssa virginity is the ideal state. This is followed by married women living a "virgin" life, and thus "celibacy becomes second in rank to the ideal state."[44] Salisbury says that "the Fathers firmly believed that the ideal life was that of dedicated virginity, followed by widowhood or chaste marriage. [Then] marriage with its carnal debt, of necessity the lowest in a hierarchy which drew such strict distinction between the flesh and the spirit."[45]

These Fathers believed that sexual perfection, i.e., virginity, could only be achieved by a man, for the essence of man was spiritual, and it was "the manliness of the virgin woman" that was able to transcend "the sexual nature itself."[46]

Therefore, Schulenburg and McNamara are reminding us that one of the issues facing women in early Christian communities was that of self-definition. We have already seen how women in Greek, Latin, and Jewish cultures were assigned roles by the men in these cultures. They were defined as daughters of fathers, wives of husbands, mothers of children (preferably male children) or prostitutes of male customers. Who women were was determined by their relationship to males, and only by their relationship to males. They were sexual and/or reproductive creatures who were used in the service of a patriarchal family and a patriarchal culture. Ruether says that for the ancients "Procreation, indeed, is the only purpose for the existence of a female as distinct from a male body."[47]

Further, any attempts by women to define themselves apart from the standard definitions given to them by men were met with suspicion, anger, and threats of violence. Corrington says that "the graphic sexual mutilation that appears in [Persian martyr] stories, rare in martyrologies of men, serve, as does the transvestism in the stories of penitents, to destroy their identity as women and take on that of men."[48] We read in the Gnostic literature how families and rulers responded to women who, upon conversion, decided to be either virginal or celibate. Early female monastic communities, which allowed these women a degree of autonomy, were quickly brought under control of their male counterparts. And although Kraemer argues that "ascetic Christianity . . . offered women a new measure of worth which involved a rejection of their traditional roles," in reality, to be a "sister in Christ" did not change her status vis-à-vis autonomy and freedom.[49] Although Paul had written to the Galatian believers (Gal 3.28) that in Christ there were no longer the categories of "male and female," in practice, those categories continued to exist. And in the early Christian communities, which were patriarchal to the core, women were still being defined by men.

Therefore, although all Christian women should aspire to the designation of virgin, not all could. Further, whereas in the wider cultures women who submitted to the imposed roles of wife and mother were honored and blessed, in the writings of some early Christian Fathers, those women who chose to be wives and mothers were considered weaker then virgins. Ruether reminds us that "marriage .. is seen as intrinsically inferior to virginity" and "to marry at all is seen as choosing the lower course, [and] not living in the resurrected order."[50] The strongest women, the most devoted and committed women, were now given the designation of "saint." With very few (but notable) early exceptions, only women who devoted both body and soul to Christ could aspire to sainthood. Only the virginal women were allowed a degree of equality with the men in the Christian communities. These women, by disassociating themselves completely from their sexual selves, were worthy of praise. These sexless women, because they were sexless, were no longer a threat to the Christian men. They could no longer tempt, seduce, and bring to ruin the men who had devoted themselves to Christ. The inference is that the allure of a woman's sexuality is so powerful that it could undermine a life devoted to Christ. The attraction of female sexuality was viewed as stronger than the attraction of Christ. Indeed, Ruether points out that Augustine speaks of the "hideous" male erection, and of his "horrified description of the male erection and its key role in his doctrine of sin."[51] However, "if the male erection was the essence of sin, woman as its source, became peculiarly the cause, object and extension of it."[52]

Ruether also speaks powerfully to this issue of imposed definitions of women. She notes that Augustine engaged in this process of definition for women, and concludes with the following:

[The] assimilation of male-female dualism into soul-body dualism in patristic theology conditions basically the definition of woman, both in terms of her

subordination to the male in the order of nature and her "carnality" in the disorder of sin. The result of this assimilation is that woman is not really seen as a
self-sufficient, whole person with equal honor, as the image of God in her own
right, but is seen, ethically, as dangerous to the male . . . This double definition
of woman, as submissive body in the order of nature and "revolting body in the
disorder of sin, allows the Fathers to slide somewhat inconsistently from
the second to the first and attribute woman's inferiority first to sin and then to
nature. In Augustine the stress falls decidedly on the side of woman's natural inferiority as body in relation to mind in the right ordering of nature.[53]

Salisbury agrees with Ruether, and tells us that for Tertullian it was the
"carnality of her sexuality, which had been the primary definition of [a
woman's] nature."[54] And because it was the carnality of a woman's nature
that defined her, "Tertullian demands an abasement of woman and the cover-
ing of her shameful female nature as the consequence of her continuing im-
aging of [the] guilty nature of Eve."[55]

## THE POLITICS OF VIRGINITY:
## CONTROLLING VIRGINITY = CONTROLLING VIRGINS

There are over twenty-five documents written by Christian writers (letters,
epistles, apologies, commentaries) from the early second century to the early
sixth century specifically dealing with some aspect of virginity. The authors
that scholars can identify, Tertullian, Cyprian of Carthage, Methodius of
Olympus, Basil of Caesarea, Gregory of Nyssa, Ambrose, Jerome, John
Chrysostom, Augustine of Hippo, Sulpitius Severus, and Leander of Seville
are all males. The authors of the documents which cannot be identified either
claim to be written by men (*The Epistle of Titus, the Disciple of Paul, on the
State of Chastity*) or have been given male pseudopigraphical designations
(Pseudo-Clement; Pseudo-Athanasius). The topics range from the dress of
virgins to how and where and with whom virgins could live, to theological
treatises on the superiority of virginity over against marriage, to assurances of
salvation to those strong enough to commit to a life of virginity, to warnings
of damnation to those who either have "fallen" from a life of virginity or
would even consider leaving that life. And while some of the arguments are
more theologically sophisticated than others, all of the authors lean heavily
on Scripture, the divine Word of God, to support their arguments.

Many of these documents are addressed to particular women (wives or sisters). Others, though not addressed to women exclusively, are unmistakenly
directed toward women rather than men. The directions given to virgins on
how to live their lives—what to wear, how to appear in public, who to live

with, how to travel, who to associate with, what to think, how to pray—are almost exclusively directed toward women. Very little attention is given to male virgins, and none of the authors delineate how male virgins are to live to the degree that they do for women. This lack of attention to male virginity, coupled with an obsession with the female body and female virginity, point quite clearly to issues of control, autonomy and fear. Put simply, in all ancient Mediterranean cultures, both political and religious, female sexuality must be controlled. She must never have control of her own body, for if she gains control over her own body, she has begun to move toward control over her own identity.[56] As a child she is under the control of her family, and in particular her father. And in ideal situations, she moves directly from the control of her father to the control of her husband. She is forbidden to engage in any sexual activity, under penalty of the severest punishment, until she marries the man chosen by her father to be her husband. Of course it is naive to believe that this pattern was always followed. There were options for women, but all of them either came with the high price of peril or shame or both.

Some women became adulterous. To believe that only husbands engaged in extramarital relations is wrong. To believe that wives either had the desire or the opportunities to engage in these relations to the degree that husbands did is also wrong. But there are too many stories of cuckolds in ancient Greek and Roman histories and plays to deny that some married women took on other lovers.

Some women became prostitutes, or more correctly, were forced into prostitution, either through slavery, abandonment, or poverty. However, to claim that these women had gained a degree of sexual autonomy is to ignore the evidence that this was a perilous life, a short life, of extreme danger and degradation.[57]

Other women, refusing to follow the pattern of passing from the control of one man to another refused to marry. Some women became ascetics, and either lived in isolation or lived with fellow ascetics. Yet we have already seen how a woman who chose that life was viewed. Corrington reminds us that "conversion to celibacy was an affront to the Greco-Roman social order because it appeared to be a denial of heteronomy (outside control) and an assertion of autonomy (self-control)."[58] She lists stories in the *Apocryphal Acts of the Apostles* where women, by taking control of their own sexual identity assume either authority or power over their own lives.[59] And Salisbury notes that "for these women, the renunciation of their sexuality and the preservation of their virginity or even chastity was enough to confer some measure of power, power over their own bodies and, by extension, over their own lives." [60] These women were breaking with traditions that were ancient and sacred. To allow this to proceed unchecked was not an option in a patriarchal society, for not only were these women living lives with no reference to males, there was the possibility that they would influence other women to live autonomous lives, free from the control of men.

However, to argue, as Ruether does, that the women who did not follow the ancient traditions practiced by their mothers for generations beyond memory for the specific reason of, or even primarily to gain *sexual* autonomy is asking too much of these women. Ross Kraemer argues, more correctly, that "ascetic Christianity, in fact, offered women a new measure of worth which involved a rejection of their traditional sociosexual roles."[61] That the end result of this decision was a degree of sexual autonomy does not allow scholars to assume that sexual autonomy was the *raison d'etre* for these alternate life choices. The fact does remain that the women who choose celibacy did, for a time, and in some places, gain a degree of autonomy. How modern scholars have interpreted this freedom is where we next turn our attention.

Many of the Fathers write of the horrors of child-birth and motherhood; of the dangers and inevitable separation and death that must follow marriage and motherhood. The alternative to all of this death and sorrow was virginity. Cyprian of Carthage, for example, writes, "What else is virginity than the freedom of liberty? It has no husband for a master. Virginity is freed from all affections: it is not given up to marriage, nor to the world, nor to children."[62] Therefore, while it is true that the church Fathers who wrote on virginity do extol the virtues of being childless, to suggest that these same men are also praising virginity because frees women from male domination is not defensible. While the Fathers were not only interested and even desirous of women becoming virgins, they were also interested and insistent on controlling not only individual virgins, but the growing virgin communities as well. Joyce Salisbury in her exploration of this issue in her excellent book *Church Fathers, Independent Virgins* says:

> Church Fathers were placed in a curious dilemma when they explored the ideal of virginity and considered the position of women living a chaste life. On the one hand, they strongly supported the ideal of virginity. There was a sufficiently strong bias against the flesh in the Scriptures, particularly in the writings of Paul, to provide a theoretical basis for advocating celibacy. However, the advocacy of virginity and ascetic renunciation in general was leading to the presence of holy women assuming an independence that was unacceptable to the Fathers.[63]

Salisbury argues that some of these women were, in fact, "claiming freedom from ecclesiastical authority" and that they seemed "to have believed that such independence also exempted them from expected women's social roles."[64] She goes on to say that these women were claiming "power over their own bodies and, by extension, over their own lives."[65] McNamara comes to the same conclusion and states, "the unstructured new religion that spread through the Empire offered, among its other attractions, a strong individualistic message which some women used . . . to create a positive new identity grounded in celibacy, and transcending the gender system."[66]

However, decisions by Christian ascetic women which freed them from traditional sociosexual roles cannot be globalized to read that they were free from the control of men. It was, in fact, male authors who wrote reams and reams of paper on what virgins could and could not do, think, dress, and act. And these were not suggestions which the virgins were free to dismiss. Not following these directives resulted in dire consequences in this life and in the next. The virgins who chose to live in convents in the company only of other women, and who lived under the leadership of an Abbess, were still dependent on male priests to administer God's grace through the sacraments. In a religion whose soteriology was becoming more and more sacramental, the administration of these sacraments was indispensable, and only male priests were authorized to bring God's grace to His people, including virgins. Therefore, their link to heaven, their link to God, their access to salvific grace was administered through male priests.

Further, Ruether's statement that "in the fourth century . . . many women were taking literally the Church's ascetic preaching as a mandate for woman's liberation." is anachronistic.[67] The whole idea of "women's liberation," and its theological, academic sister, feminist theology, is a late 20th century ideology. There simply is no evidence, nor can any evidence be interpreted which allows us in the 21st century to read back into the fourth century, 20th century ideology. It can be argued that some of the women who opted for a life of virginity did so to escape the vicissitudes of a life as wife and mother. But that is a long way from saying that many women in the fourth century were taking the Church's ascetic preaching as a mandate for women's liberation.

Some of the Fathers' instructions to virgins included warnings against spiritual pride. Ambrose writes, "for if women are bidden to keep silence in churches, even about divine things, and to ask their husbands at home, what do we think should be the caution of virgins, in whom modesty adorns their age, and silence commends their modesty."[68] Virgins have no husbands to ask about divine things. Therefore, their silence must be absolute, and by remaining silent they will demonstrate their modesty. Augustine tells virgins that "virginity is not only to be set forth, that it may be loved, but also to be admonished, that it be not puffed up,"[69] and McNamara says that Augustine *In Praise of Marriage* warns "that the marriage of the faithful is to be set up above the virginity of the impious."[70] Sulpitius Severus asks, "Do you flatter yourself on account of the attribute of virginity? Remember Adam and Eve fell when they were virgins, and that the perfect purity of their bodies did not profit them when they sinned."[71]

One of two tentative conclusions can be drawn from these warnings. Some virgins were, either by actions or words, declaring themselves to be superior to the married women in the congregations in which they worshiped. In other words they were "rubbing their noses in it." The other possible conclusion is that these men were suspicious that virgins were in fact gaining a degree of autonomy, acting and making decisions for themselves, and these warnings are rearguard actions to keep this degree of autonomy from becoming something that they (the men) would not know how to handle. It was unthinkable that these women, who were already regarded as Christ like and angelic, would have complete control over their own spirituality. Yet Simpson says that "from the time of Cyprian and of Methodius in the middle of the third century to the time of Chrysostom and Gregory the Great in the fifth and sixth centuries and later, thousands and thousands of virgins in all churches in the East and in the West lived in their own homes without being subjected to a superior and a rule."[72] Still, these virgins lived "under the general supervision of a bishop."[73] To combat the possibility that these women might gain control over their own spiritual lives they must be reminded that they are to keep silent, and their status as virgins is not a license nor a freedom from the male hierarchy of the church.

Jerome, for one, made sure virgins remained under, and lived by the rules established by the catholic church. In reading his letters one is struck with his absolute obsession with controlling every aspect of a virgins life, from the time she emerges from her mother's womb to the grave.[74] He orders the virgins to "diligently open your ears and keep your modesty closed; open your hands that you recognize paupers; close your door so dishonor doesn't creep in; open you mind and keep pure."[75] Virgins are to "never look upon a man, especially upon a young man," and "you should never hear an improper word" for "one in your position ought to be serious."[76] Salisbury drawing on works from Jerome, Tertullian, and Ambrose says that instructions to virgins included "avoid[ing] worldly society . . . she was to . . . 'avoid the market place and the city squares,' attend no weddings, and certainly she was not to travel to 'visit the daughters of a strange land.'"[77]

Issues of autonomy and control are also evidenced in language to describe the consequences of the virgins who later repudiated their vows. Virgins were to understand that if they chose to no longer remain eternally virginal, they were placing themselves back under the control of earthly men. Sulpitius Severus writes that, "The virgin who sins is to be compared to Eve, and not to Mary."[78] The implication of comparing the fallen virgin to Eve over against

Mary could not be more pointed. Eve was seen by many of the early church Fathers, and not just the ones writing about virginity, as the mother of all sorrow and separation from God. And Severus is saying that just as God placed Eve under the control and authority of her husband, so the fallen virgin has voluntarily placed herself under the control and authority of a man, rather than God. She has chosen to care for the things of this world, rather than the things of God. Therefore, women in early Christianity were never totally freed from the control of men. Female virgins depended on male priests for the sacraments, and married women, because they had followed Eve, were under the control of their husbands.

Early Christianity's theology of "the fall" was laid squarely at the feet of Adam and Eve, with Eve receiving, from some, more than equal blame. Therefore, the guilt of a fallen virgin resonates and mirrors the guilt of Eve. Eve was given the gift of virginity, but because of the fall she forced herself and Adam from the Paradise God had given them, and they were to populate the world, now, through sexual intercourse. Chrysostom argues that God could have continued to populate the world without having to resort to sexual intercourse. In *On Virginity* he says:

> Tell me, what sort of marriage produced Adam? What kind of birth pains produced Eve? You could not say. Therefore why have groundless fears? Why tremble at the thought of the end of marriage, and thus the end of the human race? An infinite number of angels are at the service of God, thousands upon thousands of archangels are beside him, and none of them have come into being from the succession of generations, none from childbirth, labor pains and conception. Could he not , then, have created many more men without marriage? Just as he created the first two from whom all men descend.[79]

Feelings of lust, then, in both men and women, were foreign to Adam and Eve before the fall. But part of the price of that fall was living lives in which feelings of lust must be constantly wrestled with. This struggle kept God's creation from devoting their full energies and minds on God.

## THE POLITICS OF VIRGINITY: LEGISLATED CONTROL OF VIRGINITY

In the fourth century church councils and synods began to address questions concerning virginity. The effect of these deliberations was greater control over both the lives and sexuality of female Christians whether married or virginal (there are even canons concerning prostitutes). We can assume from this that the vocation of virginity was not being practiced by just a few. More and more believers, both men and women, consecrated themselves to a life of virginity. But for some the early flush of commitment to this life faded, and they found themselves repudiating their vows either through marriage or fornication. As early as 305 C.E., sixteen years before the legalization of Christianity in the Roman Empire, at the Council of Elvira, thirty-four of the eighty-one (c. 2/5) of the canons "involved imposing greater control than heretofore on the women of the Christian community."[80] Two canons, numbers thirteen and fourteen, were promulgated concerning virginity.

Canon 13. Virgins who have been consecrated to God shall not commune even as death approaches if they have broken the vow of virginity and do not repent. If, however, they repent and do not engage in intercourse again, they may commune when death approaches.

Canon 14. If a virgin does not preserve her virginity, but she then marries a man, she may commune after one year, without doing penance, for she only broke the laws of marriage. If she has been sexually active with other men, she must complete a penance of five years before being readmitted to communion.

One of the concerns here involves the openly unholy or "polluted" (the lapsed virgin) eating the body and drinking the blood of Christ. Since sexual intercourse was inherently polluting, and since the bread and wine became the holy body and blood of Christ, those engaging in polluting intercourse, through fornication or adultery, may not approach that which is holy. The mingling of the profane and the sacred is sacrilege, and must not be allowed in the community of believers for fear that the entire community will share in the sin and guilt associated with the sacrilege. Just as the fallen Vestal Virgin compromised the military security of the Roman empire, so the fallen Christian virgin compromises the eternal security of the Christian community, and jeopardizes their entrance into the eternal Kingdom of God. In any case, these two canons are evidence that the lives of those who were recognized as virgins, and who most likely had taken open vows of virginity, had gotten the attention of the leaders of the church, and these leaders began to answer questions concerning their status through piecemeal church legislation. No matter how this is read, it addresses, in the end, issues of authority, autonomy and control.

Nine year later (314 C.E.) the leaders of the Christian communities in the vicinities around Ancyra met, and also turned their attention to matters of virginity.

Canon 11. It is decreed that virgins who have been betrothed, who have afterwards been carried off by others, shall be restored to those to whom they had formerly been betrothed, even though they may have suffered violence from the ravisher.

Canon 19. If any persons who profess virginity shall disregard their profession, let them fulfill the term of bigamists. And, moreover, we prohibit women who are virgins from living with men as sisters.

It seems questions had been raised by situations of what to do with betrothed, young, virgins who are raped. They can no longer offer to their husbands their virginity, and one has to wonder if this caused some of the men to have second thoughts about marrying a women who was no longer (in his eyes) sexually pure. It is curious that nothing appears in the canons concerning discipline of the "ravisher." Perhaps, in 314 CE, when much of the population was still non-Christian, they could not conceive that a Christian man would ever commit this sin, so the "ravisher" is left to the authorities. Years later when the Empire became officially Christian, the "ravisher" would be dealt with by Christian authorities whether he was a Christian or not.[81]

Canon 19 seems to just throw two disparate concern together in one canon. To "fulfill the term of bigamists" is unfamiliar to me, but it appears to be some sort of discipline that is imposed on lapsed virgins, and their sin warrants the same discipline as those who have engaged in bigamy.

## THE PROBLEM OF "SPIRITUAL MARRIAGES" AND SHARED LIVING

The second part of Canon 19 deserves more attention. There is a growing concern about female virgins practicing and living out their virginity while living in the same house with men. We have evidence that this was a growing practice. Fee and others define this relationship as virgin men and women "who are committed to one another in "spiritual marriage."[82] Fee argues that "although unknown this early [middle of first century] elsewhere, this practice prevailed in several quarters of the church from the second century to the fifth."[83] Elm points out that Origen, in the third century "spent two years in Caesarea 'hidden in the house of the virgin Juliana.'"[84]

Ben Witherington III gives the following description:

By the time the *Shepherd of Hermas* was written, we already appear to have indications of the strange practice of the *virgines subintroductae*. As Tavard points out, there were unmarried deacons, priests, monks, and apparently bishops, who were sharing homes, and even beds 'chastely' with these virgins. Paul of Samasota, Bishop of Antioch in AD 260, apparently lived with several such women, and Cyprian in Africa also knew of this practice (*Epistle* 61 [62] to

Pomponius). Paul, however, was deposed for aberrant Christology in AD 268, whereas Cyprian seems to be writing to orthodox Christians. This practice was considered suspect and was condemned not only by Cyprian, but also by Chrysostom, Ambrose of Milan, and the Council of Antioch.[85]

The bishops assembled at the Council of Nicea turned their attention to this issue, and Canon 3 reads, "The great Synod has stringently forbidden any bishop, presbyter, deacon or anyone of the clergy whatever, to have a subintroducta dwelling with him except only a mother, or sister, or aunt, or such persons only as are beyond all suspicion." However, in spite of these injunctions, the practice persisted. Susanna Elm writes that ascetic Christian communities "consisted of male and female ascetics who cohabited."[86] She says that the reasoning might have sounded something like the following:

> If the ascetic life transforms humans into angels, [and] if angels neither marry nor are given in marriage (Mt 22.30), and if there is neither male nor female in Jesus Christ, then the symbiosis of male and female ascetics represents the highest form of ascetic perfection.[87]

Brown writes that "a persistent campaign of preaching and canonical legislation came to be directed against monks and members of the clergy who sought female spiritual companions of this kind, . . . and the most exhaustive cautionary [work] came from . . . Basil, Bishop of Ancyra."[88] Apparently Basil believed that "in this life, there could be no such thing as sexual innocence, and hence no such thing as an innocent asexual relationship between a man and a women."[89] Jerome voices his suspicions in his letter to Eustochium.

> Whence come these unwedded wives, these novel concubines, these harlots, so I will call them, though they cling to a single partner? One house holds them and one chamber. They often occupy the same bed, and yet they call us suspicious if we fancy anything amiss. A brother leaves his virgin sister; a virgin, slighting her unmarried brother, seeks a brother in a stranger. Both alike profess to have but one object, to find spiritual consolation for those not of their kin; but their real aim is to indulge in sexual intercourse.[90]

Chrysostom viewed these living arrangements as completely unholy, and threatens women who are living with men with the following imprecitations; "Just look; [living with men] leads you down from the heavens, bars you from the spiritual wedding chamber, separates you from your celestial Bridegroom, procures eternal punishment and torture without end."[91] Brown goes on to write that "only by adopting strict codes of sexual avoidance and by taking on the firm contours of a man (in walk, in tone of voice, in a general "unnatural" masculine brusqueness) could a virgin defend herself against the lure of false familiarity with fellow -militants of the opposite sex."[92] McNamara says that Augustine praised such a couple, "Aper and Amanda, especially the wife who 'did not lead her husband to effeminacy and greed but . . . to self-discipline and courage.'"[93] Augustine also advised an Ecdicia "to . . . obey [her husband] and submit to his will in all things except the carnal debt which they had both renounced."[94]

It appears that this "spiritual marriage was also practiced among the gnostics. Kraemer writes "Maximilla in the *Acts of Andrew* continues to live a celibate life within her husband's household, despite his vigorous protestations. Drusiana in the *Acts of John*, however, lives chastely and harmoniously with her husband, Andronicus, an instance of the 'virgin marriage' apparently practiced by some early Christians."[95]

Finally Brown reminds us that the relationship between female virgins and male leaders of the Christian communities in which they lived was not only one of control, but of protection as well; protection from either local non-Christians or the virgins' own families.

Brown writes that "dedicated virgins of the church of Alexandria had been subjected to ritual humiliation by [the enemies of the Patriarch Athanasius]."[96] He goes on to talk about how young girls, no matter what their desires vis-à-vis virginity, were still under the control of their families. And these families, often for reasons other than a desire to see their daughters serve Christ as one of His brides, would offer their daughters as candidates. Brown says that "in many regions, the girls resolution was not given final, public ratification, through the bestowing of a veil, until . . . the woman was safely past childbearing age, and was no longer a pawn in the game of family alliances."[97]

## NOTES

1. Jerome *To Demetrias* 2.
2. ibid., 10.
3. Tertullian *On the Veiling of Virgins* 15.
4. Jerome *Commentary on the Epistle to Ephesus* 3.5.
5. Ambrose *Exposition on the Gospel According to Luke* 10.161.
6. Jo Ann McNamara, "Sexual Equality and the Cult of Virginity in Early Christian Thought," in *Women in Early Christianity* ed. David M. Scholer (New York: Garland Press, 1993), 154.
7. Susanna Elm, *Virgins of God: The Making of Asceticism in Late Antiquity* (New York: Clarendon Press, 1994), ix.
8. Gregory of Nazianzus *Epitaph for His Mother* 70.

9. Gregory of Nyssa *The Life of Macrina*
10. McNamara, "Sexual Equality and the Cult of Virginity," 153.
11. Brown, *Body and Society* 10.
12. ibid., 13.
13. *Gospel of Mary* 5.
14. Hoffman, *Status of Women and Gnosticism*, 41.
15. Brown, *Body and Society*, 111.
16. ibid., 113.
17. Hoffman, *Status of Women and Gnosticism*, 119, n.31. See Patricia Wilson-Kastner, *A Lost Tradition: Women Writers of the Early Church* (Washington, D.C.: University Press of America, 1981), v-xv.
18. Rosemary Radford Ruether, ed., *Religion and Sexism* (New York: Simon and Schuster, 1974), 157.
19. ibid., 159.
20. Joyce Salisbury, *Church Fathers, Independent Virgins* (New York: Verso Publishing, 1991), 26.
21. ibid.
22. ibid.
23. Corrington, "Propaganda and the Power of Celibacy," 210. A dissenting voice, though hardly a complimentary one, came from Tertullian who Salisbury argues concluded that "a virgin continued to be a woman even though she renounced the carnality of her sexuality, which had been the primary definition of her gender."
24. Ruether, *Religion and Sexism* 160.
25. Brown, *Body and Society* 260. Quote from Eusebius of Emesa, *Homily 6.18*.
26. ibid., 164, 165.
27. Salisbury, *Church Fathers, Independent Virgins*, 22.
28. see n.196.
29. Jerome *Against Helvidius* 22.
30. ibid.
31. Ruether, *Religion and Sexism* 161.
32. Salisbury, *Church Fathers, Independent Virgins*, 22.
33. ibid.
34. Jerome *To Eustochium* 27.
35. Ruether, *Religion and Sexism* 159.
36. ibid.
37. J.T. Schulenburg, *Forgetful of Their Sex: Female Sanctity and Society, ca. 500-1100*, (Chicago: University of Chicago Press, 1998), 129.
38. ibid., 128.
39. Eusebius, *Proof of the Gospel* 1.8. From Brown, *Body and Society* 205.
40. Tertullian *On the Veiling of Virgins* 17.
41. Cyprian of Carthage *Of the Discipline and Advantage of Chastity* 4.
42. Methodius of Olympus *On Virginity* (To Marcella) 2.
43. Jerome *To Pammachius* 9.
44. Ruether, *Religion and Sexism*, 177.
45. Salisbury, *Church Fathers, Independent Virgins*, 28.

46. McNamara, "Sexual Equality and the Cult of Virginity," 228.

47. Ruether, *Religion and Sexism* 162.

48. Corrington, "Propaganda and the Power of Celibacy," 211.

49. Kraemer, "The Conversion of Women to Ascetic Forms of Christianity," 301.

50. Ruether, *Religion and Sexism*, 164.

51. ibid., 162.

52. ibid.

53. ibid., 156, 157.

54. Salisbury, *Church Fathers, Independent Virgins* 27.

55. Ruether, *Religion and Sexism* 157.

56. Corrington argues that even in the Greek romance plays "the miraculous oc-currences connected with the chastity of the Greek romantic heroine do not function as 'dramas of authority' by which she takes control of her own identity, but as 'res-cue' miracles, which preserve her chastity for its proper destiny; marriage." Corring-ton, "Propaganda and the Power of Celibacy," 216.

57. The wish of some modern scholars to sanitize and even glamorize ancient prostitution as a noble choice made by women simply does not have any supporting evidence. These women were often brutalized, and lived in constant fear of death.

58. ibid., 214.

59. ibid., 219-220. She points to stories in *Acts of John, Acts of Peter, Acts of Paul and Thecla, Acts of Paul, Acts of Andrew, and Acts of Thomas.*

60. Salisbury, *Church Fathers, Independent Virgins*, 4.

61. Kraemer, "The Conversion of Women to Ascetic Forms of Christianity," 300.

62. Cyprian of Carthage *Of the Discipline and Advantage of Chastity* 7.

63. Salisbury, *Church Fathers, Independent Virgins*, 5.

64. ibid., 3.

65. ibid., 4.

66. McNamara, "Sexual Equality and the Cult of Virginity in Early Christian Thought,"

67. ibid.

68. Ambrose, *Concerning Virginity* 3.9

69. Augustine, *Of Holy Virginity* 1.

70. McNamara, "Sexual Equality and the Cult of Virginity in Early Christian Thought," 230, n.60.

71. Sulpitius Severus, *Concerning Virginity* 10.

72. Simpson, "Women and Asceticism in the fourth Century," 42.

73. ibid.

74. Ruether, on pp.170-171, lists some of the restrictions Jerome places on young women as they grow into womanhood which are designed to keep her mind and body free from any turning away from a life devoted to virginity. Her explanation of this obsession as a "violent libidinal repression that generates its own opposite in vivid sensual fantasizing under the guise of antisensual polemics" seems to be the most plausible explanation. 174.

75. Jerome, *To Eustochium* 28.

76. Jerome *To Demetrias* 12, 13.

77. Salisbury, *Church Fathers, Independent Virgins*, 33. Quotes taken from Jerome, *To Rusticus*; Tertullian, *On the Apparel of Women*; and Ambrose, *On the Institution of Virginity*.

78. Sulpitius Severus, *Concerning Virginity* 10.

79. John Chrysostom, *On Virginity* 14.6.

80. Brown, *The Body and Society* 206.

81. Pope Leo I (440-461) in a letter to the Bishops of Africa "maintains that the servants of God who lost the purity of chastity through the violence of the barbarians are not to be punished." Schulenburg, *Forgetful of Their Sex*, 133.

82. Fee, *The First Epistle to the Corinthians*, 326. In n.16 Fee says that Hurd, in *The Origin of I Corinthians* (169-182) argues that Paul is speaking of "spiritual marriages" here, and that other "commentaries by Thrass, Ruef, and Murphy-O'Connor, and esp. R.H.A. Sebolt, 'Spiritual Marriage in the Early Church: A Suggested Interpretation of 1 Cor 7:36-38,' *CTM* 30 (1959), 103-19, 176-89) also support this definition. Other Bible Commentaries who believe that Paul, in 1 Cor 7.36-38, is talking about a "spiritual marriage" are *The Anchor Bible: I Corinthians* (1976), 223; *The New Jerome Bible Commentary* (1990), 805; *Women's Bible Commentary* (1992), 415; and *The Abingdon Bible Commentary* (1929), 1181.

83. ibid., 327.

84. Elm, *Virgins of God*, 30.

85. Ben Witherington III, *Women in the Earliest Churches* (New York, NY: Cambridge University Press, 1988), 203.

86. Elm. *Virgins of God*, ix.

87. ibid.

88. Brown, *Body and Society* 267.

89. ibid.

90. Jerome *To Eustochium* 14.

91. John Chrysostom *On the Necessity of Guarding Virginity* 6.

92. Brown, *Body and Society* 267.

93. McNamara, "Sexual Equality and the Cult of Virginity," 154.

94. Salisbury, *Church Fathers, Independent Virgins*, 1.

95. Kraemer, 300.

96. Brown, *Body and Society* 259.

97. ibid., 260.

# Chapter Seven

# The Growth of Virginity in Early Christianity

Chapter 7 of the Apostle Paul's first letter to the Corinthians is testament to an early practice of virginity in the ancient church. Ignatius of Antioch (c.35-c.107), in his Epistle to the Smyrnians says, "I salute the families of my brethren, with their wives and children, and those that are ever virgins, and the widows."[1] Polycarp (c.69-c.155) tells the leaders of the church to "Admonish virgins to walk in a spotless and pure conscience."[2] Tertullian (c.160-c.225) also mentions "many virgins married to Christ."[3]

Virginity also began to be very popular with non-catholic Christian communities. Goehring writes that in the second century gnostic "women discovered in the ascetic life style a path through which to escape from the gender-defined constraints imposed upon them by Roman society," and that participation in "the ascetic branches of gnosticism" was extensive.[4] Also in the second century "Marcion demanded absolute continence within marriage, and Marcionite communities in Syria admitted to their congregation as full members only celibates and continent married persons."[5] Tertullian writes that Marcion thought of "marriage as an evil and unchaste thing."[6] Montanists, a Christian sect that flourished in the late second and early third centuries "encouraged virginity within marriage, and many made themselves eunuchs voluntarily and by mutual consent."[7]

In catholic Christian communities we have evidence that as early as the third century there are hundreds of virgins living either singly or in communities. Simpson writes that "From the time of Cyprian [c.200-258] and of Methodius [d. c. 311] in the middle of the third century to the time of Chrysostom [c.347-407] and Gregory the Great [c.540-604] in the fifth and sixth centuries and later, thousands and thousands of virgins in all churches in the East and the West lived in their own homes."[8] There were thousands of others who lived in communities. Salisbury writes that "the persistent practice of female asceticism was

well established by the second century, when enough women had chosen to remain celibate for orders of virgins and widows to be accepted, albeit at times
reluctantly, by established Church authorities."[9] However, Jean LaPorte's argument that established communities of virgins came a century later is better supported by the evidence, and says that virgins "did not constitute an order or a
rank in the Church before the second half of the third century."[10]

Simpson argues that "women were the pioneers of the communal approach."[11] In support of her argument she points to Athanasius who, in his
*Life of Anthony* writes that Anthony of Egypt (c.251-c.356), who is credited
as being the founder of Encriatic monasticism, "could find no communities
for ascetic men when he renounced the world. Yet he was able to place his
sister in a 'house of virgins.'"[12] Further, "Pachomius [290-346], the founder
of coenobitic monasticism proper, built a convent for his sister Mary opposite
his own monastery on the bank of the Nile."[13] And in *The Lusaic History* we
read that these women numbered 400.[14]

Yet it is the fourth century when a commitment to virginity in the Christian community exploded. Elizabeth Clark writes that "their number multiplied steadily through the fourth and fifth centuries when really large
communities of such women were beginning to be established. The reward
of their self-denial was social honor and a promise that they would be first
in the ranks of the saints in heaven."[15] In what might be considered an ex-
aggeration of the figures, Palladius (c.365-425) "reported finding 20,000
virgins and 10,000 monks in the city of Oxyrhynchus alone."[16] John
Chrysostom (c.347-407) speaks of 3,000 virgins and widows enrolled in
the Antioch church.[17] Susanna Elm writes that "by the end of the third century and the beginning of the fourth century A.D. ascetic communities had
developed in urban centers and gained an important voice in ecclesiastical
decisions and doctrinal disputes."[18]

Simpson writes that "properly organized monasteries in the West came
only in the early years of the fifth century,"[19] and Jerome (c.342-420) says
that he "had the joy of seeing Rome transformed into another Jerusalem.
Monastic establishments for virgins became numerous, and of hermits there
were countless numbers."[20]

We can see, then, that virginity became respectable in the fourth century.
It was no longer just the bearded monks living in the desert, but women,
often of high rank, who lived in or near cities, who caused the life of virginity to be a permanent part of the Christian landscape, both in the East
and the West.

Another development which ensured that virginity would become a major
component of the Christian cosmos was the growing practice of celibacy of
the Christian clergy. John Chrysostom (c.347-407) writes that in his day

some, in an effort to give clerical celibacy a pedigree, were saying that Paul's discussion of virginity in 1 Corinthians 7 was addressed to priests, "but I, judging from what follows, could not affirm that it was so."[21] In the fourth century Eusebius[22], Cyril of Jerusalem[23], Jerome[24], and Epiphanius of Salamis[25] testify to the existence of Bishops and/or priests who are celibate. Jerome, argues that the words in 1 Timothy 3.12 about bishops being "the husband of one wife," refers to the situation "in the past, not in the present."[26] In his letter to Pammachius he urges men who have made vows of celibacy to "keep your wife for a little, and do not try too hastily to overcome her re- luctance. Wait till she follows your example. If you only have patience, your wife will some day become your sister."[27] Finally, Socrates Scholasticus, writing in the fifth century, says that "In the East, indeed, all clergymen, and even the bishops themselves, abstain from their wives."[28]

One of the earliest proposals for clerical celibacy was brought to the bish- ops at the council of Nicea (325 C.E.). Bishop Hosius of Cordova proposed a decree mandating clerical celibacy, but was opposed by the Egyptian Bishop Paphnutius, and the decree failed to pass. However, in the following years, several Popes (Damasus I (384), Siricius (385), Innocent I (404), and Leo I (458)) issued decrees on clerical celibacy. It needs to be pointed out that in the seventy-four years between the decree of Damasus and Leo, the decree was reissued twice. It can be implied from this that not all of the clergy were adhering to these decrees.

Not only were the Popes interested in making the clergy celibate, but local councils all over the Empire were issuing similar decrees, including Carthage (390; 401-419), Orange (441), Tours (461), and Turin (398). Canons 3 and 4 of the Council of Carthage in 419 read:

Canon 3: It [is] becoming that the sacred rulers and priests of God . . . or those who served at the divine sacraments should be continent altogether.

Can 4: It seems good that a bishop, a presbyter, and a deacon, or whoever per- form the sacraments, should be keepers of modesty and should abstain from their wives.

Epiphanius of Salamis (d.403) stated that the "Holy church respects the dignity of the priesthood to such a point that she does not admit to the dea- conate, the priesthood, or the episcopate, or even to the subdeaconate, anyone still living in marriage and begetting children. She accepts only him who if married gives up his wife or has lost her by death, especially in those places where the ecclesiastical commands are strictly attended to." And we are told that "by the time of Leo I no bishop, priest, deacon, or subdeacon could be married.[29]

However, the issuance of these decrees did not go unopposed, especially among some "good Romans" who "tended to assume that the sons of clergymen would follow the profession of their fathers. In many regions, little clerical dynasties, where son followed father or nephew followed uncle, formed the backbone of the Church."[30] Further, many of these men were recruited from high-ranking families, and to ask them to either forego marriage or to cease from having relations with their wives, who were also from high-ranking families, was not universally accepted. Clement of Alexandria, Paphnutius, Jovinianus and Augustine, among others, accepted married clergy. Ambrose also, early in his career, accepted marriage, but soon fell into line with Jerome and others who opposed married clergy. Jerome's most bellicose letter was occasioned by learning that Jovinianus was declaring that all baptized Christians were equally holy in God's sight. His letter in response, which has come to be known as *Against Jovinianus*, was extremely vitriolic against marriage when comparing it to virginity. For Jerome and his supporters, it was a matter of logic. If, in fact, virginity is the highest possible state that a devoted Christian can attain, and if marriage comes in a poor second or third, then it seems only right that the leaders of the Christian communities should be models of that perfection.

It is on this stage, then, and in this context that the great explosion of literature on virginity pours forth. It was a topic, and there were issues at hand that occupied the thoughts and hearts of many Christians in the fourth century. As we look at these issues we will discover that the conclusions drawn in these tracts continued to resonate throughout the Middle Ages, and to today.

## NOTES

1. Ignatius of Antioch *Epistle to the Smyrnians* 13.1
2. *Epistle of Polycarp* 2.24
3. Tertullian *On the Resurrection of the Body* 61.
4. Goehring, "Libertine or Liberated," 329, 330.
5. Simpson, "Women and Asceticism in the Fourth Century," 40.
6. Tertullian *Five Books Against Marcion* 1.29. In continuing his argument against the position of Marcion on marriage he asks, "For how could he desire the salvation of man, whom he forbids to be born, when he takes away that institution from which his birth arises? ibid.
7. Simpson, "Women and Asceticism in the Fourth Century," 41.
8. ibid., 42.
9. Salisbury, *Church Fathers, Independent Virgins,* 4.
10. LaPorte, *The Role of Women in Early Christianity*, 70.
11. Simpson, "Women and Asceticism in the Fourth Century," 42.

12. ibid., 41. From *The Life of Anthony* 54.

13. ibid., 43.

14. *The Lusaic History* 32-33.

15. Elizabeth Clark, "Sexual Politics in the Writings of John Chrysostom," in *Women in Early Christianity*, (New York: Garland Press, 1993), 152.

16. Simpson, "Women and Asceticism in the Fourth Century," 43. From Palladius, *Paradise of the Fathers* 1.337.

17. John Chrysostom *Homily on Matthew 66.3.*

18. Elm, *Virgins of God*, viii.

19. Simpson "Women and Asceticism in the Fourth Century," 44.

20. Jerome *To Principia* 8.

21. John Chrysostom *Homily 19 on 1 Corinthians* 1.

22. Eusebius of Caesarea *Proof of the Gospel* 1.9

23. Cyril of Jerusalem *Catechetical Lectures* 12.25

24. Jerome, *Against Vigilantius* 2

25. Epiphanius of Salamis *Panarion* 59.4

26. Jerome *Against Jovinianus* 35.

27. Jerome *To Pammachius* 5.

28. Socrates *History of the Church* 5.22

29. William P. Saunders, "Clerical Celibacy," in *The Catholic Herald,* April 25, 2002.

30. Brown, *Body and Society* 357.

# Conclusion

The cultures in which Christianity was born and grew were fairly unified in their views on female virginity. For political and/or familial and/or military reasons the Greek, Roman, and Jewish cultures expected and even demanded that all young maidens remain virgins until they were married. These same young maidens were then, usually by the age of fourteen, entered into pre-arranged marriages, and were expected to produce legal heirs for the state and their families. Neither divorce from a husband, nor even the death of a husband, released women from these expectations. Widows of childbearing age were expected to remarry. Women were of value as long as they could continue to produce children. They had to be able (or at least willing) to give birth to as many children as their bodies could withstand. If these women were, for some reason, unable to procreate, then the gods were called on to help them become fertile. And if after appealing to the gods the women became pregnant, and had a successful pregnancy, then it was the will of the gods.

In both the Greek and Roman cultures the only women who were expected to remain virginal past the usual marrying age were priestesses at many, though not all, sacred temples. Some of these women were set aside at an early age and were expected to maintain their virginity to their death, while others were to remain virgins during the length of their service to the gods.

The primary reason for this demand for virginity was fear of sacral pollution. The widespread belief that sexual intercourse was somehow polluting demanded that these women, who represented their communities to the gods, remain free from acts which would bring pollution to the holy, sacred places.

These women stood in the presence of the gods to represent the people who had chosen them. They were, in very real ways, symbolized through ritual services, the intermediaries between the society and the gods of that society. These women became "sacred women" when they were chosen to serve their gods. Yet they remained sacred only as long as they maintained their virginity.

Women who were chosen by the people to represent them to the gods stood apart. They were pure, untainted, and without pollution. Dedicated virgins who engaged in sexual intercourse brought pollution, and to bring that pollution into the gods' presence was a grave crime; a crime in Rome punishable by death. It might be stated otherwise like this: Those who are the closest to the gods; those who represent the people to the gods, cannot, under any circumstances, become unclean. Therefore, the virgins that served in the Greek temples, and the Vestal Virgins of Rome, had to remain virginal. Virginity and service to the gods were seen as natural partners. As the gods were different from humans, so those who served the gods must be different from the rest of the people. Both Greek and Roman societies chose virginity to be that point of difference. Service to the gods meant virginity to and for the gods. This coupling of virginity and service to God, in Christian communities, takes on imports and meanings never imagined in either the Greek or Roman worlds.

Therefore, virginity in the ancient pagan world, for the general populace, was an anomaly. In Greek and Roman cultures, where women had limited options as to their contributions to the societies in which they lived, their destinies were often chosen for them.

The evidence from the Hebrew Scriptures, Philo, Josephus, the Essenes, Roman and Rabbinic literature, strongly suggest, that in the Jewish culture, as in the Greek and Roman cultures, while virginity was valued, and even expected in young, single maidens, the practice of virginity throughout ones entire life, would have been seen as abnormal. In the Jewish culture there was only one holy place, the Temple at Jerusalem, where only males served as priests, and their only marital injunction was that they marry virgins.

These cultures—Greek Roman, and Jewish—provided the historical and literary context for early Christianity, and, there simply are no pre-Common Era documents which call for a life of virginity for the general populace. Even in the writings of the growing and various ascetic groups do we hear a call for absolute and complete sexual abstinence. Soranus of Ephesus's call for life-long virginity for both men and women for health (and for women gynecological) reasons, written c. 2nd c. C.E., although copied and found in later Greek and Latin texts, seems to have fallen on deaf ears, and does not seem to have had much impact on the lives of the common people. Also, the later, growing corpus of Christian literature calling for lives of virginity does not draw on Soranus to support their arguments.

In all three cultures, those who followed an ascetic lifestyle, wrote about lives, and endeavored to live lives above the control of passions, but even in the writings of these ascetics we do not find calls for lives of virginity. It was a life too extreme for most people, and one which was not supported by authorities.

Which is precisely the point of the early Christian Fathers who called on men and women to live virginal lives. They were not to live ordinary lives, for as possessions of Christ they were no longer ordinary people, and these authors were out to prove that a life of virginity, while extreme, was not too extreme, and that self-will and determination would allow these followers of Christ to live lives of purity and holiness, looking toward great promises from their Divine Father as their reward.

Earlier arguments in favor of virginity begin to be repeated, and in all of these works, the single most important biblical text for the support of the practice of lifelong virginity was 1 Corinthians 7; more especially vv.25-38. The Fathers recognized that they could not build their arguments simply on tradition (especially the earlier Fathers), or simply as a reaction to the profligacy and debauchery of the Roman culture. For their arguments to be taken seriously, and to be listened to by an even greater audience, they needed to justify their beliefs from what was established by the fourth century as the Word of God. And while they combed the entire Holy Writ, both Hebrew Scripture and New Testament, it soon became clear that Paul's council to the Corinthian Christians in his first letter to that church was going to be their greatest ally. And when their views on virginity, and its superiority over marriage was challenged, men like Jerome and Augustine, fought back. And as often happened in early theological battles, extreme views were taken in efforts to defend their own positions. This may explain why we hear and read some of the more radical views being expressed by some of the later Fathers on 1 Corinthians 7.

If we ask the question, "Did Paul prefer virginity to marriage?" the best we can say is "Probably." The evidence from 1 Corinthians is that he did. But it seems that Paul preferred virginity to marriage, not on moral grounds, but out of pastoral and eschatological concerns. Paul never suggests that those who do decide to marry are in some way morally inferior to those who choose to remain virgins. Those who seek to find Paul saying that will look in vain. In fact, it is because of the fear of sexual immorality that he urges husbands and wives not to deprive each other sexually. His preference for virginity is to save the believers from the more human concerns that come with marriage and children. The married "will have trouble in this life, and I am trying to spare you." He speaks of the "present distress" and that "the form of this world is passing away [and] I want you to be free from concern." Paul's concern is pastoral and not theological. He is not presenting a theological maxim. That Paul is concerned about morals in the Corinthian church is clear, but the cure for this immorality is not choosing virginity.

The early church Fathers who did write on the subject of virginity did not speak with one voice. Their writings cover c. five centuries, from the early second century to the early sixth century. They wrote their letters, apologies and epistles in the varying cultures of Asia, Africa and Europe. They wrote about virginity when Christianity was still being subjected to periodical persecutions, when Christianity was legalized, and when Christianity became the only recognized religion of the Empire. Therefore, their political and cultural contexts varied greatly. And although theological concerns, i.e., Christology, spiritual dualism, the trinity, etc., occupied many more pens than virginity, the idea and the issues surrounding virginity continued to reappear as a major concern. This is witnessed in the amount of literature devoted to the issues of marriage, sex and virginity. Letters, both general and personal, epistles, diatribes, apologies, even canon law are found in the ancient sources to support the conclusion that the idea and practice of virginity was never far from their minds. The value of virginity, the superiority of virginity over marriage, the eventual legislation of virginity in church synods and councils, and how and where virgins were supposed to live their lives continued to be a subject of interest.

The writings of these men came to be revered, and their writings (that were preserved) soon took on a status that caused them to be seen as authoritative. These men (later) became "saints," and as saints, their writings, especially their commentaries on the Scriptures, were, of course, seen as the most trustworthy and reliable readings of the Scriptures. Therefore, if these men said that the Apostle Paul, in unequivocal language, urged virginity on the followers of Christ, and relegated married Christians to some lesser status, with lesser rewards from God, and/or even disappointment from God, the status of those who did choose virginity rose to holy status. Augustine's tract from the fifth century is not titled *Of Virginity*, but it is titled *Of Holy Virginity*.

The gnostic literature, which abounds with calls to virginity, praise for virgins, and virgin heroes and heroines, is only one example of non-catholic beliefs which also supported (or even demanded) virginity from its followers. And as one reads the stories told in gnostic literature it is hard to miss the realization, even by the gnostic authors themselves, that this call for virginity is both unintelligible to and opposed by the non-gnostic (or at least the non-Christian) populace. Hosts of demons, kings, princes, fathers, mothers, and grooms are presented as being violently opposed to the new, faithful, female, disciples of Christ who urge this life upon their hearers. The gnostic writers tell how the young people who came to listen to these gnostic evangelists were being lied to and led astray. The gnostic writers clearly understood that on this count; that the disciples of Christ would be hated by the world, were all too true. And even though gnostic Christians and catholic Christians found a great deal to argue and fight over theologically, their mutual calls for virginity resonated with each other.

In the early church, then, the practice of virginity grew from a few isolated commitments to a major movement. This drew the attention of more and more church leaders. Those who wrote about virginity were now not only praising virgins and virginity, but voicing warnings and concerns to those practicing virginity, especially female virgins. Apparently not all of the virgins were living in strict obedience to as yet standardized codes to which all virgins needed to submit. Virgins were subjected to the dual commands of living unseen lives, and at the same time having every aspect of their daily lives unceasingly, meticulously examined by the "virginal police." That these women escaped the vicissitudes of married life is certain. But their lives were now lived under a microscope, and the slightest infraction of the "rules of virginity" were met with outbursts of laments and hostility all out of keeping with the severity of the infractions. Many of these virgins, in fact, had less freedom than they would have had as married women with children. Their lives were dissected and legislated by the male leaders of the church.

Written counsels which paraded as concerns for the welfare of the virgins, are now unmasked, often seen as obsessions with and fears of female sexuality. The female body, by its very existence, is the great undoing of God's eternal plans for His creation. Therefore, the only safe women were women who became men, and they could only become men by completely sacrificing and abandoning their femininity. As long as there was a possibility that a woman was able to engage in sexual activity she was unsafe, or at best to be pitied. She was the weaker vessel, and was not worthy of the rich rewards awaiting those who had miraculously and heroically overcome their urges, their nature, their essence. But these "otherwise men" were like the *conversos* of the Middle Ages. Some of the men who wrote about virginity were never quite satisfied that these female virgins had truly, and completely given up their other life. These women were named and controlled, and for many their virginity became a burden far more odious than a life of marriage and childbearing.

Christian life-long virginity was an asceticism that other non-Christian ascetics might admire, and even try to emulate. However, this Christian form of asceticism was not an asceticism for asceticism's sake. Its *raison d'etre* was to please God. This was not based on philosophical virtues, but on the belief that this life would lead them to eternal salvation. This was religious, not philosophical. This was a religion that placed moral demands on its followers. This was a religion that called on its adherents to make a personal commitment to the One God. This was a religion that declared open war on the lusts of the flesh. And while this might have been applauded in some non-Christian circles, the call for life-long virginity was threatening to undo civilization as the people in the Roman Empire knew it. If the numbers quoted by Jerome and others are true; if cities were the homes of hundreds and even thousands of Christian virgins, then something new was happening. These were not a few scattered ascetics quietly living lives divorced from the passions that occupied others. It was one thing to not be controlled by ones passions. It was an entirely different thing to witness throngs of people living lives completely outside of what was considered normal. If the "virgin evangelists" were successful, the empire would soon be powerless to either maintain control over conquered peoples, or conquer as yet unconquered peoples. These Christian virgins were a threat to the *Pax Romana.* It became apparent, then, that these followers of Jesus of Nazareth were not just another bothersome sect of Jews, but a movement, a religion, that raised fears of national survival. Further, whereas pagan ascetics were seen as a rather odd group of people, the virgins were being held up, by the Christians, as people who had the highest honor among the Christians. Not only would these Christians not bow to Caesar, but these mostly female virgins delivered Christians from the hands of the authorities, both natural and supernatural.

Christian virginity, then, in its catholic and non-catholic manifestations, was a new culture. And it was not a new culture that was content to live alongside the established culture, but by its very existence was threatening to destroy the culture it lived in.

In the next section of the book, we will look at how virgins were perceived in their own communities, and what the non-virgin Christians expected from them.

# Part Two

# Virginity in the
# Writings of the Church Fathers

## INTRODUCTION

Variations of the question, "What must I do to be saved?" have been asked by Christians from the very beginning of Christianity.[1] As early Christian authors began to articulate what is was that Christians did believe or ought to believe, they would often, even while discussing some other aspect of doctrine, reveal what they believed concerning issues of salvation. Scholars of early Christian theology who have looked at this question of salvation in the early church have discovered a number of soteriological paradigms.[2] Questions around the stories of the incarnation, the purpose of the incarnation, the essence of the person, substance, and natures of Jesus Christ, the role of faith, grace and obedience to the demands of God all received their share of attention. Salvation as an act of God, a series of acts of God, a process in which God and the saved both worked at together and other possibilities were proposed, read and accepted.

The role that each individual Christian played in his/her salvation appears in most of the early Christian documents. One only needs to read excerpts from the Apostolic Fathers and/or the Second Century Apologists to see that Christians were being taught and told that if they expected to win salvation, they must aid God and Christ in this endeavor.[3]

One of the demands that early Christians of all ilks understood that they must meet was a life of moral purity. This particular demand is first voiced in the canonical epistles and constantly repeated in other contemporary and later Christian documents. The message to the early Christians was that they had two choices. They could choose the world which was portrayed as being unredeemingly evil or they could choose God who was offering an escape from this world to an eternal life of peace and safety. They were told, and they believed, that if they did not escape this world they were doomed to eternal damnation. Christians, once they made the commitment to follow God and Jesus Christ, understood that they had, in some deep and profound ways, turned their backs on this world with its woes. They could no longer live lives as they had. They were called not to just live changed lives, but new lives. And as they began to think about what that meant in practical terms, it occurred to some that one of the ways they could demonstrate to God and the world that they no longer belonged to this world, was to live lives of absolute moral purity; including, or more especially, sexual purity. Many of the early Christians felt the need to fully abandon the pull of the lusts of this world. The lusts of the flesh, which began to be railed against, beginning with the Apostle Paul, continued to be the main tool used by Satan and his servants to pull Christians back into his pits of suffering in this world and the next. Some of these early Christians reasoned that since even sexual intercourse between faithful husbands and wives was in some ways polluting, a life devoted to virginity, of never being polluted, was the best way to thwart the pull of the lusts of the flesh. Not surprisingly the idea and practice of virginity by Christians gained some very powerful allies. These men took the concept of virginity, and tied it to God and salvation in ways that, apparently, appealed to hundreds, and then thousands of early Christians.

This section of this book will explore the ways in which the very idea of virginity, and the practice of virginity was viewed in early Christianity. And we will discover that this idea of Christian virginity, and those practicing virginity gained access to God, were intimate with God, and were the recipients of God's blessings and grace in ways that other Christians could only imagine.

## NOTES

1. cf. Acts 2.37-41.

2. See Roger S. Evans, "Soteriological Paradigms of Early Christianity Within the Intellectual Context of the Early Roman Empire" (Ph.D. diss., Ohio State University, 1996).

3. I am not suggesting that the early Christian authors dismissed God's grace or the blood of Jesus. These were entirely necessary for salvation, and indeed opened the door of salvation. But equally important was the necessity of the Christian cooperating with the grace and will of God in his/her salvation.

# Chapter One

# Virginity:
# A Gift From God/A Gift to God

I should begin by saying a few words about the early Christian understanding of "the call." Perhaps beginning with Paul, but certainly strengthened by Paul, early Christians attached extraordinary importance to a "call" from God. The New Testament canonical writers wrote that God called (καλέω) sinners to repentance (Mt 9.13), believers to discipleship (Mt.4.21), laborers to receive their reward (Mt.20.8), invited guests to the wedding (Mt 22.3), the poor, maimed, lame and blind (Lk 14.13), both Jews and Gentiles (Rm 9.24), and believers to both justification and glorification (Rm 8.30), peace (1 Cor 7.15), God's kingdom and glory (1 Thess 2.12), in holiness (1 Thess 4.7), to obtain the glory of our Lord Jesus Christ (2 Thess 2.14), with a holy calling (2 Tim 1.9), and out of darkness into His marvelous light (1 Pet 2.9). In essence all that Christians were and could be spiritually was traceable back to a call from God. It was a call from death to life. Therefore, the early Christian authors who supported life-long virginity needed to include the "call to virginity" alongside God's other callings. And, although, neither Paul nor any of the other New Testament canonical writers wrote about God calling people to virginity, because of the writings of some early Fathers, virginity was viewed by many in the ancient church as a divine calling and a divine blessing. It was a special gift from God, and as such needed to be cherished. From Cyprian of Carthage in the early second century to Leander of Seville in the sixth century, the early Fathers continued to view this way of life as a calling from God. People did not just choose to be virgins. The anonymous fourth century document *On Virginity* says, "If you are a virgin for Christ, you must not be so according to your own wishes, but according to the wishes of Him, for whose sake you are virgin."[1]

All whom God calls to virginity, according to Cyprian, are called without regard to their sex. Cyprian though, perhaps as a reflection of those who were practicing virginity in the second century, placed the emphasis on men. He says that "indeed not to men only does the Lord promise the grace of continence, disregarding women."[2] Indeed, although some of the literature about virginity in the early church was addressed to both sexes, the language of most of these documents (not to mention the addressees) suggest that the authors had women in mind. Jerome, for example, when discussing the gift of virginity argues that, "Death came through Eve, but life through Mary. And thus the gift of virginity has been bestowed most richly upon women, seeing that it has had its beginning from a woman."[3] Jerome is writing at least 200 years after Cyprian, and perhaps, by the fourth century, the majority of virgins were, in fact, women, and Jerome is simply reporting what he knows. Cyprian, in the second century, is one of the few writers that includes men in his thoughts about virginity.

What Cyprian is also saying is that not only does God call both men and women to virginity, but God also provides the necessary grace to live this life. In other words, this is not a life which can be lived without the strengthening grace from God. Further, once the person is called, he/she begins to cooperate with God in maintaining this gift in purity, and it is their sexual purity that is their gift to God. Cyprian writes:

> Nor is this an empty precaution and a vain fear which takes thought of the way of salvation, which guards the life-giving precepts of the Lord, so that those who have consecrated their lives to Christ, and, renouncing the concupisciences of the flesh, have dedicated themselves to God in body as well as in spirit, may perfect their work, destined as it is for a great reward, and may not be solicitous to adorn themselves nor to please anyone except their Lord, from whom in truth they await the reward of virginity.[4]

The gift of virginity brings in its train divine rewards. By dedicating themselves to God and by accepting the call to virginity these believers are promised salvation and the ability to "perfect their work."

Virginity is God's plan for Christians, and in an effort to explain why virginity has not always been God's plan, Methodius of Olympus writes, "For truly by a great stretch of power the plant of virginity was sent down to men from heaven, and for this reason it was not revealed to the first generations."[5] John Chrysostom, writing in the fourth century, argues that God never intended Adam and Eve to "be fruitful and multiply" through sexual intercourse. For Methodius, it was enough to say that virginity was God's plan for later generations. The point that he is arguing is that making virginity part of humanity's experience was initiated from heaven; not from earth. Humans, left to themselves, would never have thought of practicing life-long virginity, but naturally give themselves over to marriage and intercourse. They do not condemn marriage and even speak of marriage as a gift from God. As Ambrose, Jerome and Augustine discuss the gift of virginity, they often do so in the context of the gift of marriage.

> Ambrose *Concerning Virginity* 6.35—I do not then discourage marriage, but recapitulate the advantages of holy virginity. [Virginity] is the gift of few only, [marriage] is of all.

> Jerome *To Pammachius* 3—Reflect, too, that the gift of virginity is one thing, that of marriage another . . . I allow that marriage, as well as virginity, is the gift of God, but there is a great difference between gift and gift.

> Jerome *Against Jovinianus* 8—But since in the church there is a diversity of gifts, I acquiesce in marriage, lest I should seem to condemn nature. At the same time consider that the gift of virginity is one, that of marriage, another . . . I grant that even marriage is a gift of God, but between gift and gift there is a great diversity.

> Augustine *Of Holy Virginity* 1—We admonished and admonish the virgins of Christ, not, on account of that greater gift which they have received, to despise, in comparison of themselves, the fathers and mothers of the people of God.

These are just four passages where the Fathers reveal their ambivalence concerning marriage. Marriage is also a gift from God, but it is to be understood that it is a far inferior gift when compared to the gift of virginity.

Ambrose argues that virgins live in rarified air. Only they can both receive and truly appreciate this gift. God sees in them a strength and commitment to the call to purity that most Christians simply do not have. So while all can hope for the more common gift of marriage, only a select few are able to respond to the call to virginity.

Jerome "allow[s] that marriage . . . is the gift of God," and he will "grant that even marriage is a gift of God," and, after what seems to be some arm twisting, he will "acquiesce" that marriage is a gift from God. But one can hear the reluctance in his language; that he does not really want to "allow" or "grant" that marriage is a gift from God. In these passages he hastens to remind his readers that there is "a great difference between gift and gift." There is not just a difference between the gift of marriage and the gift of virginity, but a "great difference." Virginity is so far superior to marriage, and the superiority is so obvious, that it seems almost superfluous to even articulate the difference. Jerome is paraphrasing Paul's words in 1 Cor 7.7, but in that passage Paul uses language that does not imply that one gift is superior to the other. He simply says "each one has his own gift from God, one in this manner and another in that." If Paul had wanted to say that the gift of virginity was superior to the gift of marriage he had opportunity to do it in this passage, but he does not assign gradations to the gifts of virginity and marriage, and one can assume that he did not say it, because he did not believe it. For Jerome, however, while he will not allow himself to condemn marriage, he argues that God has clearly demonstrated his preference to virgins.

Augustine falls in line with Jerome, and even more clearly than Jerome, writes unequivocally about "that greater gift which [virgins] have received." What Jerome says implicitly, Augustine says explicitly.

Virgins are not to be numbered with those who are married, nor are the married to be perceived as having equal status before God. Virgins are connected with divinity in ways that the rest of the Christians are not. Sulpitius Severus elevates virginity to an even higher realm. He talks about the gift of virginity being a "heavenly gift," and that "it is above the skies that we must look" for the source of the gift of virginity, and that this is "an ineffable gift, concealed from the eyes, hidden from the ears, veiled from the understanding." Virginity is a divinely appointed, esoteric gift for the select, elected few. Severus is suggesting that the ways in which humans perceive the world, through the senses of sight and sound, and through the workings of the mind, are ineffectual in the face of this gift; particularly in understanding this gift. It is beyond the pale of human reason. It arrives in a divine light that we cannot see, hear, or understand. It is, in fact, "ineffable." It is "too overwhelming to be expressed or described in words."[6] It is "too awesome or sacred to be spoken." So while the gift of God's Son was seen and heard, and He attempted to make Himself understood, the gift of virginity is more akin to the gift of the Holy Spirit. It is a divine gift, from the Divine Saviour, which, as we will see later, has soteriological implications.

However, not only was virginity a gift from God, but it was also a gift to God. While God chose virgins, some chose virginity and offered that virginity as a gift to God.

The author of Pseudo-Clement seems to be writing to persons who have already made known to him or who have publicly announced their decision to adopt life-long virginity. Pseudo-Clement responds by asking them a series of questions.

> You desire, then, to be a virgin? Do you know what hardship and irksomeness there is in true virginity—that stands constantly at all seasons before God, and does not withdraw from His service, and "is anxious how it may please its Lord with a holy body, and with its spirit?" Do you know what great glory pertains to virginity? Is it for this that you set yourself forth to practice it? Do you really know and understand what it is you are eager to do? Are you acquainted with the noble task of holy virginity? Do you know how, like a man, to enter "lawfully" upon this contest and "strive," that, in the might of the Holy Spirit, you choose this for yourself, that you may be crowned with a crown of light, and that they may lead you about in triumph through "the Jerusalem above?"[7]

In the context of our discussion around the issues of "virginity" and "gift," Pseudo-Clement addresses women who have chosen life-long virginity for God. He speaks of her "desire," her eagerness, and notes that she "chose this for herself," and that she has "set herself to practice it." And it may be because she has chosen the life of a virgin (rather than God choosing her), and that the choice of this was accompanied with both desire and eagerness, that he cautions her about the "hardship and irksomeness" of this task. It is interesting that the absence of the word "gift" and the use of the words "task" and "strive" belies the belief that virginity is more of a good work for God rather than a gift to God. In this passage practicing virginity is something that she is going "to do." Virginity, then, becomes more of a duty than a state of being.

We can also assume that he is addressing women, for he says that she needs to understand that to accomplish this "noble task" she needs to do it "like a man." He uses the verb "strive" and the adverb "lawfully," which he associates with male tasks.

Pseudo-Clement also notes that now that she has made this choice, she is not expected to practice life-long virginity unaided. God will honor the choice that she has made. She is promised the "might of the Holy Spirit," and because God the Holy Spirit is involved in this endeavor she is also told that she will prevail, and be "crowned with a crown of light" and be led about "in triumph through 'the Jerusalem above.'" Not only, then, is she assured of salvation, but she will receive special recognition in the courts above. This is a very powerful message to Christian women in the late second century. The male clergy had already established a male monopoly on the positions of leadership in the church. Women had already been relegated to positions of service to these male leaders. One of the few ways open to women to publicly express their spirituality was through the public announcement and public living of virginity. Pseudo-Clement, in this passage has endowed this virginal life with a degree of power and recognition that was, for Christian women, unparalleled. No other group of Christians, clergy or lay, to this point, was promised a "heavenly parade" in their honor. This hope must have been a very appealing call to virginity, and a very powerful motivation to live that life to its completion.

In three passages from two different works Jerome expresses similar thoughts. In *Against Jovinianus* 12, in a paraphrase of Mt 19.12 he writes "some are eunuchs by nature, others by the violence of men." To this paraphrase Jerome, putting words into the mouth of God, adds, "Those eunuchs please me who are such not of necessity, but of free choice." The point he seems to be making is that a life of virginity is only of value to God if it is chosen. Those who are eunuchs by nature have no choice but to be virginal.[8]

The commitment to life-long virginity must be made voluntarily. It is not just a commitment to sexual abstinence, but commitment to sexual abstinence for God. This is why, for Jerome, the virginity of the pagans and heretics are of no value. Their virginity is not a gift from God or to God, but simply a choice which they have made without the proper motivation. Jerome is saying that only the free choice of catholic Christians to devote their lives to virginity in response to this gift of virginity from God, pleases God, and is, therefore, acceptable to God.

In his letter to his friend Demetrius, Jerome, invoking terms which in the Hebrew Scriptures were reserved for the services in the Temple, i.e., "the Holy of Holies and the altar of incense," speaks of another altar upon which a sacrifice is offered to God. Jerome says that "upon [this altar] I might consecrate to eternal chastity a living offering acceptable to God."[9]

In the Hebrew Scriptures (and most especially in Exodus and Leviticus) we find descriptions of the activities that are to take place at the Temple, on a daily and annual basis. There were two altars at the Temple. To the altar, standing at the entrance to the Holy Place, sin offerings were brought by both the children of Israel and the priests. The animals were slain, blood was spilt, and forgiveness was both asked for and granted.

The altar of incense stood before the curtain separating the Holy Place from the Most Holy Place (or the Holy of Holies). On it the High Priest Aaron, and his descendants, were to burn "a perpetual incense before the Lord throughout your generations" (Ex 30.9).

Behind the veil, in the Holy of Holies, was the Ark of the Covenant, or the Mercy Seat. Into the Holy of Holies went the High Priest, but only on the Day of Atonement, and only with the blood of the sacrificial goat. Ex 30.10 says that "Aaron shall make atonement upon its horns once a year with the blood of the sin offering of atonement; once a year he shall make atonement upon it throughout your generations. It is most holy to the Lord."

Jerome was aware that the primary purpose of the Temple in the Hebrew Scriptures was as a place where forgiveness from sin and cleansing from sin was found. If those reading this letter from Jerome staid with the imagery it is difficult to see how they could have misinterpret his intent. He says that he is passing "from [the altar of incense] to this [altar of sacrifice], that upon it I might consecrate to eternal chastity a living offering acceptable to God." The bloodless sacrifice of the virgin (the "living offering") has replaced the bloody sacrifice of the Hebrew Scriptures as the remedy for the stain of sin. Further, what happened in the Holy of Holies was not just for individual followers of Jehovah, but for all of the children of God. The only time a priest passed the altar of incense to go to the altar of sacrifice was to complete the work on the Day of Atonement. It was on that day that all of Israel found relief from sin. It was efficacious for all who believed.

We hear, here, then, the mature Jerome, not arguing for virginity, but explaining the benefits of virginity. He has married the practice of virginity and the assurance of salvation in a very powerful way. Not only is virginity salvific for the virgin, but it carries with it soteriological properties for the rest of the believers. The virgin has entered into the presence of God to offer her virginity to God, and God has declared that this "living offering" is acceptable.

In *To Demetrius* 4 Jerome again places a virgin in the presence of God. He writes that "night after night she cast herself in thought at the Savior's knees and implored Him to accept her choice." Choosing to adopt the life of the virgin was not done with a cavalier attitude. And with the growing list of requirements being placed on virgins by Jerome and others, Demetrius was unsure if she had met all of those requirements. In the fourth century we are past the time when a woman could simply declare herself committed to a life of virginity, and live that life as she understood it to be lived. By the fourth century virgins had been reigned in. And the growing complexity of "dos" and "don'ts" were being multiplied. Virgins were watched very carefully. An uncharitable interpretation of this situation would suggest that these "virgin watchers" were waiting for the virgins to slip up, which would give these "watchers" even more ammunition to rail against unfaithful virgins.

In any case, the very fact that Jerome imagines Demetrius in the presence of God, suggests that she was already pure and undefiled.

## NOTES

1. Anonymous, *On Virginity* 7.81-85. Found in Elm, *Virgins of God* 36.
2. Cyprian of Carthage *The Dress of Virgins* 4.
3. Jerome *To Eustochium* 21.
4. ibid.
5. Methodius of Olympus *On Virginity* 1.2.
6. *Webster's New World Dictionary of the American Language*, 10th ed., "Ineffable."
7. Pseudo-Clement *On Virginity* 1.5.
8. This is true, of course, if virginity is understood only as abstinence from the sexual intercourse which involves both the penis and the vagina.
9. Jerome *To Demetrius* 2.

*Chapter Two*

# Virginity and the Divine

The Early Church Fathers who penned documents concerning virginity, employed images and language to help portray what they believed to be the extraordinary intimacy that virgins, and virgins alone, enjoyed with both God the Father and God the Son.

## VIRGINS ARE THE BRIDES OF CHRIST

New Testament canonical writers use the language of the bride and the bridegroom to portray certain truths concerning the relationship between Christ and His Church. In Jhn 3.29, in an obvious reference to Jesus, John the Baptist, when asked about his relationship to Jesus of Nazareth, says that he (John) is only the friend of the bridegroom; the friend who stands, hears and rejoices greatly "because of the bridegroom's voice." John is not the bridegroom, for only the bridegroom "has the bride."[1] In Mt 9.15, when Jesus is questioned by the disciples of John, refers to himself as the bridegroom, and says "the friends of the bridegroom [cannot] mourn (Mk 2.19; Lk 5.34 "fast") as long as the bridegroom is with them."

The language in Jhn 3 of the "voice of the bridegroom" is found elsewhere in both the Hebrew Scriptures and in the New Testament. The phrase is repeated four times in the book of Jeremiah, where the "voice of the Bridegroom and the voice of the bride," along with mirth and gladness, will be stilled in Judah and/or Jerusalem because of their unrepentant state. The "voice of the Bridegroom and the bride" are here, symbolically, associated with God's blessings, protection, and approbation. In the closing chapters of Revelation, when spiritual Babylon is visited with God's judgment, it says that "the voice of the bridegroom and the bride shall not be heard in you anymore" (18.23). And twice in Rev 21 (vv.2,9) the bride is the new Jerusalem who is now adorned "for her husband" (v.2) who is the Lamb (v.9).

However, for Tertullian, Gregory of Nyssa, Jerome, John Chrysostom, Sulpitius Severus, Leander of Seville, and the anonymous fourth century author of the *On Virginity*, the virgin is the glorious bride of the bridegroom Christ.

Using the language of his culture (and his own theology) of women surrendering or sacrificing their virginity to their husbands, Tertullian says to the virgin, "For wedded you are to Christ: to Him you have surrendered your flesh; to Him you have espoused your maturity."[2] The language of Tertullian here suggests that virgins, even though they have rejected marriage, have not taken control over their own bodies. Their bodies now belong to Christ. Their bodies are, therefore, still subject to a male figure. The virgins are not free to use or "disuse" their own bodies as they deem fit. Just as the Christian wife of a Christian man "does not have authority over her own body" (1 Cor 7.3), likewise the spiritual wife of the heavenly husband has surrendered her body to the male Christ. And this surrender is for eternity, for "to Him you have espoused your maturity."

However, the virgins are not to be deprived of intimacy, but it is an intimacy of a different sort. Jerome reminds his readers that sexual intimacy was never part of God's original ideal for creation. It was only because Eve listened to the seductions of the serpent that Eve and her descendants would, from thenceforth, bear children in pain and sorrow. Not only that, but she will bear the disease of sexual desire for her husband. Jerome writes:

> When God says to Eve, "In pain and in sorrow you shall bring forth children," say to yourself, "That is a vow for a married woman, not for me." And when He continues, "Your desire shall be for your husband," say again, "Let her desire be to her husband who has not Christ for her spouse."

This tête-à-tête between God and the virgin highlights the differences between virgins and all other women. She is different spiritually and she is even different anthropologically. She is able to challenge God and His will for all women. By making a commitment to virginity the virgin is transported back to a pre-fall state. The prophesies of doom pronounced on Eve do not apply to the virgin. She is not "under the law" of married women. She has risen above the cares and desires of all other women. The only husband she will recognize, the only other person that she will be intimate with, the only person she will "desire," her only spouse, is Christ. And Leander reminds the virgin that because she is intimate with Christ, she will "thus be held in the Bridegroom's embraces."[3]

Further, Christ, as the Bridegroom, will not allow Himself to be wed, to be intimate, with anyone who has been "polluted" because of sexual intercourse.

Ambrose says that "she is a virgin who is the bride of God."[4] Just as the Jewish priests in the Hebrew Scriptures were to only marry virgins, so Jesus Christ, the ante-typical High Priest (cf. Heb 5.10), will only accept a virgin for His bride. The distinguishing attribute of the bride of God is that she is a virgin. Therefore, not only has the virgin entered into a different state, but an exalted state as well. Jerome says that the virginal bride "rejoices and says: 'the king has brought me into his chambers.'"[5] And Leander observes that "a nun may claim as her Bridegroom One before whom angels tremble."[6]

Becoming the bride of Christ is a valuable gift which must be appreciated. In an attempt to reveal to the virgin how absolutely precious she is in the sight of God, and to speak of the value that God places on the virgin, Leander tells the maiden bride that "your Bridegroom . . . gave you His blood for a dowry."[7] Jerome reminds the mother of a virgin that "he has conferred on you a high privilege; you are now the mother-in-law of God."[8] While this is not quite the title of θεότοκος ("Mother of God") given to Mary by the ecclesiastical dignitaries in the fifth century, by the sixth century, not just a few writers viewed virgins as the brides of Christ, as other "ecclesiastical authorit[ies] permit us to style virgins also the brides of Christ."[9] This is, again, another piece of evidence which speaks to the gradual but inexorable exertion of control over the virgins. In societies, both ancient and modern, the person or persons who claim the right to name another or others, has, to some degree, laid claim to that person or those persons.

Jerome's words to Eustochium reminds us that some of the Fathers believed that a commitment to life-long virginity by a Christian woman created a "circle of influence" which was beneficial to all who stood inside. The mother of a virgin was no longer just another married Christian woman, but, because of her daughter's commitment to virginity, because her daughter was now the bride of Christ, the mother of the virgin was given an exalted title. And Leander tells his sister that while she is being held in the embraces of her Bridegroom, she "may ask and obtain pardon for me."[10] The requests of the pure, beloved, precious, and faithful bride are granted by the faithful Bridegroom. The virgin bride may bring into the bride chamber whom she wishes, and those who are brought in are the recipients of God's graces.

That the commitment to virginity by the virginal bride is a life-long commitment is taken up by Gregory of Nyssa. He says that not only must the virgin be pure at the time of her commitment to her Bridegroom, but she "must keep herself pure for the Husband who has married her, 'not having spot or any such thing.'"[11]

It is not surprising, then, to read that more than one of the Fathers believed that female virgins were capable of being unfaithful to their Bridegroom. Jerome warns the virgin to not "seek the Bridegroom in the streets; do not go around the corners of the city. Jesus is jealous. He does not choose that your face should be seen of others . . . Unless also you avoid the eyes of young men, you will be turned out of my bride chamber to feed the goats, which shall be set on the left hand."[12] In the ancient cities, it was in the streets and on street corners that prostitutes plied their wares, where they sought to attract "the eyes of young men." One suspects that, for Jerome, women seen on the streets of the city did not even have to have the appearance of a prostitute or be acting in a seductive manner to be guilty of some sort of sexual misconduct. Simply being seen on the streets was enough to arouse suspicion, in his eyes (and in the eyes of God), and call into question the virgin's commitment to her Holy Husband. God, the Bridegroom, would dismiss His bride in shame and disgrace. To avoid this spiritual disgrace Sulpitius Severus exhorts the virgin to "realize your state, realize your position, realize your purpose. You are called the bride of Christ; see that you commit no act which is un worthy of Him to whom you profess to be betrothed."[13]

Finally, we hear that being the bride of Christ imparts immortality not only to the virgin, but to others in her family who aided her in her path towards the life of virginity. The virgin can be the Saviour of her household. In the anonymous *On Virginity* it reads:

> [Your daughter] will progress with generosity towards the immaculate bridal chamber of Christ, where she will dwell in the company of the wise virgins, so that you, who guided her as well will be admitted to the bridal chamber of the heavenly kingdom, and that she, on her part will receive the crown of immortality.

## VIRGINS ARE THE MOTHERS OF CHRIST

It can be argued, and quite convincingly, that the title θεότοκος was being applied to Mary before the Council of Chalcedon in 451 C.E. The Christological and Trinitarian controversies which the Bishops at Chalcedon attempted to resolve, included a sweeping condemnation of the teachings of Nestorius, who insisted, ostensibly because of his own Christology and Trinitarian beliefs, that Mary could be called the "Mother of Christ," but not the "Mother of God."

However, a few decades before this controversy erupted, Augustine was already naming, not only Mary as the "mother of Christ," but, in ch. 5 of *Of Holy Virginity* other virgins, and in ch. 6 all faithful Christian women. The two texts where he speaks to this are as follows:

> However, that birth of the Holy Virgin is the ornament of all holy virgins, and they themselves, together with Mary, are mothers of Christ, if they do the will of His Father.[14]

> Forsooth, both faithful women who are married, and virgins dedicated to God,
> by holy manners, and charity out of a pure heart, and good conscience, and faith
> unfeigned, because they do the will of the Father, are, after a spiritual sense,
> mothers of Christ.[15]

Mary, both experientially and ontologically, seems to be the spiritual
progenitor, not only of all Christian virgins, but of all Christian women.
However, whereas Mary was chosen by God to be the physical mother of
Christ, Christian virgins and Christian women can also, "after a spiritual
sense," become mothers of Christ. In ch.5 all Christian virgins, together
with Mary, become the mothers of Christ "*If* they do the will of His Father." (emphasis mine). In ch.6 all faithful women, both virginal and married, become the mothers of Christ, "*Because* they do the will of the Father." (emphasis mine). In other words, in ch.5 being awarded the title
"Mother of Christ" is conditional on obedience to the will of God. In ch.6
it is a *fait accompli*. There is an assumption that *because* these faithful
women have followed the will of the Father, they have been awarded the
title Mother of Christ.

More important for our purposes here, though, is the inclusion of married
women in the ranks of the exalted. We will explore the attitude of these particular Father's attitudes toward marriage in great detail later in this book, but
what we can say here, is that Augustine is the only Father who allows married women, at least in this text, a place alongside, and equal to virgins. It is
anomalous not only to the other Fathers, but it is anomalous to what Augustine has to say elsewhere as well.

Also of interest is that Augustine, the "Doctor of Grace," here, plainly
holds out the gifts of God to those who because of pure hearts, good con-
sciences, and faith unfeigned, do the will of the Father. There is, curiously, no
mention of the grace of God at work in the lives of these women.

## VIRGINS ARE THE CONSTANT COMPANIONS OF CHRIST

Cyprian of Carthage, Methodius of Olympus, Augustine, and Sulpitius
Severus quote either part or all of Rev 14.4-5. Beginning with v.3b it reads:

> . . . the hundred and forty-four thousand who were redeemed from the earth.
> These are the ones who were not defiled with women, for they are virgins.
> These are the ones who follow the Lamb wherever He goes. These were re-
> deemed from among men, being the first fruits to God and to the Lamb. And
> in their mouth was found no guile, for they are without fault before the throne
> of God.

It is impossible to know if they viewed the 144,000 as literal, but it seems that, for these authors, the virgins spoken of in Rev 14 are not figurative. What is important is that these verses are being used to highlight the contrast between Christian virgins and the rest of the Christian population. Sulpitius Severus says as much.

> For the blessed Apostle John also speaks concerning these, saying that "they follow the Lamb wherever He goes." This, I think, is to be understood to the following effect, that there will be no place in the court of heaven closed against them, but that all the habitations of the divine mansions will be thrown open before them.[16]

This privilege is not extended to any other group, but is restricted to virgins alone, and Severus along with the others use Rev 14.4 as the justification for this belief.

Augustine, twice in ch.28 of his work *Of Holy Virginity*, puts a finer point on the verse. He says, "Therefore let the rest of the faithful, who have lost virginity, follow the Lamb, not wherever He shall have gone, but so far as ever they shall have been able." And later in the same chapter he decides to be more magnanimous, and says, "But surely even married persons may go in those steps (of Christ), although not setting their foot perfectly in the same print, yet walking in the same paths." In the earlier quote Augustine clearly gives virgins an access to Christ that married Christians do not have. However, in the second quote he seems to be saying that Christians who have lost or sacrificed their virginity may follow Christ, but their following will, in some manner, be less perfect. This is a hierarchy less severe than that of Severus, but a hierarchy nonetheless.

Gregory of Nyssa and John Chrysostom also declare that virgins are the constant companions of Christ, but they do not quote Scripture to support their views. Gregory of Nyssa uses logic and reason, while John Chrysostom, being the orator, uses his imagination.

Gregory writes, "[Virgins are] always present with the powers above; their purity and their incorruptibility being the means of bringing them into relationship with Him."[17] Gregory reasons that since only purity and incorruptibility can enter into the presence of the Godhead ("the powers above"), and since these are the qualities that define virgins, then, the relationship with God is never broken. Gregory does not state whether this union with the divine is in heaven or on earth, but in either case it is a present reality. Are the virgins, in this life, continually, spiritually, present with God, or does the purity and incorruptibility of the virgins have the power to call the divine down to the earth? Perhaps it is both.

John Chrysostom exhibits his title "Chrysostom" ("the golden tongued") in his description of the union between the virgins and Christ.

> Those who wear golden robes, are borne upon horses decorated with gilded or-
> naments, and carry golden shields set with precious stones are not obliged to
> manifest the presence of the emperor as much as the virgin is the presence of
> Christ. For those men appear near the royal chariot but the virgin, if she desires,
> truly becomes a royal chariot, like the cherubim, and stands at Christ's side, like
> the seraphim.[18]

Chrysostom is saying that the attendants of kings, who by their dress attempt to portray the dignity and majesty of the king, are shouldering less
responsibility than virgins who are to correctly portray the divine majesty
of the presence of Christ. And this is not the dying Jesus on the cross of the
New Testament. This is the reigning God sitting on His throne in heaven
portrayed in the Hebrew Scriptures. Isaiah, in vision, "saw the Lord sitting
on a throne, high and lifted up . . . and above [the throne] stood seraphim;
each one had six wings: with two he covered his face, with two he covered
his feet, and with two he flew" (Isa 6.2). And Ezekiel, in vision, also sees
God sitting on a chariot which had "the appearance of the likeness of a
throne" (Eze 10.1). This chariot/throne is surrounded with cherubim, on all
sides, and even seem to be part of the chariot, or at least control the wheels
of the chariot. Both visions are of God sitting on His throne, and these are
the visions Chrysostom calls on to speak to the union between the virgin
and God. The virgin is not just near the chariot of God, but symbolically,
she becomes the chariot, and if the chariot of God in Eze 10 is also God's
throne, then, virgins are the means by which God moves (again symbolically), while sitting on His throne, in heaven. Not only that, but in
Chrysostom's vision, virgins are also, like the seraphim, the only beings
that are called on to shield the divine glory, for they cried to one another,
"Holy, holy, holy is the Lord of hosts; The whole earth is full of his
glory" (Isa 6.3). Therefore, while the writer of the epistle to the Hebrews
has thrown open the veil to the Holy of Holies to all Christians (see Heb
10.19), virgins appear to have an even more exalted place in God's
presence.

This language does not sound quite correct to our 21st century egalitarian
ears. Therefore, those who study the paradigms of salvation in the first few
centuries of Christianity must either allow that there are a group of Christians
(virgins) who, by virtue of the language heard in Rev , have access to God in
ways that other saved Christians do not, or find interpretations which blunt
those claims.

## VIRGINITY IS PLEASING TO GOD

While most, if not all, of the early church Fathers proclaimed that their God was a God of love, and through letters, sermons, and epistles kept reminding the believers that God loved them, in these documents, beginning with Methodius and carrying through to Pseudo-Titus, the believers are told that God loves some more than others.

While Methodius's words to his readers to ("mark . . . how very great in the sight of God is the dignity of virginity") does not explicitly say that God loves virgins more than the rest of the believers, this approbation is reserved only for virgins, and perhaps martyrs.[19] All Christians believed that they lived their lives in the sight of God, but virgins are singled out as those whose lives, because of the dignity of their virginity, are especially pleasing to God.

Jerome is especially desirous to let believers know that there are gradations of God's love, with virgins receiving the greatest portion of that love. We hear this from Jerome, in various ways, either explicitly or implicitly, in his letters to Eustochium and Pammachius, and in his diatribe against Jovinianus. His words are as follows:

> Assuredly no gold or silver vessel was ever so dear to God as is the temple of a virgin's body.[20]

> Christ loves virgins more than others, because they willingly give what was not commanded of them.[21]

> Some are eunuchs by nature, others by the violence of men. Those eunuchs please Me who are such not of necessity, but of free choice.[22]

> John, one of the disciples, who is related to have been the youngest of the Apostles, and who was a virgin when he embraced Christianity, remained a virgin, and on that account was more beloved by our Lord.[23]

> If, however, Jovinianus should obstinately contend that John was not a virgin (whereas we have maintained that his virginity was the cause of the special love our Lord bore to him), let him explain, if he was not a virgin, why it was that he was loved more than the other Apostles.[24]

> If virgins are the first fruits unto God, then widows and wives who live in continence must come after the first fruits—that is to say, in the second and third place.[25]

We can assume that Jerome believes that God loves the spirit of virgins, but it is the "virgin's body" that is referenced here. And in language that, again places the virgins in the throne room of God, the body of the virgin is compared to "the temple." The New Testament writers make it abundantly clear that the temple of the new covenant is either the body of Christ (see Jhn 2.21) or the body of the believers (see 1 Cor 3.16, 6.19; 2 Cor 6.16; Eph 2.21). Jerome enlarges on this imagery, and says that the "gold [and] sliver vessels" used in the Tabernacle and Temples used by the Hebrews, Israelites, and Jews in the Hebrew Scriptures, some of which held the sacrificial blood and incense, offered as part of cleansing and propitiation rituals to God (see Ex 29, 30), and which are copies of the ones used in the temple in heaven (see Heb 9.23-24), are of less value, in God's eyes, than the bodies of virgins.

In *Against Jovinianus* 12 it is the willingness of the virgins to commit to this life that causes Christ to "love virgins more than others." They did not respond to a command (which does not exist), but theirs was "a free choice." Jerome does not identify who these "others" are, but we can assume that he is talking about other Christians. If this is so, then, one has to wonder how this belief was received by all of the "other" Christians. How, for instance, would this be received by a married couple newly converted to Christianity, who are now made aware that they are somehow viewed by this God, whom they have committed their lives to, as less desirable than the virgins in the community? Or how would this be viewed by a young person, or young persons in the church who do not have any desire or inclination to devote the entire rest of their life to virginity? Are they being told that, by going through this marriage, they are somehow lessening their value to God. Jerome seems unconcerned with these possible scenarios, and continues to repeat this belief in ch.26 where he, twice, points to the example of John the Evangelist, who, because he was a virgin when he came to Christ, and remained a virgin for the rest of his life, "was loved more than the other Apostles." Jerome, here, has interpreted the phrase, "the disciple whom Jesus loved," to mean that John was more loved than the rest of the Apostles, and Jerome has attributed to John a life for which we have no evidence.

Augustine, in discussing the virginity of Mary says, "her virginity also was on this account more pleasing and accepted, in that it was not that Christ being conceived in her, rescued it from a husband who would violate it."[26] Augustine seems to be suggesting, here, that those women whom God chooses to rescue from the burden of marriage, like Mary, are in God's eyes "more pleasing and accepted." But to whom are these women being compared? Are they being compared to other virgins who of themselves choose to devote themselves to God by living a life of virginity? Or are these women, as in Jerome, being compared to the rest of the Christian community? Augustine's words do no lend themselves to a clear understanding. However, what can be said is that Augustine, by using the word "violate" to express the loss of virginity, is suggesting that women, in fact, are not guilty (as many of the other Fathers declare) of sexual aggressiveness, but that they are often the victims of sexually aggressive males. Augustine might, here, be reflecting on his own rather complicated dealings with his own sexuality, and his struggles with himself and with God to bring his sexual urges under control. Given that history, one can easily imagine Augustine, much more than any of the other Fathers, attributing sexual aggressiveness to the male rather than the female.

It is in his reflections on the virginity of Mary that causes Sulpitius Severus, like Augustine, to conclude that virginity is especially pleasing to God. However, unlike Augustine, it is the incarnation of God in the virgin womb of Mary that demonstrates God's pleasure with virginity. He says:

> But that the merit of virginity may shine forth more clearly, and that there may
> be a better understanding as to how worthy it is of God, let this be considered,
> that the Lord God, our Saviour, when, for the salvation of the human race, he
> condescended to assume mankind, chose no other than a virgin's womb, that he
> might show how virtue of this kind especially pleased him.[27]

While the virginity of Jesus is always held out as an example to follow, the two passages here, in Augustine and Sulpitius Severus, are evidence that the virginity of Mary is receiving more and more attention, and her virginity is also (or even more so?) put forth as an example of God's preference of virginity as the quintessential life for Christians. The point is being made that God purposefully did not choose a married women who had already had sexual relations with her husband to be the physical mother of the incarnate God. In other words, did God choose a virgin, because a married women would have already been "polluted" by having sexual intercourse with her husband? Or was the virgin birth story not essentially about the virginity of Mary, but primarily about the miraculousness of such a birth? It is possible that such a question would not have even occurred to the early Christians, who simply found comfort in the story that God had become man to save His creation from sin and ruin. And this is part of Severus's message here: God, "for the salvation of the human race, . . . condescended to assume mankind."

Neither Leander of Seville nor Pseudo-Titus add anything new to what has already been discussed. Leander simply says that "virginity wins special favor for itself in Christ,"[28] and Pseudo-Titus, in what almost sounds like some sort of formulaic recitation writes, "Blessed are those who have kept themselves from the unchastity of this world, for they will be pleasing to Christ, the Son of God, and to the Father, the Lord."[29]

## VIRGINITY BRINGS REWARDS FROM GOD

The authors of these pieces of literature hold out the promise of a "reward" from God that is only offered to those who maintain their virginity to the end

of their lives. However, for most of the authors, the specifics of these "rewards" are not forthcoming. Notice the following examples. Cyprian of
Carthage says that those who have renounced "the concupiscences of the
flesh" are destined for "a great reward," and they "await the reward of virginity."[30] Later, in the same document, these rewards are called "the rewards
of God,"[31] and he tells the virgins that "a great recompense is reserved for
you, a glorious prize for virtue, a most excellent reward for purity."[32] Jerome
writes of Demetrius's mother and grandmother that "the prize was so great
that they did not venture to hope for it, or to aspire to it."[33] John Chrysostom
is also vague about these rewards when he asks rhetorically of the virgin,
what goods shall she not enjoy, what reward shall she not reap, she who ri-
vals the spiritual powers themselves?[34] And in another work he reasons that,
"by decreeing that marriage is bad, [the Greeks] have robbed themselves of
the prizes of virginity in advance."[35] Sulpitius Severus urges the virgin to
"maintain your purpose which is destined for a great reward."[36] And, finally,
Leander of Seville writes to his sister that "it is above the skies that we must
seek, where you received your gift of virginity, that you may also find there
the reward and inheritance of that virginity."[37] Later, in the same work, he
says that he is not even worthy "to speak of the rewards of virginity," and that
Christ has "prepared [the virgin] for the rewards of chastity."[38] The important
point that needs to be made here is that these virgins—and the language suggests that these are female virgins—are promised rewards exceeding the general reward of redemption. These rewards are "great," and a "great recompense." It would be crass to suggest that these male authors are telling these
women that there is a pay-off for the toils and tribulations of a life of virginity. It is more of a *quid pro quo*. God will not only honor their devotion to
Him, but theirs will be rewarded more than others. What are these rewards?

Some of the authors have allowed themselves to imagine what, specifically, these rewards might be. Pseudo-Clement says that God "will give to
virgins a notable place in the house of God, which is something 'better than
sons and daughters,' and better than the place of those who have passed a
wedded life in sanctity, and whose 'bed is not defiled.'"[39] As early as the early
third century a hierarchy of heavenly rewards has emerged in Christian soteriology. Some Christians will be rewarded by God for their extraordinary and
exemplary life. One expects the Apostles and martyrs are also offered special
rewards from God. But the reward for the virgins is specifically "better than
sons and daughters," and if that was not a strong enough clue as to his meaning, he says that the reward of the virgins are greater than those Christians
who were married, even those "whose 'bed is not defiled.'" Whether "the
house of God" is a reference to all of heaven or that special place in heaven
reserved for the most loved saints is not clear. But even if it is a reference to

all of heaven, there are places in that "house of God" that are more "notable." Therefore, if this epistle received a general reading in the churches who were in possession of it, (and we have no reason to believe that it was not), it is easy to see how this passage could cause some tension in these churches. It is one thing to honor those who have chosen what, in all honesty, must have been a difficult life of sacrifice and denial. It is an entirely other matter for married Christians to read (or hear) that it is impossible for them to receive these "great rewards." You cannot undo sexual intercourse. Once virginity was lost; once the hymen was broken, an irretrievable step had been taken, which could not be undone. And the loss of the intact hymen, according to Pseudo-Clement and others, meant the loss of the greatest reward from God. God had favorites, and you, because you chose marriage, are not one of them. Living a life of married purity was of no value if you were interested in receiving the same rewards as those promised to the virgins. Even the crown that was promised to all faithful Christians (I Cor 9.25) is not the same as the "crown of virginity, which is great in its toil and great in its reward."[40]

Jerome believes that "Anna, the prophetess" of Lk 2.36, was a virgin, together with the four virgin daughters of Philip the Evangelist (Acts 21.9), who also prophesied, is enough evidence to reason that all virgins receive the reward of prophesy. He says of Demetrius that she "longed to join their band and be numbered with those who by their virginal purity have attained the grace of prophesy."[41] However, no extant evidence has survived which reveals that early Christian virgins were known to be prophetesses. Perhaps their prophesies were kept to themselves since they were not allowed to speak in church, and were discouraged from being in the company of men, who could tell the congregations of the prophesies of the virgins.

Finally, Leander of Seville says to his sister that her reward, like that of all Christians, is Christ Himself. He writes "[Christ] is your inheritance. He is your reward . . . You have in Him the inheritance, which you may embrace . . . You have in Him the reward which you may recognize, for His blood is your redemption."[42]

## VIRGINS ARE ANGELIC

Most, if not all, of the early Christians believed that there existed an incorporeal world that was just as real as the physical world that defined their existence. This "other" world was populated by God (Jhn 4.24), angels, Satan, and demons. In this incorporeal world God the Father, Son and Holy Spirit, along with the heavenly angels were in constant war with Satan and his demons, and this war had spilled over into the world in which the Christians

lived (Eph 6.12). This was a war that was fought for the souls of human beings, and many of the battles were fought on the battleground of morality.
And while Satan and his demons represented all that was impure and unholy,
the angels, as the representatives of God, represented all that was pure and
holy.

It was these qualities of purity and holiness that the early Fathers ascribed
to the Christian virgins. This particular vision of virgins is seen as early as the
third century with Pseudo-Clement, and runs through the sixth century with
Pseudo-Titus. However, the virgins that the Fathers describe as either angels
or angelic, are, for the most part, male virgins. To this point the focus has been
on female virgins, but here, the references are overwhelmingly either male or
gender neutral.

Pseudo-Clement writes, "For he who covets for himself these things so
great and excellent, withdraws and severs himself on this account from all
the world, that he may go and live a life divine and heavenly, like the holy
angels, in work pure and holy, and 'in the holiness of the Spirit of God.'"[43]
For Pseudo-Clement the virgin no longer lives just in this world. He has,
in a very real and profound way, escaped this world and its cares. He has
gone to live a "live divine and heavenly." And just as the angels are untouched by the miasma of this world, so the virgin, who has "sever[ed]
himself" from this world escapes to another reality.

Ambrose posits as a maxim that "they who marry not nor are given in
marriage are as the angels in heaven."[44] Married Christians have sacrificed
the blessedness of being compared to the angels of God. Later, in the same
letter, Ambrose reconsiders his earlier comments comparing virgins to angels, and says that virgins are not just angelic, but angels. He writes,
"chastity has made even angels. He who has preserved it is an angel; he
who has lost it a devil . . . she is a virgin who is the bride of God, a harlot
who makes gods for herself."[45] Although Ambrose changes gender in the
middle of his discussion here, the message is the same to both male and female virgins, *viz*, there are profound and eternal consequences for those
who choose a live of virginity.

Perseverance to the vow of virginity earns one a title. For the male virgin
he earns the title of "angel," while the female virgin earns the title "bride of
God." And perseverance is needed, for a repudiation of this vow, once taken,
also earns titles -different titles. The male virgin who succumbs to lust
changes from an angel to "a devil," and the female virgin has sacrificed her
title as "bride of God" for that of "harlot."

It seems reasonable to ask who these believers are who have repudiated
vows of virginity. Earlier Ambrose sets up a dichotomy between virgins and
those who are married. Therefore, is the label of "devil" and "harlot" reserved

for those former virgins who have engaged in some sort of fornication, or does the label also describe those former virgins who have decided to marry, and to live as a Christian husband and wife? Ambrose doe not tell us.

For Jerome it matters not if sexual intercourse takes place between husbands and wives or outside of the marriage vow, for the vow of virginity trumps all other vows. In his letter to Pammachius he writes, "I am not expounding the law as to husbands and wives, but simply discussing the general question of sexual intercourse—how in comparison with chastity and virginity, the life of angels, "it is good for a man not to touch a woman."[46] Husbands, wives, fornicators are all regarded as living lives that are somehow less virtuous than that of the virgins, for the virgins are, in comparison, living "the life of angels."

Jerome's obsession with female sexuality, coupled with his belief that all women, by nature, are sexually aggressive reappears in his comments to Demetrius. The goal and the promise to virgins is to "live the angelic life." This goal is attainable, but not without sacrifices. Jerome tells Demetrius that "the dew of heaven and severe fasting quench in a girl the flame of passion and enable her soul even in its earthly tenement to live the angelic life."[47] Female sensuality is a constant threat even to those females who have taken the vow of virginity. But there are ways to tame that passion that is so very much a part of all females; even female Christians and female virgins. God, in His mercy, provides "the dew of heaven." Jerome doe not tell his readers what that "dew" is, but we can assume it is some type of heavenly encouragement, strength or grace. But that is not enough. Even God, by Himself, cannot overcome what has become an integral part of all women since the fall, i.e. sexual lust. Therefore, virgins who hope to quench this passion so that it does not torture them, must also engage in severe fasting. Whether fasting had already been proven to lessen or completely undo a woman's sexual passion, or if this was a theory that Jerome believed worked is not revealed. It is also not revealed whether God needed to continually apply the dew of heaven, and if the virgin needed to continually, periodically, engage in "severe fasting" for her to maintain the angelic life, but it certainly was a goal to be wished for.

John Chrysostom tells his readers that the destiny of angels is "bright torches, and the sum total of all goodness: life with the Bridegroom."[48] This he contrasts with the virginity practiced by the heretics which "means fetters, tears, lamentations, and unending punishment."[49] The implication, of course, is that virgins need to be both doctrinally and physically pure. Physical purity is not enough. The life of the virgins that is beginning to emerge in the Christian communities is one of severity and seriousness. Spiritual perseverance, the ability to withstand severe fasting, and maintaining doctrinal purity are parts of the life of the virgin that needed constant attention. These exhortations, coupled with all of

the other instructions regarding how virgins are to live their lives reveals a life
so devoid of any pleasure, that it is a wonder that so many Christian women
choose this life over marriage. This is especially true of the anchorites. The virgins who lived communally at least had constant human contact. But the anchorites lived lives, while not of complete isolation, fairly close to it. Yet
Chrysostom insists that this is a life of light, goodness and communion with
Christ as His bride. The virgins, indeed all Christians, are being told that the
"normal" life of marriage and children, weddings and celebrations, is looked on
with less favor than the "unnatural" life of virginity. Therefore, just as angels
are not a part of the natural, physical world, so virgins, in becoming angelic, are
also not part of the normal, natural world.

One of the things we can extrapolate from this passage is that virginity was
not just being practiced by catholic Christians, but by non-catholic Christians
as well. Chrysostom either knows of these "heretical" virgins or has heard of
them. He is incensed that these pseudo-Christians have appropriated something which has reached holy status in the catholic Christian communities,
and condemns their pseudo-virginity; a virginity that is vanity. The virginity
practiced by the non-catholics is an affront to Chrysostom. It is the same effrontery that Jewish believers in the second century might have felt when
Barnabas, Tertullian and others insisted that the Torah, along with the rest of
the Hebrew Scriptures, was in fact, always intended for Christians, for they,
unlike the Jews, had not turned their backs on and abandoned God. Appro-
priating what is holy in another's religion often elicits hostile and even violent responses.

Chrysostom recognizes that virgins are "stuck" in their bodies in this
world, but their bodies should not be an impediment to their rise to angelic
status. He asks, "Do you grasp the value of virginity? That it makes those who
spend time on earth live like the angels dwelling in heaven? It does not allow
those endowed with bodies to be inferior to the incorporeal powers and spurs
all men to rival the angels."[50]

It seems to be generally understood among the early Christians that the
angels of heaven are not only sexually continent, but are also free from any
sexual desires. Augustine writes, "but virginal chastity and freedom through
pious continence from all sexual intercourse is the portion of angels."[51] Augustine does not explain what "freedom" he is referring to here, but given his
self-revealed struggles with his personal sexual history, this "freedom" might
include freedom from the emotional and spiritual trauma brought about by
sexual lust. If that is the case, then, he is saying that virgins, like the angels,
are free from the tortures of sexual lust.

In his argument that the heavenly and final rewards of the "eunuchs" and
the "married persons in the house of God" are dissimilar, and chastising those

who "madly oppose" this truth, Augustine says that virgins are "practicing an heavenly and angelic life in an earthly state."[52] Although the argument here, as with some of the passages above, is not specifically about virgins becoming angelic, it does give us insight as to the Christian's belief about the sacredness that virginity had assumed by the fifth century. All faithful Christians will receive their "deserts" from God, and it is unwise to "contend" that the deserts of the virgins are "on a level with the deserts of the married."[53]

Therefore, Christians in the fifth century have been assigned different degrees of salvation, and their assignations are based on their sexual history. Christians in the fifth century are to understand that God values some Christians more than others. Certainly the clergy, with little or no discouragement from the clergy themselves, have risen to a different status than the laity. Martyrs of the past, monks and nuns, all enjoy a superior status with God than the rest of the believers. Physical martyrdom, at least in the Roman Empire, at least by the Roman authorities has ended. So if you are a married adult, unless you abandon your family and enter a monastery or convent, you have little to no chance of raising your stock in the eyes of God. It is only the "heroes" of the faith that enjoy the exalted status of being angelic.

Finally, Pseudo-Titus understands Rev 14.4 to say that , "Those, then, who are not defiled with women He calls an angelic host."[54] The scene in Rev 14 is God's throne in heaven, described as Mount Zion.

> And I looked and behold, a Lamb standing on Mount Zion, and with Him 144,000, having His Father's name written on their foreheads . . . and they sang . . . a new song . . . and no one could learn that song except the 144,000 who were redeemed from the earth. These are the ones who were not defiled with women, for they are virgins. These are the ones who follow the Lamb wherever He goes. These were redeemed from among men, being the first-fruits to God and to the Lamb. And in their mouths was found no guile, for they are without fault before the throne of God.

Certainly all of the redeemed are redeemed from among men, but Pseudo-Titus is making Rev 14 say that the virgins who are redeemed from among men are an "angelic host." This is a designation reserved for the redeemed virgins, which, again, places them on a higher level, not only on this earth, but in heaven as well.


## VIRGINS ARE HOLY

It is not surprising to hear the Fathers declare that virgins are holy. It was taken as fact that the virgins in the communities (or in the deserts) were holy men and women. What we hear in these passages, however, is that the epithet of "holy" be applied only to virgins. This is, yet, more evidence that the Christian community had been striated into different levels of holiness; each level being dependent on the persons own sexual history.

We begin with Pseudo-Clement who writes, "[The Apostle] John . . . reclined on the bosom of our Lord, and whom He greatly loved—he, too, was a holy person . . . Moreover, also, Elijah and Elisha, and many other holy men, we find to have lived a holy and spotless life."[55] In his attempt to equate holiness with virginity Pseudo-Clement points to men who were heroes of the faith. He draws on both imagery ("reclined on the bosom of our Lord') and a declarative statement ("whom He greatly loved") to separate the Apostle John from the rest of the Apostles; John's separateness being a result of his virginity.[56] It was specifically his virginity that made him a holy person.

Pseudo-Clement also either assumes or knows that those who will read this document will be familiar with the Hebrew Scriptures, and argues that it was the virginity of Elijah and Elisha that allowed each of them to live "a holy and spotless life," comparing them to the "spotless" and "without blemish" sacrifices brought to the Temple. Only those sacrifices which were unpolluted were acceptable to God, for only those sacrifices brought the promise of the forgiveness of sin. Therefore, in the Hebrew Scriptures, the ideal of a spotless sacrifice was associated with the hope of forgiveness of sin from God, and a resumption of communion with God. The "holy and spotless" virgin lives of Elijah and Elisha represent this relationship with God. Therefore, "every [Christian] virgin who is in God is holy in her body and in her spirit, and is constant in the service of her Lord."[57]

Gregory of Nyssa, like Pseudo-Clement, uses phraseology from the Hebrew Scriptures to speak to the holiness of virgins.

> [God] only styles as "holy and without blemish" her who has this grace [of virginity] for her ornament. Now if the achievement of this saintly virtue consists in making one "without blemish and holy," and these epithets are adopted in their first and fullest force to glorify the incorruptible Deity, what greater praise of virginity can there be than thus to be shown in a manner deifying those who share in her pure mysteries, so that they become partakers of His glory . . . Their purity and their incorruptibility being the means of bringing them into relationship with Him.[58]

In what seems to be a wordy and complicated argument, Gregory's contention is that virgins, because of their virginity, are, among other things, holy in a way that is close to the way God is holy. First, notice his language. Gregory uses the phrases "holy and without blemish," "this grace [of virginity]," "this saintly virtue," "without blemish and holy," "the incorruptible Deity," "deifying those who share in [virginity's] pure mysteries," "they become partakers of [God's] glory," and "their purity and incorruptibility." Virgins are un-like other Christians. Virgins do not just become godly; they become "Godlike." Just as the "incorruptible Deity" is "without blemish and holy," so, also, God "styles as holy and without blemish," because of "their purity and incorruptibility" those who possess the "saintly virtue" of "this grace [of virginity]." Virgins, in fact, "become partakers in [God's] glory." And while Gregory would not deny that other Christians partake in God's glory and are in a relationship with God, his argument, here, suggests that virgins, because of their virginity, are not only incorruptible, but deified. They are holy in the way God is holy. They are pure in the way God is pure. Virgins are, finally, incorruptible in the way God is incorruptible. Indeed, Gregory says in the next chapter that "when you have named the pure and incorruptible, you have named virginity."[59] In other words, "these epithets" of purity and incorruptibility, in an ontological sense, are reserved only for virgins. Married Christians, Christians who presently are or formerly were sexually active, even widows, cannot bring to God sacrifices that are "holy and without blemish."

This deification of virginity using imagery from the Hebrew Scriptures is also seen in the writings of Ambrose. He asks, "For if the virgin's body be a temple of God, what is her soul, which, the ashes, as it were, of the body being shaken off, once more uncovered by the hand of the Eternal Priest, exhales the vapor of the divine fire?"[60] Ambrose's use of this metaphor would bring to the mind of the believers who knew about the history of the children of Israel, images of sacrifices for sin and the place where God communicated the divine will to the chosen people. For those less informed they would understand that it is in temples where divinity dwells. This is, for Ambrose, metaphorically, the body of the virgin. However, it is also her soul, which can only be "uncovered by the hand of the Eternal Priest," that "exhales the vapor of the divine fire." This divine fire, as an image of the soul of the virgin, in the context of the temple, could represent the fire used to burn the sacrifices, or the fire burning the candles in the Holy Place, or even the fire used to burn the incense before the veil separating the Holy Place and the Most Holy Place. However, the language of uncovering might suggest the act of the High Priest uncovering the Most Holy Place when he pulls back the curtain to enter the Most Holy Place on the Day of Atonement. In that place dwelt the Shekinah glory of God, which only the High Priest might approach, and only on the Day of Atonement, and only with the blood of the sacrificial goat. Therefore, the act of the Eternal Priest (read Christ) uncovering the body of the virgin to reveal her soul, and there discovering the "vapor of the divine fire," is a very powerful image. In the Hebrew Scriptures this act involved a holy man going into a holy place on a holy day with consecrated, holy blood

to meet a holy God, there to cleanse the "camp" from sin. For the readers of
Ambrose, then, if the body of the virgin is the temple of God, and her soul
contains the "divine vapor," either the virgin, or the idea of virginity begins
to be closely and intimately associated with forgiveness and redemption. Virgins, of course, do not replace God and Christ as the Saviours of humanity,
but they are, here, metaphorically, being linked with the hope of salvation for
the believers of God.

Jerome, addressing female virgins, and those females interested in becoming virgins, reminds his readers that "a virgin is defined as she that is holy in
body and in spirit, for it is no good to have virgin flesh if a women be married in mind."[61] This statement is, of course, in keeping with what was now a
well worn groove in the record of all of the Father's statements that virginity
is not just a state of physical being, but a state of spiritual being as well.
Methodius, earlier in the fourth century tells virgins that "it is not enough to
keep the body only undefiled."[62] However, it is John Chrysostom, also in the
fourth century, and Sulpitius in the sixth century that are most adamant about
virgins keeping watch over their minds and their souls as well as their bodies.
Notice these three statements from Chrysostom's *On Virginity*.

> 5.2. For the virgin must be pure not only in the body, but also in soul if she is
> going to receive the holy Bridegroom.
>
> 6.1. If, then, virginity is defined by holiness of body and soul, but a woman is
> unholy and impure in each respect, how could she be a virgin?
>
> 7.1. You say that her clothes are shabby, but virginity resides not in clothing, nor
> in one's complexion, but in the body and soul.

We cannot of course conclude what prompted these statements, but it can
be inferred that there were some who were claiming the title of virginity, but
were not living their lives according to what the Fathers were expecting. The
Fathers, by the fourth century saw virgins not just as sexually pure women,
but holy women. And as holy women they were expected to lead, not just exemplary lives, but lives which were completely above reproach. To make sure
these virgins knew what was, therefore, expected of them, the Fathers did not
fail to articulate these expectations, sometimes in great detail.

This desire to control the lives of the virgins did not abate with the passing
of time, and in the sixth century Sulpitius Severus takes up the subject again
in his letter to his sister, *On the Training of Nuns*.

> 4. Desiring to fulfill the divine counsel, that that, above all things, you keep the
> commandment: wishing to attain to the reward of virginity, see that you keep
> fast hold of what is necessary to merit life, that your chastity may be such as can

receive a recompense. For as the observance of the commandments ensures life, so, on the other hand, does the violation give rise to death. And he who through disobedience has been doomed to death cannot hope for the crown pertaining to virginity; nor, when really handed over to punishment, can he expect the reward promised to chastity.

9. There follows the clause "how may she please God,"—God, I say, not men,— "that she may be holy in both body and spirit." He does not say that she may be holy only in a member of the body, but that she may be holy in body and spirit.

10. Wherefore, I beseech you, O virgin, do not flatter yourself on the ground of your purity along, and do not trust in the perfection of one member; but according to the Apostle, maintain the sanctity of your body throughout.

Severus' main concern seems to be that there either are, or there is the possibility that there are, female virgins who are comparing their life with that of their married sisters, and wondering if they made the right choice. These thoughts, according to Severus, disqualifies the virgin from the blessings of virginity. She can no longer enjoy "the happiness of that state" where "even the distinction of sex is lost."[63] The female virgin must so totally disassociate herself from her femaleness that she "is no longer called a woman."[64] Both the body and the soul must be sexless for virginity to be of any value to God.

For Jerome there is something inherently ennobling in virginity. Choosing virginity, or having God choose you for virginity, raises the virgins status on earth as well as in heaven. Jerome tells Demetrius that her virginity gives her a "holiness [which] ennobles her as much as her rank."[65] As has been suggested before, this sort of language to female Christians, especially to female Christians with a very strong sense of their calling, could prove to be a very powerful incentive to become a virgin. Both in this life and the next they can raise themselves to a status that is otherwise almost certainly closed to them. To women of noble families, like Demetrius, this may not be quite as appealing, but even these women are forbidden to lead a congregation or express spiritual understandings contrary (or even different) to those of their brothers in Christ.

Finally, Augustine, extolling the benefits of virginity, makes the same appeal as Jerome, and asks his readers why God would "promise temporal advantage only to holy persons exercising continence."[66] Jerome's contention is that the benefits of virginity are not just for the heavenly world, but for this world as well. Augustine's contention is that the benefits of virginity are not just for this world, but for the heavenly world as well. This is part of Augustine's ongoing argument about the greater divine gifts afforded virgins, over against the divine gifts to the married.

## NOTES

1. Jhn 3.29.
2. Tertullian *On the Veiling of Virgins* 26.
3. Leander of Seville *The Training of Nuns* 4.
4. Ambrose *Concerning Virginity* 1.9.52.
5. Jerome *To Demetrius* 2.
6. Leander of Seville *The Training of Nuns* 5.
7. ibid.
8. Jerome *To Eustochium* 20.
9. Sulpitius Severus *Concerning Virginity* 1.
10. Leander of Seville *The Training of Nuns* 9.
11. Gregory of Nyssa *On Virginity* 15.
12. Jerome *To Eustochium* 18.
13. Sulpitius Severus *Concerning Virginity* 12.
14. Augustine *Of Holy Virginity* 5.
15. ibid., 6.
16. Sulpitius Severus *Concerning Virginity* 2.
17. Gregory of Nyssa *On Virginity* 2.
18. John Chrysostom *On the Necessity of Guarding Virginity* 9.
19. Methodius of Olympus *On Virginity* 1.5.
20. Jerome *To Eustochium* 23.
21. Jerome *Against Jovinianus* 12.
22. ibid.
23. ibid., 26.
24. ibid.
25. Jerome *To Pammachius* 10.
26. Augustine *Of Holy Virginity* 4.
27. Sulpitius Severus *Concerning Virginity* 3.
28. Leander of Seville *The Training of Nuns* 5.
29. Pseudo-Titus *On the State of Chastity* 36.
30. Cyprian of Carthage *The Dress of Virgins* 4.
31. ibid., 11.
32. ibid., 22.
33. Jerome *To Demetrius* 4.
34. John Chrysostom *On the Necessity of Guarding Virginity* 7.
35. John Chrysostom *On Virginity* 1.2.
36. Sulpitius Severus *Concerning Virginity* 12.
37. Leander of Seville *The Training of Nuns* 4.
38. ibid., 7.
39. Pseudo-Clement *On Virginity* 1.4.
40. ibid., 1.5.
41. Jerome *To Demetrius* 4.
42. Leander of Seville *The Training of Nuns* 4.
43. Pseudo-Clement *On Virginity* 1.4.

44. Ambrose *Concerning Virginity* 1.3.11.

45. ibid., 1.9.52.

46. Jerome *To Pammachius* 14.

47. Jerome *To Demetrius* 10.

48. John Chrysostom *On Virginity* 2.1.

49. ibid.

50. ibid., 11.2

51. Augustine *Of Holy Virginity* 12.

52. ibid., 24.

53. ibid.

54. Pseudo-Titus *On the State of Chastity* 3.

55. Pseudo-Clement *On Virginity* 1.6.

56. Jerome makes the same argument in *Against Jovinianus* 26 where he says that it was because of John's virginity that he "was more beloved by our Lord."

57. Pseudo-Clement *On Virginity* 1.7.

58. Gregory of Nyssa *On Virginity* 1.

59. ibid., 2.

60. Ambrose *Concerning Virgins* 2.18.

61. Jerome *Against Helvidius* 22.

62. Methodius *On Virginity* 1.1.

63. Jerome *Against Helvidius* 22.

64. ibid.

65. Jerome *To Demetrius* 7.

66. Augustine *Of Holy Virginity* 25

## Chapter Three

# Virginity and Marriage

The range of attitudes towards marriage in the examined writings fall some-where between begrudging tolerance to tepid approval. All of the Fathers read here, from the earliest to the latest, who compare marriage to virginity agree that marriage is a poor second choice, reserved only for the morally and spir-itually weak. Ambrose argues that a women "sins not if she marries, . . . [how-ever] if she marries not it is for eternity. In the former is the remedy for weak-ness, in the latter the glory of chastity."[1] The Fathers cannot afford to condemn marriage outright, and they attack other heterodox groups, i.e., Gnostics, Marcionites, Manicheans, Tatian, and the Encratites, for doing so. Marriage simply demonstrates the superiority of virginity, is a cure for un-controllable sexual lust, and carries the possibility of producing more virgins for Christ. At least one passage from each of the Fathers on this subject will suffice.

Methodius *On Virginity* 1.3: Lest, however, we should seem prolix in collecting the testimonies of the prophets, let us again point out how chastity succeeded to marriage with one wife, taking away by degrees the lusts of the flesh, until it re-moved entirely the inclination for sexual intercourse engendered by habit.

Ambrose *Concerning Virginity* 6.24: I am not discouraging marriage, but am en-larging upon the benefits of virginity . . . The former is not reproved, the latter is praised.

—— 6.34: Some one may say, "Do you, then, discourage marriage?" Nay, I encourage it, and condemn those who are wont to discourage it . . . I do not then discourage marriage, but recapitulate the advantages of holy virginity.

Jerome *Against Helvidius* 22: And now that I am about to institute a comparison between virginity and marriage, I ask my readers not to suppose that in praising virginity I have in the least disparaged marriage.

Jerome *To Eustochium* 19: Wedded women may congratulate themselves that they come next to virgins.

———— 19-20: To show that virginity is natural while wedlock only follows guilt, what is born of wedlock is virgin flesh, and it gives back in fruit what in root it has lost. I praise wedlock, I praise marriage, but it is because they give me virgins.

Jerome *Against Jovinianus* 8: And do we still hesitate to speak of marriage as a concession to weakness.

———— 29: They who in Paradise remained in perpetual virginity, when they were expelled from Paradise were joined together. Or if Paradise admits marriage, and there is no difference between marriage and virginity, what prevented their previous intercourse even in Paradise? They were driven out of Paradise; and what they did not do there, they do on earth; so that from the very earliest days of humanity virginity was consecrated by Paradise, and marriage by earth . . . Let us, therefore, who served marriage under the law, serve virginity under the Gospel.

Jerome *To Pammachius* 2: If a virgin and a wife are to be looked on as the same, why has Rome refused to listen to this impious doctrine . . . Either my view of the matter must be embraced, or that of Jovinianus.

———— 7: We have summed up the discussion thus: When one thing is good and another thing is better; when that which is good has a different reward from that which is better; and when there are more rewards then one, then, obviously, there exists a diversity of gifts. The difference between marriage and virginity is as great as that between not doing evil and doing good—or, to speak more favorably still, as that between what is good and what is still better.

———— 14: I call virginity fine corn, wedlock barley, and fornication cow-dung.

———— 17: it is only good to marry, because it is bad to burn.

John Chrysostom *On the Necessity of Guarding Virginity* 1: A matter so important and full of such wisdom as virginity is despitefully treated, the veil which separates it from marriage has been destroyed, torn asunder by shameless hands, the holy of holies is trod underfoot, and that which is august and full of terror has become impure, exposed to all. The state which is more honorable than marriage has been degraded and dashed to the ground so that those women who marry are considered more fortunate. As compared with marriage, virginity always was assigned the first place.

John Chrysostom *On Virginity* 10.2: Is marriage a good? Then virginity is admirable because it is better than a good, as much better as a helmsman is than his sailors, and a general to his army.

Augustine *Of Holy Virginity* 1: by divine right continence is preferred to wedded life, and pious virginity to marriage.

Augustine *On the Good of Marriage* 19: Both by sure reason and authority of holy Scriptures, we both discover that marriage is not a sin, and yet equal it not to the good either of virginal or even of widowed chastity.

Leander of Seville *The Training of Nuns* 15: A virgin may marry, but she who does not is numbered among the angels.

Pseudo-Titus *On the State of Chastity* 3: Why should a virgin who is already betrothed to Christ be united with a carnal man?

We begin with Pseudo-Clement who reminds his readers that God " will give to virgins a notable place in the house of God, . . . and better than those who have passed a wedded life in sanctity, and whose 'bed is undefiled.'"[2] The message here is that while God loves all of the redeemed, virgins are loved more than others. All Christians who have not committed themselves to virginity—all non-virgins—regardless of any other considerations, will receive a less notable place in the house of God. The question of how much of a reading Pseudo-Clement was given remains, but the existence of extant copies of his epistles suggest that some considered his writings of some value. If this is true, then by the second century some Christians are beginning to believe that God does not love all impartially, but reserves His special approbations for those committed to virginity.

It is difficult to know exactly where Jerome stands on some of the issues of marriage and virginity. We hear Jerome reasoning that because marriages might produce more virgins for Christ, God does not condemn marriage outright. He writes, "If the Lord had commanded virginity He would have seemed to condemn marriage, and to do away with the seed-plot of mankind, of which virginity itself is a growth."[3] But even this gift given back to God of more virgins falls far short of the more excellent choice. Jerome writes "we keep to the King's highway if we aspire to virginity yet refrain from condemning marriage."[4] Throughout his writings he speaks of "allow[ing] marriage,"[5] that "even marriage is a gift of God,"[6] that "in praising virginity" he is not "in the least disparag[ing] marriage."[7] He even says in one place that "we honor marriage."[8] Yet, each of these statements come with a caveat. While Jerome can say that we "allow marriage," it is to be understood that "we prefer the virginity which springs from it." And though he may "grant that even marriage is a gift from God," the reader is to also know that "between gift and gift there is great diversity." And "while we honor marriage we prefer virginity which is the offspring of marriage." The only Christian marriages that Jerome condemns outright are the marriages of those who have fallen from the ranks of publicly confessed virgins. Of those, "When they have begun to wax wanton against Christ they will marry, having condemnation because they have rejected their first faith."[9]

Jerome professes, in his letter to Eustochium, that he is writing neither to "praise the virginity which you follow," nor to "recount the drawback of marriage." However, he, not taking his own advice, lists "pregnancy [and] the crying of infants" among the troubles encountered by wives.[10] In his broadside against Helvidius he writes that the virgin "is not subject to the anxiety and pain of childbearing, and having passed the change of life, has ceased to perform the functions of a woman [and] is freed from the curse of God."[11] The only way to escape the curse of childbearing in pain and sorrow—a "curse from God," and the lot of all women because of Eve—is to either remain virginal or live long enough to become barren. Jerome even goes as far as to condemn procreation altogether. We read in his work against Jovinianus the following:

> What is this distress which, in contempt of the marriage tie, long for the liberty of virginity? "Woe unto them that are with child and to them that give suck in those days." We have not here a condemnation of harlots and brothels, of whose damnation there is no doubt, but [a condemnation] of the swelling of the womb, and wailing of infancy, the fruit as well as the work of marriage.[12]

A solution for Jerome was "spiritual marriages." In *Against Helvidius* 23 he writes, "I do not deny that holy women are found both among widows and those who have husbands; but they are such as have ceased to be wives, or such as even in the close bond of marriage, imitate virgin chastity."

However, Augustine, in an attempt to give encouragement to the married, advises them to "let the gain of children make up for our lost virginity."[13] Still, he confesses in the very next chapter that there is "no fruitfulness of the flesh [that] can be compared to holy virginity of the flesh."[14] Ambrose says that virginity "is the gift of a few, that [of marriage] is of all."[15] Leander begrudgingly admits to his sister that while "it is true that God instituted marriage, . . . it was in order that virginity might spring there from, that, by increasing the number of virgins, married women might gain offspring, what they had lost in marriage."[16]

That marriage might act as a hedge against fornication is only for "those who cannot contain." Jerome even compares marriage to the works of the law that Paul condemns in Galatians. After quoting Gal 2.16b, "by the works of the law shall no flesh be justified.," he writes, "I have spoken to the following effect: Marriages also are works of the law. And for this reason there is a curse upon such as do not produce offspring." In other words, if you are going to marry, and if you are going to engage in sexual intercourse, you must produce children, or you will be proven to be a person who is controlled by your lust. This passage in Galatians has traditionally been understood to carry soteriological significance. The context of v.16 is as follows:

> Knowing that a man is not justified by the works of the law, but by faith in Jesus Christ, even we have believed in Christ Jesus, that we might be justified by faith in Christ and not by the works of the law; for by the works of the law no

flesh will be justified . . . I have been crucified with Christ; it is no longer I who live, but Christ lives in me; and the life which I now live in the flesh I live by faith in the Son of God, who loved me and gave himself for me. I do not set aside the grace of God; for if righteousness comes through the law, then Christ died in vain.

Therefore, when Jerome is comparing marriage with the works of the law, it is possible to suggest that marriage is of no use in the issues surrounding salvation. If marriage is the works of the law, then, virginity can be thought of as justification through Christ. Further, a coupling of this passage in Galatians with Eph 2.8-9 makes Jerome's comments even more interesting. And yet, Jerome still allows a place for marriage, for he says in his writing against Jovinianus that "We are not ignorant of the words, 'Marriage is honorable among all, and the bed undefiled.' We have read God's first command, 'Be fruitful and multiply, and replenish the earth;' but while we honor marriage we prefer virginity."[17]

We have already established, through his own writings, that Jerome believes all women, left to their own devices, even after publicly taking vows, are almost incapable of restraining the lust the burns in their flesh. Therefore, it is not surprising to read this passage to Pammachius.

> As marriage is permitted to virgins by reason of the danger of fornication, and what in itself is not desirable is thus made excusable, so be reason of the same danger widows are permitted to marry a second time. For it is better that a woman should know one man (though he should be a second or a third) than that she should know several. In other words, it is preferable that she should prostitute herself to one rather than to many."[18]

This is not subtle. A widow who remarries is no better than a prostitute whose condemnation is already a known fact.[19] This is simply another revelation of how conflicted Jerome is about his own sexuality and the sexuality of others; especially women, and Christian women in particular. He can only see women as either saints or whores, and they are not allowed to be saints unless they become spiritual men.

It is the disruption of prayer that is one of Jerome's major concerns concerning marriage, and, more particularly, the marriage act. He believes that engaging in sex disqualifies a person from coming to God in prayer. It is interesting that the other things that might occupy a married persons day, i.e., work, preparing meals, washing clothes and kitchen utensils, caring for children, helping a neighbor, are not condemned. Perhaps he believes that a person could continue to pray while engaged in these activities. And while he rejects the position taken by others that "all intercourse is impure," it is utterly impossible to pray while engaging in sex with one's spouse. Sex and prayer are like oil and water. Jerome returns to this argument in four different documents.

> *Against Helvidius* 22. thus they begin to have time for prayer. For so long as the debt of marriage is paid, earnest prayer is neglected.
>
> *To Eustochium* 22. I will just say that the Apostle bids us pray without ceasing, and that he who in the married state renders his wife her due cannot so pray. Either we pray always and are virgins, or we cease to pray that we may fulfill the claims of marriage.
>
> *Against Jovinianus* 7. The same Apostle in another place commands us to pray always. If we are to pray always, it follows that we must never be in the bondage of wedlock, for as often as I render my wife her due, I cannot pray.
>
> *To Pammachius* 15. The same Apostle, in another place, commands us to pray always. But if we are always to pray we must never yield to the claims of wedlock, for, as often as I render her doe to my wife, I incapacitate myself for prayer.

Jerome is not the only church Father afflicted with this equivocation concerning marriage. John Chrysostom can only bring himself to admit that marriage is "less honorable than virginity." Further, he has a rather tepid warning against those who detract from marriage, but only because they "also reduce the glory of virginity."[20] On the other hand, he seems to be horrified that there are those who dare to compare marriage with virginity, and says that the very act of comparing that which "is august and full of terror has become impure, [and] exposed to all." [21] He goes on to ask women, "what is more burdensome than having a husband and being anxious about his affairs? . . . Why do you welcome slavery after Christ has made you free?"[22] Pseudo-Titus also asks, "Why should a virgin who is already betrothed to Christ be united with a carnal man?"[23] Chrysostom's arguments reveal that neither he nor the Apostle Paul nor God has any use for marriage, and declares that, "he who has Christ speaking within him testifies that God wishes all men to refrain from marriage,"[24] for while virginity has the power to make people saints, marriage does not. The risk of losing an exalted state in heaven is echoed by Leander by writing, "a virgin may marry, but she who does not is numbered among the angels."[25]

Marriage, then, is either a wrong choice or an inferior choice. Marriage can never be considered equal to virginity. Naturally, then, the question arises, "Why?" What are the imagined consequences of allowing marriage to stand on an equal footing with virginity? It seems that there are at least four.

1) *Allowing marriage to be equal to virginity contradicts the word of God.* The Fathers' exegeses of Paul's councils in 1 Cor 7.7,8,34, and 38 allowed

them to read these verses as moral absolutes. "He who gives in marriage does well, *but* he who does not give in marriage does better." Therefore, since, according to Paul, the action of either marrying or not marrying falls along a continuum between good and better (or "not sinning" and "praising"), the ontological status of a person *vis-à-vis* marriage also falls along that continuum; a continuum revealed by God through the Apostle Paul. The sexual hierarchy, with virginity at the top, was ordained by God. And, if on Earth, virginity surpasses marriage, then, it can be assumed that, in the eyes of God, the rewards for virgins surpass the rewards for married Christians in heaven.

2) *Allowing marriage to be equal to virginity removes an important motivation for choosing virginity.* It is important to remember that the Fathers were intent on eradicating as much sex from the Christian communities as possible. Sex and lust were just plain bad, both for the male and female Christians, and the only morally acceptable situation for Christian to engage in sex at all was in marriage for the procreation of children. And, although, sexual intercourse was forgivable in marriage, those who fell victim to their own lust, or the lusts of others, were seen, in the eyes of God, as weaker than the heroic virgins. If the heavenly, divine, rewards for the married Christians and the virgins were the same, and if the married Christians and the virgins were equal to each other, then there is very little reason to choose, what the Fathers themselves admitted, was a life of sacrifice and denial. The Fathers let their readers know that in reality, on the whole, public acknowledgment of the spirituality of a married Christian women was non-existent.

3) *Allowing marriage to be equal to virginity meant there would be fewer "safe" women in the Christian communities.* The Fathers believed that the powerful pull of sexual lust was demonic. Also, it is difficult to read these documents and not sense that some of these men, Augustine for one, were struggling with sexual lust themselves. Some, even felt that that pull was even stronger than the pull of Christ. They also believed that the "trigger" for sexual lust in men was women. And women did not even have to dress or act seductively. Simply appearing in public could cause men to forget their devotion to Christ and their commitment to Him. For some of the Fathers, women, simply by their existence, were dangerous to men. Therefore, women who publicly made a commitment to life-long virginity to the Almighty God in Heaven, were seen as sexually inviolate. To even think about engaging in sex with one of these women would be an unforgivable effrontery to God. Virgins were the only women that were safe, because they were the only women who had never, and would never, engage in any sex act. The Fathers, then, in their calls for virginity, and praising it above marriage, were protecting themselves from dangerous females. Sexually active females were the true enemy, for they could cause a man to loose control over his own sexual urges and

awaken sexual lusts that would almost certainly run riot, and ruin his status with Christ.

4) *Allowing marriage to be equal to virginity would mean a loss of a degree of control over tens of thousands of women.*[26] We have earlier revealed in the texts on virginity clear evidence that the Fathers, through warnings, threats, and admonitions, were insistent on maintaining control over every aspect of the virgins' lives. Whether the women practicing virginity actually followed all of these rules and regulations is another matter. The point that needs to be made is that the Fathers could not imagine tens or hundreds of thousands of women being left to themselves, to practice and maintain their own Christianity either by themselves or in the company of other women only. Two fears that are consistently voiced by the Fathers concerning virgins are spiritual pride and heresy. Women, even virgins who follow Christ wherever he goes, who are blessed with special gifts from God, who have become "men" in the spiritual sense, cannot possibly practice true Christianity in the context of other women only. Women, if allowed to form and articulate their own spirituality, by that very act, would be guilty of spiritual pride. Women, all women, even virgins, must be kept in subjection to men. To allow otherwise would cause spiritual and theological chaos and anarchy. The patriarchy must know what Christian women are doing and thinking so that they can be corrected, which they will undoubtedly, consistently need. Further, if they are married, they are undoubtedly having sex with their husbands, and undoubtedly enjoying it, for women, are, by nature, sensual. This, I believe, is the Father's greatest fear; that Christians who are married are having sex, and secretly enjoying it. And the sexual rush from engaging in the sex act is addictive and will cause the married Christians to engage in sex more and more frequently with no thought of procreation at all. They simply, like animals, are satisfying their sexual urges. The Fathers knew that they had no weapons to control those who were victims of the disease of sexual addiction, which they believed all to be capable of. Sexual urges were just under the surface of all people, ready at the slightest provocation, to bust out and ruin lives, and, for Christians, endanger their salvation. Married Christians had already demonstrated their weakness regarding sexual lust. There was still hope for the virgins, but they must be kept under the tightest control.

## NOTES

1. Ambrose *Concerning Virginity* 6.24.
2. Pseudo-Clement *On Virginity* 1.4.
3. Jerome *Against Jovinianus* 12.

4. Jerome *To Pammachius* 8.

5. ibid., 2.

6. Jerome *Against Jovinianus* 8.

7. Jerome *Against Helvidius* 22.

8. Jerome *Against Jovinianus* 3.

9. Jerome *To Eustochium* 29.

10. ibid., 2.

11. Jerome *Against Helvidius* 22.

12. Jerome *Against Jovinianus* 12.

13. Augustine *Of Holy Virginity* 7.

14. ibid., 8.

15. Ambrose *Concerning Virginity* 6.35.

16. Leander of Seville *The Training of Nuns* 11.

17. Jerome *Against Jovinianus* 3.

18. Jerome *To Pammachius* 8.

19. cf. Jerome *Against Jovinianus* 12.

20. John Chrysostom *On Virginity* 10.1.

21. John Chrysostom *On the Necessity of Guarding Virginity* 1.

22. ibid., 10.

23. Pseudo-Titus *On the State of Chastity* 3.

24. John Chrysostom *On the Necessity of Guarding Virginity* 1; see also 2.2, 30.2.

25. Leander of Seville *The Training of Nuns* 11.

26. I recognize that this argument runs counter to the arguments of some feminist historians. However, those objections have been addressed earlier.

# Chapter Four

# Virginity in the Economy of Salvation

## VIRGINS ARE SAVED

The Apostle Paul often speaks of salvation in the past tense, i.e. it is something that has already been provided through the substitutional death of Jesus Christ. Therefore, telling virgins that they have the assurance of salvation is to be expected. But it appears that the redemption that the virgins receive is essentially different from that of the rest of the Christian community. Beginning with Pseudo-Clement we read that the salvation awaiting virgins is uniquely theirs. It is, in fact, a short-cut to heaven. However, unlike the soteriology of Paul which was decidedly centered on the reception of grace over against the "works of the law," the soteriology revealed in these writings speak of a righteousness that the virgin must earn, and in some of the writings it is the virgin's virginity that gains her that meritorious righteousness. In other words virgins must not only *be* virginal, they must also *act* virginal.

Pseudo-Clement states that virgins have chosen virginity and, perhaps more importantly, persevere in virginity specifically for the sake of the "kingdom of heaven." In some passages Pseudo-Clement tells the virgins that they must be holy in all things, and in others he assumes that virgins, by virtue of their choice, are holy in all things. In either case there seems to be a distinct *virginal* holiness that is part of perpetual virginity.

The passages in Pseudo-Clement's letters where virginity and salvation intersect are as follows:

> 1.1-2: . . . to the blessed brother virgins who devote themselves to preserve virginity "for the sake of the kingdom of heaven" . . . [and to] all virgins of either sex who have truly resolved to preserve virginity for the sake of the kingdom of heaven.

1.4: For he who covets for himself these things so great and excellent, with-draws and severs himself on this account from all the world, that he may go and live a life divine and heavenly, like the holy angels, in work pure and holy, and "in the holiness of the Spirit of God," and that he may serve God Almighty through Jesus Christ for the sake of the kingdom of heaven.

1.4: He will give to virgins a notable place in the house of God, which is some-thing "better than sons and daughters," and better then the place of those who have passed a wedded life in sanctity, and whose "bed has not been defiled. For God will give to virgins the kingdom of heaven, as to the holy angels, by reason of this great and noble profession.

1.5: Do you know how, like a man, to enter "lawfully" upon this contest and "strive," that, in the might of the Holy Spirit, you choose this for yourself that you may be crowned with a crown of light, and that they may lead you about in triumph through "the Jerusalem above."

The assurance of salvation, or, for Pseudo-Clement, "the kingdom of heaven" (ἡ βασιλεία τῶν οὐρανῶν) is repeated throughout his first epistle to the virgins. And although scholars have no evidence that the epistles of Pseudo-Clement were ever considered canonical, there was at least a few Christians, by the early second century, that believed that salvation was as-sured for a group of people primarily (though not solely) because of their choice to renounce sexual contact. Coming at such an early date makes this belief fairly remarkable. For, although various individuals were awarded sal-vation, only the Apostles, martyrs and virgins were, *as a group*, given this as-surance.

However, it can be argued that, in some sense, this salvation was even somewhat more difficult to attain for the virgins. For when they chose vir-ginity, it was life-long virginity. Pseudo-Clement repeats that it is the virgins who "preserve virginity" who are awarded the kingdom of heaven. There was no turning back from this decision, and the stakes were high. Pseudo-Clement's language is that these virgins chose virginity precisely "for the sake of heaven." These men and women have staked their eternity on their ability to remain virginal for the rest of their lives.

We hear no such language directed to married Christians. It can be assumed that married Christians were encouraged to remain true to their spouse, but their are no extant documents written to married Christians which articulate a specific tie between preserving marital fidelity and salvation. In other words, married Christians did not choose marriage as a way to "the kingdom of heaven." For Pseudo-Clement and the rest of the authors, married Chris-tians chose marriage to escape perdition, for they could not control their sex-ual lust. Therefore, by the early second century there are Christians who have moved from the Pauline soteriology based solely on the reception of unmerited grace provided by Jesus Christ, to a soteriology based, at least partly, on the moral stamina, no doubt aided by Christ, to maintain a sexless life.

But while Pseudo-Clement maintains that the choice and maintaining of virginity is helpful in gaining "the kingdom of heaven," this vow, and the moral fortitude to preserve the vow, was still not enough. Pseudo-Clement will not let the readers of his epistles forget that merely calling yourself a virgin, and even maintaining your virginity, is vanity in and of itself. Virgins have chosen a higher calling, and because they are known in the community for their purity, they must demonstrate what it means to choose this life. There are added responsibilities which the virgins are to follow:

> 1.2. It is required that [virgins] be worthy of the kingdom of heaven in every thing.
>
> 1.3. For virgins are a beautiful pattern to believers, and to those who shall believe. The name alone, indeed, without works, does not introduce into the kingdom of heaven; but, if a man be truly a believer, such an one can be saved. For, if a person be only called a believer in name, while he is not such in works, he cannot possibly be a believer . . . For, merely because a person is called a virgin, if he be destitute of works excellent and comely, and suitable to virginity, he cannot possibly be saved. For our Lord called such virginity as that "foolish" . . . for virginity of such a kind is impure, and disowned by all good works.
>
> 1.7. No virgin, therefore, unless they be in everything as Christ, and as those "who are Christ's," can be saved.

It can be seen in these texts that the moral demands on virgins are as severe as their virginal life. Not only are they to be "worthy the kingdom of heaven in every thing," but they are to be "in everything as Christ." There is no room for error for the virgins. For if Christ is the model for the Christian, and if Christ lived a sinless life, and if the virgins must be "in everything as Christ" was, then the virgins must also live sinless lives.

> This theme is repeated in 1.5-6:
> Do you understand and know how honorable a thing is sanctity? Do you understand how great and exalted and excellent is the glory of virginity? The womb of a holy virgin carried our Lord Jesus Christ, the Son of God; and the body which our Lord wore, and in which He carried on the conflict in this world, He put on from a holy virgin. From this, therefore, understand the greatness and dignity of virginity. Do you wish to be a Christian? Imitate Christ in everything. John, the ambassador, he who came before our Lord . . . was a virgin. Imitate, therefore, the ambassador of our Lord, and be his follower in everything.

This sinless life may be what Pseudo-Clement is speaking of when he says that virgins must be known by "works excellent and comely, and suitable for virginity." Virgins, therefore, are not under obligation to produce the good works that are required of the rest of the Christian community, but are to produce good works that are "suitable to virginity," i.e., perfection. And not only does Pseudo-Clement require this of virgins, but he believes that virgins are indeed capable of the same perfection as Christ. And because he believes this, he can say that God "will give to virgins a notable place in the house of God . . . [which is] better than the place of those who have passed a wedded life in sanctity, and whose 'bed has not been defiled.'" God will give to virgins the kingdom of heaven, as to the holy angels, *by reason of this great and noble profession*. Faithful married Christians can look forward to heaven to be sure, but not the "notable place in the house of God." Sulpitius Severus writing ca. three centuries later is more explicit about the greater rewards awaiting Christian virgins.

> How great blessedness, among heavenly gifts, belongs to holy virginity, besides the testimonies of the Scriptures, we learn also from the practice of the Church, by which we are taught that a peculiar merit belongs to those who have devoted themselves to [virginity] by special consecration. For while the whole multitude of those that believe receive equal gifts of grace, and all rejoice in the same blessings of the sacraments, those who are virgins possess something above the rest, since, out of the holy and unstained company of the Church, they are chosen by the Holy Spirit, and are presented by the bishop at the alter of God, as if being more holy and pure sacrifices, on account of the merits of their voluntary dedication.[1]

Also, Leander of Seville, writing in the sixth century to his sister says, "Do you see, dearly beloved sister, how virgins hold the chief place in the kingdom of God?"[2]

Therefore, that "notable place in the house of God," which Pseudo-Clement writes about, and which was originally reserved for the perfect and sinless angels, is now also occupied by perfect and sinless virgins, "by reason of this great and noble profession . . .For every virgin who is in God is holy in her body and in her spirit, and is constant in the service of her Lord, not turning away from it in any way, but wait[s] upon him always in purity and holiness in the Spirit of God."[3]

It is possible, then, to deduce that this early belief that virgins were holy, pure, and Christ like, was partially responsible for later Christians to conclude that not only were virgins saved, but were saviours as well.

Cyprian of Carthage reasons that "if continence follows Christ, and virginity is destined for the kingdom of God, what have such maidens to do with worldly dress and adornments."[4] Here we have a recognized, catholic author saying the same thing that Pseudo-Clement also said. The qualifier for

Cyprian, here, however, is not the moral rigor that Pseudo-Clement describes, but simply a warning not to embarrass Christ, as Christ's virgins, by appearing in public in "worldly dress and adornments." This document, along with Tertullian's *On the Veiling of Virgins*, are the earliest evidences of a demand that virgins submit to a prescribed dress code, which would make them recognizable as Christian virgins. It has already been established that these men writing on virginity believe that women are naturally sensual, and as sensual beings, they are forever looking to attract the attention of men, and to be more successful in that pursuit, they wore clothes, jewelry and hairdos that attracted men's eyes, and awakened lust in their hearts (and loins). One can suppose that married women were discouraged from attracting attention to themselves by their physical appearance, and if that it true, if would be even more paramount for Christian virgins.

Methodius of Olympus tells his readers that life-long virginity has always been God's plan for humanity, and it was only because of Adam and Eve's fall into sin that the sin of sexual intercourse was introduced. But God has slowly brought His people back from their fallenness to a state of perfection and Christ likeness. The language and imagery that Methodius uses to praise virginity can hardly be exceeded. Methodius is not interested in slowly and methodically building his argument for virginity, but states, upfront, what he intends to discuss in the rest of the document. He begins his entire discourse with the following words.

> Virginity is something supernaturally great, wonderful, and glorious, and to speak plainly and in accordance with the Holy Scriptures, this best and noblest manner of life alone is the root of immortality, and also its flower and first-fruits; and for this reason the Lord promises that those shall enter in the kingdom of heaven who have made themselves eunuchs.[5]

In describing both the idea and practice of virginity, as well as the rewards of those who have devoted themselves to virginity, Methodius' use of superlatives is noteworthy. For him virginity is not just great, wonderful and glorious, but it is "supernatural" in its greatness, wonderfulness and gloriousness. For those who practice virginity, it is not just a better and noble life, but the "best and noblest" of lives. As for the rewards for those who practice virginity, it "alone" is the "root of immortality," as well as the "flower and first-fruits" of immortality. And all of these superlatives attached to virginity are witnessed, and are in "accordance with the Holy Scriptures" and the promises of God, and, therefore, cannot be gainsaid.

Virginity, then, for Methodius, is not a human institution neither in its inception nor in its completion. It is from God, for it is supernatural, its praises are found in the "Word of God," and God has made promises of rewards to

His virgins. Those who enter into the virginity of God, enter into the Kingdom of God. There are not qualifiers here, as we saw in Pseudo-Clement.
Since virginity is so imbued with supernatural, divine grace, virgins are also
imbued with this same grace, which Methodius will later tell his readers is
nothing less than perfection. And this is a perfection which only virgins can
attain. In discussing God's plan for creation following the fall, Methodius
tracks humanity's rise back to perfection through a decreasing sexual component of their lives.

> For truly by a great stretch of power the plant of virginity was sent down to men
> from heaven, and for this reason it was not revealed to the first generations. For
> the race of mankind was still very small in number; and it was necessary that it
> should first be increased in number, and then brought to perfection . . .But when
> hereafter it was colonized from end to end, the race of man spreading to a
> boundless extent, God no longer allowed man to remain in the same ways, con-
> sidering how they might now proceed from one point to another, and advance
> nearer to heaven, until, having attained to the very greatest and most exalted les-
> son of virginity, they should reach to perfection; that first they should abandon
> the intermarriage of brothers and sisters, and marry wives from other families;
> and then that they should no longer have many wives, like brute beasts, as
> though born for the mere propagation of the species; and then that they should
> not be adulterers; and then again that they should go on to continence, and from
> continence to virginity, when, having trained themselves to despise the flesh,
> they sail fearlessly into the peaceful haven of immortality.[6]

For Methodius, God had created humanity perfect and whole, and His goal
was to bring them back to perfection, and the most obvious way was through
virginity. He writes that "in old times man was not yet perfect, and for this
reason was unable to receive perfection, which is virginity."[7] That the first humans were to remain perpetually virginal, and, therefore, perfect is echoed by
Jerome.

> What really happened is plain enough—that in they who in Paradise remained in
> perpetual virginity, when they were expelled from Paradise were joined together [in
> sexual intercourse]. Or if Paradise admits marriage, and there is no difference be-
> tween marriage and virginity, what prevented their previous intercourse in Par-
> adise? They were driven out of Paradise; and what they did not there, they do on
> earth; so that from the very earliest days of humanity virginity was consecrated by
> Paradise, and marriage by earth. "Let your garments be always white." The eternal
> whiteness of our garments is the purity of virginity . . . Let us who served in mar-
> riage under the law, serve virginity under the Gospel.[8]

John Chrysostom agrees with this assessment, and argues that "Moses himself directed the Jews away from intercourse."[9]

However, God chose to wean humans both of their sexual lust and habitual sexual activity through stages, beginning with a prohibition of incest, to polygamy, to adultery, finally approaching continence, and ending with virginity. The recitation of this process is accompanied with more superlatives. With each step away from the sexual practices of the ancients, the people who followed God were advancing "nearer to heaven" until they finally gained "the very greatest and most exalted lesson of virginity."

The link between virginity and salvation is unmistakable here. Those who, in the past, did not adopt virginity, only approached heaven, but those who now practice virginity "sail fearlessly into the peaceful haven of immortality." Left to their own devices, humanity would still be practicing the most debasing sexual acts, but Methodius says that God "no longer allowed man to remain in the same ways," and, in His mercy, He brought them to a place, sexually, where they were safe for heaven, for they had been taught by God to "despise the flesh."

Methodius' language continues to be thick and rich with imagery in ch.6.2. Here he suggests that since God created humans as virgins, and since what God created was perfect, any change in their status as virgins is a deliberate marring of God's creation. Methodius urges his readers to "keep this beauty [of virginity] inviolate and unharmed" just as God "constructed, formed and fashioned it." And if they do this "they will become like a glorious and holy image, [and] will be transferred thence to heaven, the city of the blessed, and will dwell there as in a sanctuary."

By the time Methodius penned this document (late 3rd—early 4th c.) Christians already had a long history of using images and/or icons to depict heroes of their faith. Besides images of Jesus, the Apostles, and Mary, there were also images of men and women who, either because of their faith or martyrdom, were remembered through drawings or paintings. Methodius is elevating virgins to stand with these other heroes of the faith. Not only will they be praised for their purity in this life, and "transferred to . . . the city of the blessed," but they will, as "glorious and holy image[s], be remembered in perpetuity. Cyprian of Carthage describes this holiness of virgins.

> Our discourse is directed to virgins, for whom our solitude is the greater inasmuch as their glory is the more exalted. They are the flower of the tree that is the church, the beauty and adornment of spiritual grace, the image of God reflecting the holiness of the Lord, the more illustrious part of Christ's flock.[10]

Only the most exalted Christians could ever hope to attain this status, and while martyrdom was still a possibility, another way was through virginity. And while Christians, officially, did not worship any images, both the laity and the clergy prayed before these images. While we do know that in the

Middle Ages saints were seen as intermediaries between the believers and God, can it be assumed that some of that practice already existed in the fourth century? If it can, then these virgins were also possible intermediaries between the non-virgin Christians and God. They had not only become icons, but they assisted God in the work of salvation.

Their virginity must be kept "inviolate and unharmed." However, while male virgins might "suffer" from involuntary ejaculations in his dreams, for female virgins it was the hymen that must be kept inviolate and unharmed. The breaking of the hymen through sexual activity was a marring God's perfect creation; a marring which could never be undone, and those who were guilty of that defacing could not possibly be considered glorious and holy images. Pseudo-Clement pointed to the apostles John and Paul, and Barnabas and Timothy, because "they cherished and loved sanctity," as models for the virginal life.[11] Methodius is suggesting that virgins are contemporary models, "glorious and holy image[s]," that Christians may look to as well.

Methodius also tells these "glorious and holy image[s]" that once they enter into "the city of the blessed" they will "dwell there as in a sanctuary." Most fourth century Christians, whether they were converts from some pagan or mystery religion, from Judaism, or were children of Christian parents, knew that the only beings that actually dwelt in sanctuaries were gods. Therefore, Methodius is telling his readers that not only are virgins intermediaries with God, but dwell in the actual sanctuary in heaven. Does that give virgins a divine status? That we cannot answer, but that hope is not held out to any other Christians in this letter.

In 6.5 Methodius, using language and phraseology reserved for the "mystery" religions, tells his readers that just as the devotees of the various mystery religions have orgies and secret initiation rites (a commonly held belief), so do the virgins of God. He writes:

> These, O Fair virgins, are the orgies of our mysteries; these the mystic rites of those who are initiated in virginity; these the "undefiled rewards" of the conflict of virginity. I am betrothed to the Word, and receive as a reward the eternal crown of immortality and riches from the Father.

Rumors concerning the "mystery religions," which the Christians would have known about, were full of tales concerning their sexual orgies involving ritualistic rites which only the initiated knew. Further, the initiates into these religions were promised a number of gifts from their gods, always among them being salvation; often through resurrection. And just as the initiates into the mystery religions were perceived, because of the secrecy of their practices, as somehow removed from regular society, Methodius is telling his readers that virgins are not part of the rest of society. They are not like the rest of the community of Christians. However, unlike the polluted rewards of the followers of the mystery religions, the virgins receive "undefiled rewards," for they are betrothed to the Word (read "Jesus"), and the undefiled reward is an "eternal crown of immortality."

In this passage, Methodius writes about the "conflict of virginity." Methodius understood that choosing life-long virginity did not mean a peaceful, serene, and utopian existence far from the cares of this world. For many virgins, both men and women, choosing this life meant a constant struggle with their own desires. And because they were held up as models for the rest of the Christian communities, their lives were constantly put under a microscope. Those who did persevere were applauded for their tenacity. Ambrose, recognized this and writes, "How much stronger are our virgins, who overcome even those powers which they do not see; whose victory is not only over flesh and blood, but also over the prince of this world, and the ruler of this age!"[12]

Turning to Jerome, we find him allowing virgins a place in heaven, but only if they adhere completely and unquestioningly to a stringent set of guidelines that does not even allow for one stray thought. Jerome takes the metaphor of the "narrow gate" and "difficult way" that Jesus speaks of that leads to life, and which only a few find, and couples it with warnings so dire that the faint of heart dare not even try to begin the life of virginity. Indeed, Jerome spends time more warning "saved" virgins what will happen to them if they should fall from their purity than assuring them of their salvation. Heaven becomes a place that God begrudgingly allows a few blessed souls to enter. Even virgins are mistaken if they think that devoting just their body to Christ will save them, for "even real virgins . . . are not saved by their physical virginity."[13] The physical virginity that must never be assailed even once must be matched with a mind that must never be assailed even once, for "virginity may be lost even by a thought."[14] Virgins are being told, therefore, that they must take seriously the words of Paul in Phil 2.5; "Let this mind be in you which was also in Jesus Christ." In other words, the sinless life lived by Jesus must be perfectly copied by those who have committed themselves to a life of virginity. If they do they will "have a place forever in heaven."[15] Further, in harmony with both earlier and later writers, Jerome says, "but, just as widows receive a greater reward from God than wives obedient to their husbands, they, too, must be content to see virgins preferred before themselves."[16]

Finally, in *Against Jovinianus* 26 Jerome writes, "Virginity does not die . . . but [it] abides with Christ, and its sleep is not death but a passing to another state." This passage, perhaps more than any other to this point, illustrates the degree of elevation of virginity to a divine status.

This was written in the fourth century, and although there are already documents describing the joys of heaven and the horrors of hell, we are still

removed by some years from fully developed theologies concerning the ultimate disposition of the body and the soul. Nor is there a common belief concerning the resurrection. Putting that all aside, what Jerome is attempting to
say is that the death of the virgin is not the death of the rest of humanity. Nor
is it even the death of the non-virginal Christians. This "passing to another
state" is only for the privileged few. What this state is is not made clear. It is
clearly not the immortality enjoyed by Enoch and Elisha in the Hebrew Scriptures. But when their bodies ceased to function, they, because of their virginity, did not have to experience the unknown of death. This, then, was the ultimate salvation. While all Christians were promised a resurrection, virgins
did not need a resurrection, or, at least, their resurrection was not a resurrection from the dead.

The power that this hope would inspire in the early Christian community
cannot be underestimated. In a world where many babies were stillborn or
died at birth or died in infancy; and in a world where young, sometimes pre-
teen, mothers died giving birth; and in a world where the average life ex-
pectancy was less than forty years; and in a world without shelter from war,
tyranny, pestilence and natural disasters, comes a promise that you can remain untouched by death by remaining a virgin. Death and virginity are antithetical to each other. Miracles, even the ultimate miracle, a deathless life,
was the gift from God to those who dedicated both their body and soul to
God. Virgins, in this light, are not just Christians who have decided to show
their dedication to God in refraining from sex and marriage. Virgins are "others," in ways that are not available to all. Their gifts from God, their communion with God, the very essence of their humanness has been changed.

In this same passage Jerome not only makes death and virginity antithetical to each other, but he makes marriage and virginity antithetical to each
other as well; highlighting the danger that those who have chosen marriage
have placed themselves in vis-à-vis their salvation. The entire passage reads
as follows:

> Again, after hearing the prediction that he must be bound by another, and led
> whither he would not, and must suffer on the cross, Peter said, "Lord what shall
> this man do?" being unwilling to desert John, with whom he had always been
> united. Our Lord said to him, "What is that to thee if I wish him so to be?"
> Whence the saying went abroad among the brethren that that disciple should not
> die. Here we have proof that virginity does not die, that the defilement of mar-
> riage is not washed away by the blood of martyrdom, but virginity abides with
> Christ, and its sleep is not death but a passing to another state.

Jerome, extrapolating from what was most likely an oral tradition, has constructed a truth that since the virgin John did not die, no virgins actually die.

Further, Jerome has proof that John was a virgin , for if he was not, how can Jovinianus explain "the cause of the special love our Lord bore to him," and "let him explain, if [John] was not a virgin, why it was that he was loved more than the other Apostles."[17]

Before we can even begin to address the issues raised by the statement that "the defilement of marriage . . . [is] not washed away by the blood of martyrdom," other concerns must be addressed.

First, even though the tradition that John never married is ancient, it still is just that—tradition. Secondly, although there is a disciple identified in the Gospel of John as the "disciple whom Jesus loved," (see Jhn 19.26; 21.7, 20) and although tradition says that that disciple was John, we still do not know that it was John. However, even granting that the disciple is John, and that he remained a virgin, the text simply says that he is the disciple that Jesus loved. While no one would suggest that John was the only disciple that Jesus loved, the evidence does not suggest that John was more loved than the rest of the disciples. Further, even if we allow that John was more loved by Jesus, there is a complete lack of evidence that John was more beloved because of his virginity. Jerome, in an effort to build an argument against Jovinianus, has built a house of cards, which cannot stand up to scrutiny. His entire argument is built on unsubstantiated conjectures.

Therefore, for Jerome, John, not Peter, is the chief apostle because of his virginity. He writes, "Peter is an Apostle, and John is an Apostle—the one a married man, the other a virgin; but Peter is an Apostle only, John is both an Apostle and an Evangelist, and a prophet."[18] Peter, therefore, could not be the chief apostle because he was defiled. His defilement came from the fact that he was married, and even though he died a martyr's death, that defilement stayed with him. Nothing, therefore, according to Jerome, can erase the defilement (pollution) that attends marriage and the marriage act. Martyrs, then, are no longer the most honored heroes that Christians need to emulate, but it is the virgins. Even martyred apostles are less in rank to virgins if the martyred apostles were married.

Although Jerome's *Against Jovinianus* is the best known early church document arguing for the preferability, in the eyes of God, of virginity to marriage, Augustine's *On Holy Virginity* contains two passages that continue the argument. In ch.13 Augustine writes that "they are marvelously void of wisdom, who think that the good of this continence is not necessary for the sake of the kingdom of heaven." And in ch.22 he writes that "on account of that future life which is promised in the kingdom of heaven we are to choose perpetual continence.." However, in both of these passages Augustine also says that it is not just for the promise of the blessedness of the future lived in the kingdom of heaven, but virginity is to be preferred in this life as well. He writes, "The joys peculiar to the virgins of Christ, are not the same as of such as are not virgins."[19] In ch.13 after scolding those who doubt the need for virginity for entrance into heaven, he says that virginity is also to be preferred to marriage "for the sake of the present world." He goes on to remind his readers that "married persons are strained different ways by earthly cares more and more straitened, from which trouble virgins and continent persons are free." And to make sure his readers understand that these conclusions are not his, he says in ch.22 that these truths are from the "plainest witnesses of divine Scripture."

It is in the writings of Sulpitius Severus that we find the most numerous and clearest coupling of the practice of virginity and the promise of salvation. However, Severus also reveals a great deal about his own soteriological beliefs as he writes about the salvation promised to virgins. The pertinent passages in his *Concerning Virginity* are as follows:

1. How great blessedness, among heavenly gifts, belongs to holy virginity, besides the testimonies of the Scriptures, we learn also from the practice of the Church, by which we are taught that a peculiar merit belongs to those who have devoted themselves to it by special consecration. For while the whole multitude of those that believe receive equal gifts of grace, and all rejoice in the same blessings of the sacraments, those who are virgins possess something above the rest, since, out of the holy and unstained company of the Church, they are chosen by the Holy Spirit, and are presented by the bishop at the altar of God, as if being more holy and pure sacrifices, on account of the merits of their voluntary dedication.

2. [Virginity] is . . . a great and admirable virtue, and is not undeservedly destined to a vast reward, in proportion to the greatness of its labor . . . Great, indeed, is the struggle connected with chastity, but greater is the reward; the restraint is temporal, but the reward will be eternal. For the blessed Apostle John also speaks concerning these, saying that "they follow the Lamb wherever he goes." This, I think, is to be understood to the following effect, that there will be no place in the court of heaven closed against them, but that all the habitations of the divine mansions will be thrown open before them.

4. For unless I am mistaken, chastity is preserved in its entirety, for the sake of the reward to be obtained in the kingdom of heaven.

5. Now, there are three kinds of virtue, by means of which the possession of the kingdom of heaven is secured. The first is chastity, the second, contempt of the world, and the third, righteousness.

10. Acknowledge that your members were formed for you by God the Maker, not for vices, but for virtues; and, when you have cleansed the whole of your limbs from every stain of sin, and they have become sanctified throughout your whole body, then understand that this purity will profit you, and look forward with all confidence to the prize of virginity.

19. Maintain to the last that purpose of virginity which you have formed; for it is the part of virtue not merely to begin, but to finish, as the Lord says in the Gospel, "Whosoever shall endure to the end, the same shall be saved."

Severus's use of the terms "merit," "grace," and "righteousness," used in the context of how the kingdom of God is obtained deserve our attention, for it is through virginity that these "virtues" of merit, grace, and righteousness are obtained. Those looking for a single, clearly articulated, Christian, soteriology in the early fifth century will be disappointed. We only need to remember the soteriological wars still being fought by supporters of Severus's contemporaries, Augustine and Pelagius.[20] However, when Severus says that the virtues of virginity, contempt of the world, and righteousness are virtues which will secure a place in the kingdom of heaven, we do not hear any protests. There are two sets of unanswered questions concerning this particular passage which scholars are left with:

1) Is there any particular significance to the order of these virtues? Is virginity the greatest and righteousness the least? Or are these three virtues in no particular order, all being equally important?

2) Are all three virtues needed for entrance into the kingdom of heaven, or is each virtue efficacious for salvation in its own right? Or are these three virtues to be seen as parts of a single virtue which merits salvation?

This final interpretation is the most likely, given the fact that virgins were, by their choice, demonstrating contempt for the world, and its expectations on them as women. Further, the requirements of absolute righteousness placed on virgins by Jerome may not have been forgotten in the sixth century, and were still part of the active literature of which virgins needed to be aware. Severus himself tells the virgins that they needed to be cleansed from "every stain of sin," and that they were required to "become sanctified throughout [their] whole body."[21] However, Severus's crafting of this sentence does not allow us to come to anything more than a tentative conclusion.

Further soteriological questions arise at the very beginning of this letter to his sister where he mentions a special "merit" which belongs to virgins alone. His words are that "we are taught that *a peculiar merit* belongs to those who have devoted themselves to [virginity] by special consecration, . . . [virgins] are chosen by the Holy Spirit, and are presented by the bishop at the altar of God, as if being more holy and pure sacrifices, on account of *the merits* of their voluntary dedication." (emphasis mine). A number of issues need to be addressed in this passage, but let us begin with Severus's use of the term "merit."

By the time Severus wrote this letter to his sister there was already an impressive, and growing, host of documents supporting virginity as the best and most holy life a Christian could choose. Special gifts from God had previously been granted to virgins. Virgins were especially dear in God's sight, and were given access to God in ways that non-virgin Christians were not. Jerome had already urged virgins to recognize this with regards to their married sisters. He tells them "to "learn in this respect a holy pride; know that you are better than they."[22] Therefore, when Severus' readers hear him saying that there is a "peculiar merit" that belongs to virgins, and that their virginity gives them "merits" which make them a "more holy and pure sacrifice," they would not be surprised. Severus is telling his readers that virginity is meritorious for salvation, for it is because of the virginity of the virgins that they are "presented by the bishop at the altar of God." They are, in the eyes of God, a "more holy and pure sacrifice," than the rest of the community of Christians. When God gives His grace, in the fifth century represented through the sacraments, it is efficacious for all, but "virgins possess something above the rest." Therefore, Severus can say without hesitation that "great, indeed, is the struggle with chastity, but greater is the reward." And the reward is that "there will be no place in the court of heaven closed against them, but that all the habitations of the divine mansions will be thrown open before them."[23]

Finally, Severus, like many who wrote before him, reminds the virgins that taking a vow of life-long virginity is, in fact, life-long, and promises that virgins who preserve their chastity in its entirety, and who "endure to the end" will "obtain the kingdom of heaven," and the "the same shall be saved."

The language and images that these writers use to indicate the separateness of virgins from the rest of humanity, and even the rest of Christendom, begins with some of the earliest Christian authors. Some may see this as a development toward the divination of virgins, finding its greatest fulfillment in Mary the Θεότοκος (Mother of God; God-bearer). Pseudo-Clement, as early as the second century, had already declared that virgins "live a life divine and heavenly," and their work is "pure and holy."[24] He also wrote that virgins receive, and even deserve, "a better place [than] those who have passed a wedded life in sanctity."[25] The angelic life of the virgins allowed them to receive the kingdom of heaven with "the holy angels."[26]

Christian authors, even canonical authors, before Sulpitius Severus, had already declared that Jesus Christ was the fulfillment of many of the sanctuary rituals found in the Hebrew Scriptures. John (Jhn 1.29), Luke (Lk 8.32-33), Paul (Rom 3.23-25; 1 Cor 5.7), Peter (1 Pet 1.18-21), and the author of Revelations (Rev 5.9-14) had written that Jesus was the true Lamb sacrificed for the sins of His people. The author of Hebrews also says that not only was Jesus the true bloody sacrifice for sin, but He is the true High Priest who enters into the presence of God on the Day of Atonement with His own blood to cleanse the Temple from the sin offerings brought to the temple throughout the previous year. (Heb 9.7-28). Severus, evoking these images, says that the Bishop (not Christ) presents the virgins to God as the "more holy and pure sacrifices." Therefore, in light of what has already been said about virgins, we are hardly surprised to hear Leander declare that "what all the saints hope to become and what the whole church promises will happen after the resurrection, that you already have."[27] If we couple this statement with Jerome's about virgins not tasting death, but passing to another state with Christ, we can conclude that virgins escape death altogether.

Pseudo-Titus begins with the assumption that virgins are saved, but their virginity and salvation are fragile, and in constant peril from the pull of lust and marriage.

> 13. Why strive against your own salvation to find death in love?
>
> 18. [God] has commanded that salvation be preserved in lonely celibacy.
>
> 23. Why expose your eternal salvation to loss through a trifle?
>
> 28. Bridle the desires of the flesh [so that] we may be able to carry away the everlasting resurrection.

Pseudo-Titus, like many of the male authors writing about virginity before him, "exposes" his own distrust of the strength of the virgins to maintain their virginity, and are constantly wondering if they should give up their vows of virginity and become married.

For many of these authors sex is not just about satisfying the always present, ever dangerous, persistent draw of humanity's now engrained lust. Lust, since the Fall, has become part of our essence. It must be sublimated, because sex is not just about satisfying sexual urges, but it has taken on cosmic ramifications. Sex is not about sex, it is about a struggle between the forces of darkness and light. It is about decisions which will result in either eternal life or eternal damnation. Few state this in more urgent terms than Pseudo-Titus.

> 23. No one from the church will then be able to get away [from the judgment] apart from the virgins dedicated to God, whose members have not been defiled by the enemy with the infection of his evil will.[28]

> 36. Why do you think, O foolish man, that what you commit in secrecy is not forbidden, when God is Lord of the night and of the day? . . . If one knows that it is not lawful to comply with the divers desires of the flesh and does what he regards as contrary to belief, can that not be described as obstinate offence? . . . The lusts of the flesh must be deplored; this greediness must be expelled from the mind . . . Those who suffer themselves to be enticed by the human . . . of the flesh will not attain to the possession of the kingdom of God.[29]

Pseudo-Titus has voiced, in these passages, what none of the other authors dared to say, even if they believed it. He has declared that God will only be merciful to those Christians who have chosen, and maintain vows of virginity. God's grace is cut off from all of the rest of humanity. Those Christians in the various churches who are married are practicing their faith in vain, for they have already chosen death over life. Those who have publicly taken vows of virginity, but secretly fantasize about or practice unholy sex are equally condemned. All sex, marital as well as non-marital, is polluting. All non-virgins are not just passively outside of the pale of God's mercy, but they are under the active condemnation of God. God will punish all non-virgins. Pseudo-Titus says that sex is the tool of the enemy to defile and inflict his evil will. These warnings most likely come not just from a hatred of sex, but also from a deeply-seated, profound fear of sex. And this obsession with sex has led the author of Pseudo-Titus to focus on the judgment of God rather than the mercies of God. Not only is the entire world is lost, but most of the church is lost, and only those who have a tenuous hold on virginity will escape the final conflagration in God's awful judgment.

## VIRGINS ARE SAVIOURS

Diverse theories concerning the purpose of the incarnation appeared in the first few centuries of the common era. Many included the theme of Jesus as Saviour from sin; sin being part of the Judeo-Christian cosmos. The evil that people did to each other were not bad choices, nor just bad choices, but they were defiant acts of sin against God and God's creation. Following Augustine's articulation of original sin, which stated that all of Adam and Eve's progeny were born sinful, were inherently sinful, and were predispositioned toward sin, the old question, "What must I do to be saved?" gained even more urgency. Sinners needed a Saviour.

One of the dominant soteriological theories that emerged in the first century was that salvation from sin came through the perfect life and substitutionary death of Jesus Christ. His spilt blood was efficacious, He was the propitiation that God required (Rom 3;25), for He (Christ) had lived the perfect life that God had required. Christians were granted salvation from their own sinfulness by placing their faith in the blood of Jesus.

However, another soteriological paradigm that found early adherents was a variation on the need to, in cooperation with the saving work of God, earn or merit God's salvation.[30] Various good works were offered as means of earning God's favor. What we have discovered in this study is that one of the most effective ways of earning God's favor, and thereby earning salvation, was through the practice of virginity. However, by the time we get well into the first five to six centuries of the common era we hear Christian writers suggesting that not only is the practice of virginity a guarantee of salvation, but virgins themselves begin to be fashioned as saviours. We have already, earlier, quoted a few of the texts which indicate a belief that the holiness and goodness of virgins qualified them to be saviours. Two examples of this belief appears in Ambrose's document *Concerning Virginity*, and the epistle of Leander to his sister, *The Training of Nuns*. First the texts from Ambrose.

Ambrose 1.7.32: You have heard, O parents [how] you ought to train your daughters, that you may possess those by whose merits your faults may be redeemed. The virgin is an offering for her mother, by whose daily sacrifice the divine power is appeased.

2.2.16: One virgin may redeem her parents, another her brothers.

The first thing that is noticed about the two quotes from Ambrose is that both references are to female virgins. It is the "daughters" that are to be trained as virgins. The virgin is an offering for "her" mother, and the virgin may redeem "her" parents. Are we to conclude from this that the virginity of female virgins carried with it more power than that of male virgins? Was the belief that because female virgins had overcome their natural, sensual, femaleness counted as more heroic, and a more sure sign of divine power? These are questions that we cannot answer with complete certainty, but it does appear that female virgins were the virgins that were viewed as saviours.

The second thing to be noticed is that these female virgin saviours do not function as saviours of the world as did Christ. For Ambrose, the virgins' salvific work was limited to members of their own family; mothers, parents, brothers. And not all family members are guaranteed salvation through the virginity of the daughter/sister. For some it may be the parents, and for others the brothers are specifically mentioned. It is curious that sisters are not mentioned, unless it is assumed that all of the daughters/sisters are virgins.

The third, and most obvious thing that needs to be noticed is that this is salvation by virginity. We do not hear Ambrose denying the saving work of Christ; virgins are not ante-Christs. They are not substitute saviours. To use a more modern term we might call a virgin savior a co-redemtrix with Christ.

Brown reminds us that by the fourth century "women with ascetic vocations emerged in upper-class circles, where they had wealth and prestige needed to make a permanent impact on the Christian church . . . [and] it was the individual householder who was thought to benefit most directly from the piety of his virgin daughter."[31] But it was not just the individual householder who benefited. Athanasius states that "in every house of Christians, it is needful that there be a virgin, for the salvation of the whole house is [dependent on] that one virgin."[32] This and similar statements by the church Fathers illuminates the degree of sanctity afforded to those who had voluntarily sacrificed their sexual selves for the sake of Christ. Not only were they the brides of Christ, but their virginity was efficacious for salvation. Not even the saints in the fourth century were lauded with such praise and afforded such power. This is the true power of virginity; that it has the power to save, not only the individual practicing virginity, but those who simply fell under her influence. Brown says that in towns in the Mediterranean the local virgin's "continued virginity was a matter of deep concern for their neighbors; for it brought down the mercy of God on the locality."[33] Further, this was happening at a time when there were still many competing Christian paradigms of salvation, and at a time, i.e., early fourth century, when tens if not hundreds of thousands "converted" to Christianity. Emperor worship, which had been part of the religious landscape of the Roman empire since the "Divine Augustus" in the first century, was, with the "conversion" of Constantine, largely replaced with adopting the religion of the Emperor. The logical assumption was that access (or at least better access) to the Emperor could be had by practicing the religion of the Emperor.[34] Thousands flooded to the new Imperial city, Constantinople, to serve and worship with the new Emperor. Many of those who moved to or near Constantinople were monks and nuns, bringing their virginal lifestyle with them. If the new Christians at Constantinople had not been exposed to virgin Christians before their move, they certainly were following their move. Also, at the time of the "conversion" of the Emperor Constantine, many already practicing Christians, and many of the new Christians came to believe that it was not just Christ as the *logos* of God, nor it was just Christ as the Sacrifice of God, nor it was just the diligent obedience to the commands of God that brought salvation. How are we in the post-Reformation twenty-first century to interpret how new Christians in the fourth century understood the elevation of local Christian virgins as assurances of salvation? If these new Christians did not have access to the emerging sophisticated (and sometimes convoluted) soteriological arguments (egs. Arianism and Donatism) they are left with accepting the teachings of the leaders of the local churches. Many of these new Christians were hearing that the virgins in their congregations held such a degree of divine power, precisely because of their virginity, that they, in some sense, were responsible for the salvation of the community.

Also it was not just catholic Christians who were preaching the virtues of virginity. The Marcionites, Montanists, Manicheans, and the Encratites, all claiming to be the true Christianity, also had elevated views of virginity and the celibate lifestyle. The Manicheans taught that "the bodies of the believers, if kept holy by continence, could play a role in nothing less than the redemption of the universe."[35] If the leaders of these often opposing and/or competing factions of Christianity either formally or informally indicate or imply that the presence of the virgins in the community were responsible for bringing down the grace of God, and if the grace of God is necessary for their salvation, then the status of these virgins could only increase. They are no longer only holy "brides of Christ," but are holy mediators of the grace of Christ. They were not saviors in the way Christ was Saviour, but aided in the process (or act) of salvation.

Families without female virgins, therefore, are left to Christ as their only Savior. Yet I don't believe that Ambrose is suggesting that the saving work of Christ is somehow insufficient or deficient. I do not believe that he would say that the work of Christ on the cross was somehow not fully efficacious. Ambrose says that it is through the "merits" of the virgin that "faults may be redeemed." Yet how can we talk about a redeemable fault that Christ did not redeem? Does the sexual activity of the parents and the sexual activity of the married brothers need to be canceled out by the virginal life of the daughter/sister? Does the family's sexual patterns need to be kept in balance, and a virgin in the family serves that purpose?

Although we do not hear it here in Ambrose, I believe that Leander's view of virgins as mediators is a possible answer. For while Ambrose talks about the saving "merits" of the virgins, Leander talks about the virgin being an oblation, an offering, and an interceder.

Temple imagery, taken from the Hebrew Scriptures, which has already repeatedly appeared in these writings to describe different aspects of the life and promises made to virgins, makes another appearance here in Leander. Also, like the earlier authors, virgins are singled out for their relationship with God. Leander says that of all the Christians in the entire world, which he refers to as the "whole mass of Christ's body," virgins are the "oblations accepted by God and consecrated on the altars." Oblations (offerings; sacrifices) that were consecrated (set apart) on altars in the Hebrew Scriptures were offerings to God. The various offerings were part of either a daily or annual ritualistic drama which symbolized either the believer's or the nation's repentance for sins, and God's forgiveness of those sins. The procedures which were to be meticulously followed, were, according to the authors of Leviticus, revealed to Israel by God. The offerings were to be either first fruits or animal offerings, and if an animal was required, it was to be spotless and without blemish. These were the only offerings that would be acceptable to God, and, therefore, the only way to receive forgiveness from God.

Leander has taken this ritual from the Hebrew Scriptures and replaced the animal "oblations accepted by God and consecrated on the altars," with Christian virgins. Only the pure, unspoilt, unpolluted, virgins are acceptable sacrifices on God's altar. God's requirement of a sacrifice ("Without the shedding of blood there is no forgiveness of sin." Heb 9.22) was either not fully satisfied by the ante-typical "Lamb of God," or virgins, by offering their pure, unspoilt, unpolluted bodies to God are reenacting the sacrifice made by pure, unspoilt, unpolluted Christ. While the non-virgins Christians can only receive the offering of Christ in the Eucharist, virgins are a living, active participant in this cosmic drama. Both Christ and the virgins were offering their bodies as sacrifices to God. Christ, the spotless Son of God, sacrificed His body on a cross on Calvary, and by all early Christian accounts, was acceptable to God. The result was redemption for all who believed and accepted that sacrifice for their sins. Virgins, according to Leander, are offering their bodies as sacrifices to God. They are the new "lambs of God.". Ambrose writes, "For virginity is not praiseworthy because it is found in martyrs, but because itself makes martyrs."[36] They are consecrated oblations, and Leander says that these offerings are also acceptable to God. But for what purpose? Leander reveals the purpose in ch.9.

> You are my shelter in Christ; you, dearest sister, are my security; you are my most sacred offering, through which I doubt not that I shall be purified of the uncleanness of my sins. If you are acceptable to God, if you shall lie with Christ upon the chaste couch, if you shall cling to the embrace of Christ with the most fragrant odor of virginity, surely, when you recall your brother's sins, you will obtain the indulgence which you request for that brother's guilt . . . Held thus in the Bridegroom's embraces, you may ask and obtain pardon for me. The punishment that is due me for my errors may possibly be relieved by the intercession of your chastity . . . through you, perhaps, I shall be released from the spiritual debt which I have contracted . . . Even Mary herself, the Mother and guide of virgins, will intercede with her Son for your merits.

This is very powerful language, and it is a language which sixth century Christians would understand. Just as Jesus Christ stood as a mediator between the believer and God, so too does the virgin, in concert with Christ, act as a mediator between the believer and God. When Leander writes, "You are my shelter in Christ," it seems that he is speaking of the shelter that all non-virgins need from the judgment of God. This cannot be overstated. Virgins provide believers shelter from the judgment of God. Further, Leander does not seem to be speaking metaphorically. "You, dearest sister, are my security; you are my most sacred offering." And it is the offering of the body of the virgin which brings about the purification of "the uncleanness of my sins." How is this done? The virgin "shall lie with Christ on the chaste couch," and "cling to the embrace of Christ with the most fragrant odor of virginity," and "held thus in Bridegroom's embraces, you may ask and obtain pardon for me."

There is an understanding of this text which requires a major soteriological paradigmatic shift. The most Holy God can only be approached through His Sacrificial Son, and, now, further, the Holy Sacrificial Son, must also be approached through an intercessor, and that intercessor is a holy sacrificial virgin. Virgins have become an integral, indispensable piece of a soteriology that believers must pass through to obtain the pardon needed to obtain salvation. Leander, like many in his age, believed that he was still standing under the judgment of God. He says that "the punishment that is due me for my errors may possible be relieved by the intercession of your chastity.

Finally, we hear one of the earliest references to the virgin Mary acting as an intercessor. "Even Mary herself, the Mother and guide of virgins, will intercede with her Son for your merits."[37] The prayers of the believers, now, must pass through virgins, who will only consider these prayers from unholy, sinful, sorrowful, repentant believers because they are seasoned with the merits of virgins. The merits of the virgins are enough for Mary to pass these prayers along to her Son, who will pass them along to His Father. Further layers of intercessors, i.e. sacraments, priests, the Pope, were added as the Middle Ages progressed. It is no wonder, then, that Luther's doctrine of the "priesthood of all believers," where each individual believer had direct access to God, seemed such a radical thought.

## NOTES

1. Sulpitius Severus *Concerning Virginity* 1.
2. Leander of Seville *The Training of Nuns* 16.
3. Pseudo-Clement *On Virginity* 1.7.
4. Cyprian of Carthage *The Dress of Virgins* 5.
5. Methodius of Olympus *On Virginity* 1.1.
6. ibid., 1.2.
7. ibid., 4.
8. Jerome *Against Jovinianus* 29.
9. John Chrysostom *On Virginity* 30.2.
10. Cyprian of Carthage *The Dress of Virgins* 3.
11. Pseudo-Clement *On Virginity* 1.6.
12. Ambrose *Concerning Virginity* 3.19.
13. Jerome *To Eustochium* 6.
14. ibid.
15. ibid., 21.
16. Jerome *To Pammachius* 9.
17. ibid.
18. Jerome *Against Jovinianus* 26.
19. Augustine *Of Holy Virginity* 27.

*Chapter Four*

20. The main issues between Augustine and Pelagius were actually far more anthropological. However, the anthropological starting point for each determined, ultimately, their soteriology.

21. Sulpitius Severus *Concerning Virginity* 10.

22. Jerome *To Eustochium* 16.

23. ibid., 2.

24. Pseudo-Clement *On Virginity* 1.4.

25. ibid.

26. ibid.

27. Leander of Seville *The Training of Nuns* 7.

28. Pseudo-Titus *On the State of Chastity* 23.

29. ibid., 36.

30. A quick reading of the second century Apostolic Fathers; especially the *Epistle of Barnabas* and *1 Clement* provide ample evidence that as early as the second century people believed that obedience to the commands of God were meritorious toward their salvation.

31. Brown, *Body and Society* 263.

32. ibid. From *Canons of Athanasius* 98.

33. ibid., 264.

34. The ongoing debate as to the level of personal commitment to Christianity of Constantine I, and the evidences of that commitment will not be discussed here.

35. ibid., 198.

36. Ambrose *Concerning Virgins* 3.10.

37. Leander of Seville *On the Training of Nuns* 9.

# Chapter Five

# Virginity Lost

Not only were many of the church Fathers desirous of believers, both men and women, taking vows of life-long virginity, but they seemed to be in a constant state of anxiety over the ability of those who had taken these vows, especially female virgins, to maintain the vows. Because of that concern, not only do we hear these writers calling believers to commit to virginity, but reminders to persevere in virginity as well. The following is a sample of those exhortations.

> Cyprian of Carthage *The Dress of Virgins* 22: Persevere, virgins, persevere in what you have begun to be. Persevere in what you will be. A great recompense is reserved for you, a glorious prize for virtue, a most excellent reward for purity . . . Only let your virginity remain and endure substantial and uninjured; and as it began bravely, let is persevere continuously. [For] we must proceed be a different path, for our purpose is not the praise of virginity but its preservation.

> Jerome *Against Jovinianus* 36: Many begin, few persevere. And so the reward is great for those who have persevered.

> Augustine *Of Holy Virginity* 27: Therefore go on, saints of God, boys and girls, males and females, unmarried man and women; go on the persevere unto the end.

> Sulpitius Severus *Concerning Virginity* 19: Maintain to the last that purpose of virginity which you have formed; for it is the part of virtue not merely to begin, but to finish, as the Lord says in the Gospel, "whoever shall endure to the end, the same shall be saved."

These calls to persevere in virginity may be just one example of the many times in the history of the church when the leaders of the church address issues that have come to their attention. If that is the case, then, Jerome's statement that "Many begin, [but] few persevere," may be the one text of the five above which reveals what perhaps is not being explicitly said, but merely implied in the other texts. Jerome's lament to Eustochium that "I cannot bring myself to speak of the many virgins who daily fall and are lost to the bosom of the church, their mother" lends further evidence that not everyone who took vows of virginity were able to maintain it throughout their lives.[1] He further tells Eustochium, most likely as a warning, that "many veteran virgins, of a chastity never called in question, have, on the very threshold of death, let their crown fall from their hands."[2] This act of turning away from what has come to be regarded as divine virginity, speaks, therefore, not just about the virgins, but about the theology of virginity that the Fathers have endeavored to craft. Those who have taken vows of virginity have been declared deathless, more beloved by God, the recipient of greater gifts from God, heroes of the faith because of their strength, sacrifices to God greater than that of the martyrs, overcomers of the most base instincts, and followers of Christ wherever He goes. Those, therefore, who have taken vows of virginity, only to at some later date renounce that vow and all that comes with it, calls into doubt what the Fathers have openly and publicly said about virginity. Not only is the reputation of the institution of virginity called into question, but the reputations of the Fathers as well. In other words, if what the Fathers had said about virginity was not always true, it is possible that what they have said about other issues may be questioned as well. And in a time in the history of the church, i.e. second through the sixth century, when catholic orthodoxy is beginning to take shape, questions about the status of virgins vis-à-vis their relationship to God were not welcomed.

Most Fathers would find this to be intolerable, and for this reason the most extreme condemnations are directed toward those who either have or are thinking about turning from their vows.

Methodius' reflections on this problem, using a well-known parable of Jesus, are perhaps the mildest of the warnings, reminding the virgins whose they are.

> But when the oil failed, by their turning away from the faith to incontinence, the light was entirely extinguished, so that the virgins have again to kindle their lamps by light transmitted from one to another, bringing the light of incorruption to the world from above.[3]

The five foolish virgins in this parable were made to stand for virgins whose light was "entirely extinguished" because they "turn[ed] away from the faith to incontinence." Methodius posits a dichotomy between "the faith" and incontinence. This choice of words allows "the faith of virginity" to be placed in the same category as the "faith of Christology" or the "faith of redemption." It is part of "the faith." And just as turning away from the held beliefs concerning the essence of Christ, or the trinity would cause a believer to turn from the light, so virgins who turn from virginity also turn from the light. This light of virginity is the "light of incorruption to the world from above." Incontinence and corruption are the lot of those who turn from virginity. The five remaining wise virgins are called to kindle their lights again, and the light of virginity is so strong that they can transmit their light "from one to another."

The fear of the resultant theological confusion caused by virgins turning away from virginity elicited some of the sternest warnings heard in the early church. These began as early as the third century with Cyprian of Carthage.

> *On the Dress of Virgins* 20: In proportion as they had been as virgins destined to great rewards, so will they experience great punishments for the loss of their virginity . . . You have flung away the yoke of that divine union; you have fled from the undefiled chamber of the true king; you have shamefully fallen into this disgraceful and impious corruption.

Cyprian chooses language which makes his intent clear. He talks about "great punishments," "you have flung away," "you have fled from the undefiled chamber," "you have shamefully fallen into this disgraceful and impious corruption." We can only suppose that these former virgins are ones who have intentionally given up their vows of virginity, and not ones who were raped or taken by force. By the early third century virgins in the Christian communities were not just a few souls scattered in the remote parts of the desserts, but were often organized into companies, and were important, public, even high-profile, bodies in many cities. Therefore, when one of these virgins turns away from her/his vows the entire Christian community knew about it, and the reaction was swift. Virgins simply could not change their minds. Once the commitment was made, it was irreversible. And as the expected rewards were greater, so the punishments were greater. Whatever punishments were reserved for the lost, whether Christian or non-Christian, they were not as great as those awaiting the fallen virgins. The vitriolic language usually reserved for unrepentant heretics and Jews appears here in describing the fate of the fallen virgins. With the marriage imagery unmistakable, Cyprian implicitly compares them to the prostitutes in Hosea. They have flung away the "divine union" and fled from the "undefiled chamber." They are left only with "shame" and "disgrace." Further, the repeated use of the word "fallen" to describe the condition of these former virgins, removes them from the side of the Virgin Mary, and places them aside the fallen Eve. There is no concern for some sort of recovery, and, in fact, there does not seem to be even any possibility for recovery, which puts this sin on a par with other unforgivable, unpardonable sins.

Basil of Caesarea, in the fourth century, expresses his own and heaven's horror and amazement in his letter to a fallen virgin.

You have been deceived by the serpent more bitterly than Eve; and not only your mind but also your body has been defiled. Even that last horror has come to pass which I shrink from saying, and yet cannot leave unsaid, for it is as a burning and blazing fire in my bones, and I am undone and cannot endure. You have taken the members of Christ and made them members of a harlot. This is an evil with which no other can be matched . . . The heavens are astonished at this, and the earth is horribly afraid, says the Lord, for the virgin has committed two evils; she has forsaken Me, the true and holy Bridegroom of holy souls, and has betaken herself to an impious and lawless destroyer of body and soul alike. She has revolted from God her Saviour, and yielded her members [as] servants to uncleanness and to iniquity. She forgot me and went after her lover from whom she will get no good.[4]

Knowingly, and seemingly purposefully, sacrificing their perfect virginal body to uncleanness has cost these former virgins more than just a loss of bodily purity, but they have sacrificed their souls. Twice Basil mentions the double loss. Both the body and soul have been defiled for both the body and soul were willingly yielded to the lawless destroyer of both body and soul. Virgins must never think that it is only their body that is at stake. Jerome's dictum that "virginity may be lost even by a thought" makes it clear that the purity that was demanded of virgins was a purity of body, soul and mind.[5] And these three parts of each human being were so interconnected that what "stained" one stained all.

One of the more curious passages in this text is Basil's contention that Satan's (the serpent) deception of the fallen virgin is somehow more bitter than the one he perpetrated on Eve. All of the church Fathers believed that the fall of Adam and Eve had cosmic consequences for all of humanity. Further, the whole experience of sex, along with the awakening of sexual lust, which was non-existent in Paradise, had entered into the experience of the world because Adam and Eve had fallen to the deception of the Serpent. How, then, could the fall of a virgin be more bitter?

It could be argued that since Eve never knew, either cognitively or experientially, what sorrows and misery followed in the train of lust and sex, she could not possibly have the same motivation as Christian virgins to remain chaste. Along the same line of thinking, God had worked for thousands of years to bring humanity back to the perfection lost in Paradise; perfection defined as sexual abstinence. Therefore, virgins who had embraced that perfection, only to throw it away, were, in effect, undoing the eons of work God had put into the recovery of His creation.

The early church Father's inability to use the words "penis" and "vagina" is also seen here in the writings of Basil. And to even contemplate the mention of these organs, which he feels he cannot avoid, causes him "horror," and he wants to "shrink" from using these terms. He does not want to mention them, but his anguish has caused him to be undone and he can no longer endure to keep silent. He must pronounce God's judgment. The best he can do is to call the male and female sexual organs "members." However, they are not just "members" but they are referred to as "members of Christ." Therefore, it can be concluded that these "brides" of the "Holy Bridegroom" have dedicated, along with the rest of their being, their sexual organs. And true intimacy between the true brides with the "Holy Bridegroom" will always be pure and undefiled. Therefore, use of the sexual organs, especially use of the sexual organs once dedicated to Christ, is an act of harlotry. And this brand of harlotry, perpetrated against the Holy Bridegroom, is of a magnitude of which none is greater. Imagine what Basil is actually saying. In the categories of all of the sins which humans have committed; of all the atrocities, of all the slaughters; even of the sins which caused God to destroy the earth with water; none have been as great as the sin of a virgin repudiating her vows of virginity to God. And in light of the promised divine gifts of the virgins who persevere to the end, to choose "an impious and lawless destroyer of body and soul alike" causes the inhabitants of heaven to be "astonished." The choice for the vowed virgin, then, is not between God and a human spouse, but between God and Satan. The virgin should have known, and did know, that the choice is between the giver of life, and the destroyer of life. The fallen virgin has forsaken God, revolted from God, and forgotten God. This language to express the utter forsakenness of the fallen virgin is only elsewhere in the early church seen in the *Epistle of Barnabas* where he launches into his anti-Semitic diatribe against the Jews.[6] And like the virgins here, the author of that epistle places the blame of God's abandonment of the Jews squarely at their own feet, for choosing other gods, even when they were God's chosen people.

Finally, the verbs used to describe what the fallen virgin has done are all active, save one; "You have taken," you have "made them the members of a harlot," "the virgin has committed two evils," "she has forsaken," she "has betaken herself to an impious and lawless destroyer," "she has revolted from God," she "has yielded her members," "she forgot me," and she "went after her lover." What this particular virgin did was, according to Basil, purposeful and intentional. Therefore, her condemnation is just, and her lostness is sure.

We have already seen how virgins were not allowed to be just pious people. They were so connected to the supernatural that they themselves became supernatural. Once this vow to virginity was made, they were removed from common existence. And this uncommon existence was one from which, according to Ambrose, they could never return, even if they fell from their virginal state. He says, " He who has preserved [virginity] is an angel; he who has lost it is a devil."[7] The person who had taken vows of virginity could not, for any reason just return to a more "normal" existence. Succumbing to the fatigue of the struggle, or simply changing their mind about the necessity of a life of virginity; neither these, nor any other reasons for renouncing virginity was acceptable. The consequences were disastrous. "The higher [a virgin] climbs, the more terrible will be her fall."[8] A fallen virgin was no better than the very enemy of God. Virgins who, as long as they maintained their virginity, were the heroes of the faith, could with one decision, become the enemy of the faith, and were a curse to the faithful. As a devil they would, of course, be excised from the community, and banned from the sacraments. They were lost, and it was a lostness, Jerome reminds us, from which he/she could never recover. In his letter to Eustochium he tells her, "though God can do all things, He cannot raise up a virgin when once she has fallen."[9] Further, in her fallen state she is subject to the judgment of God. Jerome writes, "that virgin who has once for all dedicated herself to the service of God . . . should one of these marry, she will have damnation because she has made of no account her first faith . . . for virgins who marry after consecration are rather incestuous than adulterous."[10] Whether incestuous or adulterous was of little consequence, for both were sins in the sight of God. And for that reason Jerome, referring to his earlier works on virginity, writes, "I have tried to show that all who have not remained virgins are reckoned as defiled when compared to the perfect chastity of the angels and of our Lord Jesus Christ."[11]

This portrayal of God as a harsh, exacting judge, or as an angry revengeful cuckold, continues with John Chrysostom. He says to an imaginary fallen virgin that "God himself beckoned you toward the spiritual wedding chamber, but you have severed yourself from that glory, [and you] have plunged yourself into the devil's fire and into fatal punishment."[12]

Finally, Sulpitius Severus, though not nearly as condemnatory at the earlier writers, lets fallen virgins know that there is a divine price to pay for renouncing their virginal vows. He writes, "O virgin, maintain thy purpose which is destined for a great reward, [but] He will quickly write a bill of divorcement if he perceive in you even one act of unfaithfulness."[13]

## NOTES

1. Jerome *To Eustochium* 13. It is most likely that Jerome is referring to publicly vowed virgins rather than young girls (& boys) who are deciding on marriage rather than virginity.

2. ibid., 29.

3. Methodius *On Virginity* 6.4.

4. Basil of Caesarea *To a Fallen Virgin* 3.

5. Jerome *To Eustochium* 5.

6. Most of chs. 1-17 are given over to the author's vitriol.
7. Ambrose *Concerning Virginity* 1.9.52.
8. Jerome *To Demetrius* 7.
9. Jerome *To Eustochium* 5.
10. Jerome *Against Jovinianus* 13.
11. Jerome *To Pammachius* 14.
12. John Chrysostom *On the Necessity of Guarding Virginity* 2.
13. Sulpitius Severus *Concerning Virginity* 12.

# Conclusion

Those who wrote about virginity in the ancient Church understood it to be both a gift from God and a gift to God. However, while Ambrose and Jerome lament that virginity is a "gift of few only" and that "all men cannot receive" virginity, it can be suggested that Augustine's words that "we are to choose perpetual continence" was addressed to all Christians. Accepting this "heavenly gift" from God and choosing to offer their virginity back to God as their gift gave virgins access to God in ways that married Christians could not. The married had sacrificed their virginity to another human being, and that decision cost them blessings and assurances which only virgins could enjoy.

The early church Fathers who turned their attention to the issues of virginity believed that virgins and the practice of virginity connected these virgins with God in intimate ways that other Christians could only hope for. Only virgins were both the brides *and* mothers of Christ. Virgins were never out of the presence of Christ, both in this world and the next. They were His constant companions, and followed Him wherever He went. Also virginity was seen as more pleasing to God than any other devotion that could be offered, and because it was more pleasing, it brought greater rewards from God. Virgins were portrayed as being no longer just part of the corporeal world, but part of the "other" world as well. They were either angels or angelic. And just as all of God's angels are holy, so were the virgins. Their holiness is even compared to the holiness that is possessed by God. Therefore, virgins are different from their fellow Christians, and the difference is not just an apparent difference, it is an essential difference in their existence. It is an existence that married Christians cannot share.

What we have in these documents on virginity is a pre-disposition against not just Christian marriage, but the institution of marriage itself. It would be difficult to argue that married Christians in the first five to six centuries were more lustful or profligate than the general population. It is more likely that they were not. Therefore, we can assume that, for these Fathers, any marriage (other than "spiritual marriages") was a sign of weakness and divided loyalties at best; loss and abandonment of one's call from God at worst. It is rare in the early post-apostolic age (late first—early second century) to find a catholic author praising an institution (marriage) that was the very foundation of all past and contemporary cultures. These men, either intentionally or unintentionally, were re-creating society; a society that would be void of many standards of familial responsibilities and sensitivities. This was an extreme culture which very few could understand. Fewer still could identify the motivation for this sexless society, and fewer still were motivated enough to accept the challenge of living a virginal life. Expressing care for your husband (or wife) and children was a signal, not that you cared more for them than for the things of God, but that you cared nothing for the things of God. If you cared for the things of God you expressed that by not becoming entangled with intimate relationships in this life. Christ was your Bridegroom and heaven was "better than sons and daughters."

Married Christians were not denied the blessings of the Kingdom of God, but in the "hierarchical heaven" created by these men, the best that married Christians could hope for was entrance into the Kingdom. God, and the rest of the inhabitants of Heaven—Divine, angelic, and human—knew that God and Christ held virgins and celibate widows in far greater esteem than faithful married Christians. They were "third class" citizens, forever, in the eternal world to which they were hoping.

Based on the evidence it is safe to say that the understandings of early Christian soteriology needs to be broadened. The merits of Christ's sacrifice were not the only merits available to the believers. And while the merits of the martyrs enjoyed early popularity, the merits of virgins, which third, fourth, and fifth century Christians began to honor, has not yet been considered by modern scholars.

Salvation by grace through faith and not by works, presented by Paul (Eph 2.8), by the late first century was one of a variety of ways in which Christians might be saved. The importance of good works came to take an important, and readily accepted role in the language of salvation. Salvation was no longer only an act by God through Christ, but a process. In this process the believer, having faith in God's saving power, and trusting in God's grace, performs good works, further earning God's favor. However, the evidence makes it abundantly clear that virginity was not just another good work. Its increasing elevation in the writings of the early church Fathers, its connection with the divine, its participation in what now can be recognized as a soteriological scheme, and the promises of exceedingly greater gifts from God, demonstrate that virginity was not just a good work, but rather a way of salvation standing on its own. It can be suggested that very few early Christian believers, other than perhaps some Pelagians, believed that good works, on their own, could earn salvation. However, more than one early Christian Father author either implicitly suggested, or explicitly stated that taking the vow of virginity, and remaining true to that vow, both physically and spiritually, was enough to ensure one's salvation.

It is stated that virgins, because of their virginity, can offer to their fellow believers blessings which only they (the virgins) can offer. It may be too early to suggest that the virgins are, in some sense, saviours. However, as this language continued to be heard it becomes more and more difficult to avoid the conclusion that virgins are not just passively saved, but are also actively engaged in the act of salvation for the Christian community. By the sixth century, some writers are saying that virgins have access to God in ways that allows them to intercede, salvifically, on behalf of others.

In light of this elevation of virginity to divine heights, it is understandable why a loss of virginity, especially a voluntary abandonment seemed to be the most abhorrent of all sins. It is obvious that devoting one's life to virginity in the early church was a high stakes challenge, fraught with eternal consequences. The ultimate end of those who took virgin vows was the very heights of heaven, but if renounced the very deepest pits of hell. Virgins were portrayed as no longer being part of this world, and they enjoyed a closeness with God that the rest of the Christian communities could only imagine. And it is primarily for this reason that fallen virgins were subject to some of the harshest language and deepest animosity from the church Fathers. They pulled out their full *repertoire* to voice both their own and God's displeasure.

# Bibliography

## ANCIENT TEXTS

Cassius Dio 54.
Dio Cassius *History of Rome.*
Hippocrates *On Virginity.*
*Lex Julia de Maritandis Ordinabus.*
*Lex Papia Poppaea.*
Pliny the Elder *Natural History.*
Plutarch *On the Disappearance of the Oracles.*
———. *Life of Numa Pompilius.*
Sophicles *Antigone.*
Soranus of Ephesus *Gynecology.*
Suetonius *Life of Augustus.*
Tacitus *Annals.*
*The Twelve Tables.*

## ANCIENT JEWISH TEXTS

*Babylonian Talmud: Baba Bathra.*
Josephus *Antiquities.*
———. *Wars of the Jews.*
*Midrash Rabba: Genesis.*
Philo *Apology.*
*Testaments of the Twelve Patriarchs.*

# ANCIENT GNOSTIC AND
# NEW TESTAMENT APOCRYPHA TEXTS

*Acts of John the Evangelist.*
*Acts of Paul and Thecla.*
*Acts of Thomas.*
*Apocryphon of John.*
*The Book of Thomas the Contender.*
*The Exegesis of the Soul.*
*The Gospel of Bartholomew.*
*The Gospel of Mary.*
*The Gospel of the Nativity of Mary.*
*The Gospel of Pseudo-Matthew* (aka *Gospel of Barnabas*).
*Hypostasis of the Archons.*
*Trimorphic Protennoia.*
*Tripartite Tractat.e*

# EARLY CHRISTIAN TEXTS

Ambrose *Concerning Virgins: To His Sister Marcellina*. 3 bks.
——. *Exposition on the Gospel According to Luke.*
Ambrosiaster *Commentary on Paul's Epistles.*
Anonymous *The Epistle of Titus, the Disciple of Paul, on the State of Chastity.*
Augustine *Of Holy Virginity.*
Basil of Caesarea *To a Fallen Virgin.*
*Canons of Athanasius* 98.
Chrysostom, John *Homilies on First Corinthians (Homily XIX).*
——. *Homily on Matthew* 66.3.
——. *On the Necessity of Guarding Virginity.*
——. *On Virginity.*
Cyprian of Carthage *Of the Discipline and Advantage of Chastity.*
——. *The Dress of Virgins.*
Cyril of Jerusalem *Catechetical Lectures.*
Epiphanius of Salaimis *Panarion.*
*Epistle of Polycarp.*
Eusebius of Caesarea *Proof of the Gospel.*
Gregory of Nazianzus *Epitaph for His Mother.*
Gregory of Nyssa *The Life of Macrina.*
——. *On Virginity.*
Ignatius of Antioch *To the Magnesians; To the Smyrnians; To the Trallians.*
Irenaeus *Adversus Haersus.*
——. *Against Helvidius.*
——. *Against Javiliantus.*

———. *Against Vigiliantius.*
———. *Commentary on the Epistle to the Ephesians.*
———. *To Eustocium* (Letter 22).
———. *To Pammachius* (Letter 48).
———. *To Demetrias* (Letter 130).
Justin Martyr *First Dialogue.*
Leander of Seville *On the Training of Nuns and the Contempt of the World.*
*The Lusiac History.*
Methodius of Olympus *On Virginity: Discourse 1 To Marcella.*
———. *Discourse 6 To Agathe.*
Origen *Commentary on 1 Corinthians.*
Pseudo-Athanasius *On Virginity.*
Pseudo-Clement *Two Epistles Concerning Virginity.*
Severian of Gabala *Pauline Commentary from the Greek Church.*
Socrates *History of the Church.*
Sulpitius Severus *Concerning Virginity: To His Sister Claudia* (Letter 2).
Tertullian *On the Resurrection of the Body.*
———. *On the Veiling of Virgins.*

## MODERN TEXTS

Baab, O.J. "Sex, Sexual Behavior" In *The Interpreter's Dictionary of the Bible.* Vol. 4. Nashville: Abingdon Press, 1962.

Bauer, Walter. "The Relatives of Jesus." In *New Testament Apocrypha.* ed. and trans. by R. McL. Wilson. Vol. 1. Louisville, KY: Westminster/John Knox Press, 1959.

Beard, Mary. "The Sexual Status of Vestal Virgins." *The Journal of Roman Studies* 70(1980): 12-27.

Benko, Stephen. "Second Century References to the Mother of Jesus." In *Women in Early Christianity.* ed. David M. Scholer, 2-14. New York: Garland Publishing, 1993.

Black, Matthew. *The Scrolls and Christian Origins: Studies in the Jewish Background of the New Testament.* New York: Thomas Nelson and Sons, Ltd., 1961.

Bray, Gerald, ed. *Ancient Christian Commentary on Scripture.* Vol. 7. *1-2 Corinthians.* Downers Grove, IL: Intervarsity Press, 1998.

Brown, Peter. *The Body and Society: Men, Women and sexual Renunciation in Early-Christianity.* New York: Columbia University Press, 1988.

Brown, Raymond D., Joseph A. Fitzmyer, and Roland E. Murphy. eds. *The New Jerome Biblical Commentary.* Upper Saddle River, NJ: Prentice-Hall, Inc., 1990.

Bruce, F.F. ed. *New Century Bible: 1 and 2 Corinthians.* Greenwood, SC: The Attic-Press, Inc., 1971.

Brueggman, Walter. "Exodus." In *The New Interpreter's Bible.* ed. Leander E. Keck.Vol. 1. 691-981. Nashville: Abingdon Press, 1994.

Burrows, Millar. *The Dead Sea Scrolls.* New York: Viking Press, 1955.

————. *More Light on the Dead Sea Scrolls*. New York: Viking Press, 1958.

Clark, Elizabeth. "Sexual Politics in the Writings of John Chrysostom." In *Women in Early Christianity*, ed. David M. Scholer. New York: Garland Press, 1993.

Conzelmann, Hans. *A Commentary on the First Epistle to the Corinthians*. Translated by James W. Leitch. Philadelphia: Fortress Press, 1975.

Cooper, Kate. *The Virgin and the Bride: Idealized Womanhood in Late Antiquity*. Cambridge, MA: Harvard University Press, 1999.

Corrington, Gail Paterson. "The "Divine Woman:" Propaganda and the Power of Celibacy in the New Testament Apocrypha: A Reconsideration." In *Women in Eary Christianity*. ed. David M. Scholer. New York: Garland Press, 1993.

Ecker, Ronald. *And Adam Knew Eve: A Dictionary of Sex in the Bible*. Nov 2001. <http://www.hobrad.com/and.htm>.

Eiselen, Frederick Carl, Edwin Lewis, and David Downey, eds. *The Abingdon Bible Commentary*. New York: Abingdon-Cokesbury Press, 1929.

Fee, Gordon. *The First Epistle to the Corinthians*. Grand Rapids: Wm. B. Eerdmans Publishing, 1987.

Frymer-Kinsky, Tikva. "Sex and Sexuality." In *The Anchor Bible*. ed. David Noel Freedman. Vol. 5. 1144-1146. New York: Doubleday Publishing, 1992.

Goehring, James E. "Libertine or Liberated: Women in the So-called Libertine Gnostic Communities." In *Women in Early Christianity*, ed. David M. Scholer. New York: Garland Press, 1993.

Hauck, Friedrich. "Katharos." In *The Theological Dictionary of the New Testament*, Vol. 3. ed. Gerhard Kittle. Grand Rapids: Wm. B. Eerdmans, 1964.

Hoffman, Daniel. *The Status of Women and Gnosticism in Ireneaus and Tertullian*. Lewiston, NY: The Edwin Mellen Press, 1995.

Kee, H.C. "*Testaments of the Twelve Patriarchs*: A New Translation and Introduction." In *The Old Testament Pseudepigrapha*. Vol. 1, *Apocalyptic Literature and Testaments*. Garden City, NY: Doubleday, 1983.

Keroloss, Heshmat Fawzy. "Virginity in the Early Church: The Meanings and Motives of Sexual Renunciation in the first Four Centuries." Ph.D. diss., Fordham University, 1996.

King, Elizabeth Ann. "Virginity in Early Christian Writings." Ph.D. diss., Central Connecticut State University, 2000.

Kraemer, Ross S. "The Conversion of Women to Ascetic Forms of Christianity." *Signs* (Winter 1980): 298-307.

LaPorte, Jean. *The Role of Women in Early Christianity*. New York: The Edwin Mellen Press, 1982.

Lonie, I.M. *The Hippocratic Treatises, "On Generation," "On the Nature of the Child," " Diseases IV:" A Commentary*. New York: De Gruyter, 1981.

Loraux, Nicole. "What is a Goddess?" In *A History of Women in the West*. Vol. 1, *From Ancient Goddesses to Christian Saints*, ed. Pauline Schmitt Pantel. Cambridge, MA: The Belknap Press of Harvard University Press, 1992.

Mason, Steve. "What Josephus Says About the Essenes in His *Judean War*." In *Text and Artifact in the Religions of Mediterranean Antiquity: Essay in Honor of Peter*

*Richardson*, ed. Stephen G. Wilson and Michel Desjardins. Waterloo, IA: Wilfrid Laurier University Press, 2000.

McGuire, Anne. "Virginity and Subversion: Norea Against the Powers in the *Hypostasis of the Archons*." In *Images of the Feminine in Gnosticism*, ed. Karen L. King. Harrisburg, PA: Trinity Press International, 1988.

McNamara, Jo Ann. "Sexual Equality and the Cult of Virginity in Early Christian Thought." In *Women in Early Christianity*, ed. David M. Scholer. New York: Garland Press, 1993.

Newsom, Carol A. and Sharon H. Ringe, eds. *Women's Bible Commentary: Expanded Edition*. Louisville, KY: Westminster/John Knox Press, 1992.

Padel, Ruth. "Women: Model for Possession by Greek Daemons." In *Images of Women in Antiquity*, ed. Averil Cameron and Amilie Kuhrt. Detroit: Wayne State University Press, 1983.

Pinault, Jody Rubin. "The Medical Case for Virginity in the Early Second Century C.E.: Soranus of Ephesus, *Gynecology* 1.32." *Helios* 19 (1992): 123-139.

Pomoroy, Sarah B. *Goddesses, Whores, Wives and Slaves: Women in Classical Antiquity*. New York: Schocken Books, 1975.

Ringgren, Helmer. *The Faith of Qumran: Theology of the Dead Sea Scrolls*. Translated by Emilie T. Sander. New York: Crossroad Publishing, 1995.

Rouselle, Aline. "Body Politics in Ancient Rome." In *A History of Women in the West*. Vol. 1, *From Ancient Goddesses to Christian Saints*, ed. Pauline Schmitt Pantel. Cambridge, MA: The Belknap Press of Harvard University Press, 1992.

Ruether, Rosemary Radford, ed. *Religion and Sexism*. New York: Simon and Schuster, 1974.

Salisbury, Joyce. *Church Fathers, Independent Virgins*. New York: Verso Publishing, 1991.

Schulenburg, J.T. *Forgetful of Their Sex: Female Sanctity and Society, ca. 500-1100*. Chicago: University of Chicago Press, 1998.

Schurer, Emil. *The History of the Jewish People in the Age of Jesus Christ (175 B.C.–A.D. 135)*. Translated by T.A. Burkhill. Edinburgh: T. & T. Clark Publishing, 1973.

Sheres, Ita and Anne Kohn Blau. *The Truth About the Virgin: Sex and Ritual in the Dead Sea Scrolls*. New York: Continuum Publishing, 1995.

Simpson, Jane. "Women and Asceticism in the Fourth Century: A Question of Interpretation." *The Journal of Religious History* 15 (June 1988): 38-54.

Sissa, Guilia. *Greek Virginity*. Translated by Aarthur Goldhammer. Cambridge, MA: Harvard University Press, 1990.

Staples, Ariadne. *From Good Goddess to Vestal Virgins*. New York: Routledge Publishing, 1998.

Thomas, Yan. "The Division of the Sexes in Roman Law." In *A History of Women in the West*. Vol 1, *From Ancient Goddesses to Christian Saints*, ed. Pauline Schmitt, Pantel. Cambridge, MA: The Belknap Press of Harvard University Press, 1992.

Veyne, Paul. "The Roman Empire." In *A History of Private Life I: From Pagan Rome to Byzantium*, ed. Paul Veyne, 5-234. Cambridge, MA: Harvard University Press, 1987.

Wilson-Kastner, Patricia. *A Lost Tradition: Women Writers of the Early Church.* Washington, D.C.: University Press of America, 1981.

Wright, G. Ernest. "Deuteronomy." In *The Interpreter's Bible.* ed, George Arthur Buttrick. Vol. 2. Nashville: Abingdon Press, 1963.

Zaidman, Louise Bruit. "Pandora's Daughters and Rituals in Grecian Cities." In *A History of Women in the West.* Vol. 1, *From Ancient Goddesses to Christian Saints*, ed. Pauline Schmitt Pantel. Cambridge, MA: The Belknap Press of Harvard University Press, 1992.

# Scripture Index

# Name Index

# About the Author

Dr. Roger Steven Evans received his B.S. in Theology from Columbia Union College (1976), an M.Div from Andrews Theological Seminary (1979), an M.A. in Ancient History from The Ohio State University (1991), and a Ph.D. in Ancient History from The Ohio State University (1996) with a concentration in early Christian theology. Before his current tenure at Payne Theological Seminary (1990-2003), he pastored for fifteen years in the Ohio Conference of Seventh-Day Adventists (1976–1977; 1979–1994).

This book grew out of research for his class "Gender and Sex: Issues in Ancient Christianity," and is a continuation of explorations of soteriological themes in Ancient Christianity that began with his dissertation "Soteriologies of Early Christianity Within The Intellectual Context of The Early Roman Empire: Barnabas and Clement of Rome as Case Studies." His next two books—one on the legacy of early North African Christianity, and the other on early Christian Anti-Judaism and Anti-Semitism have also risen out of research for classes Dr. Evans teaches at Payne.